PRESIDENTIAL DEBATES

PRESIDENTIAL DEBATES
1988 AND BEYOND

Joel L. Swerdlow, editor

League of Women Voters Education Fund

WITHDRAWN

Congressional Quarterly Inc.

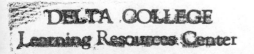

Copyright © 1987
Congressional Quarterly Inc.
1414 22nd Street N.W.
Washington, D.C. 20037

Printed in the United States of America

Gallup Poll results beginning on p. 165 are used with permission
    of the Gallup Organization, Inc., Princeton, New Jersey.

Nielsen ratings provided in Part IV are used with permission of
    Nielsen Media Research, New York. Nielsen Media Research is not
    responsible for projections of numbers of individual viewers.

Library of Congress Cataloging-in-Publication Data

Presidential debates.

   Includes index.
   1. Presidents—United States—Election. 2. Campaign debates—United
States. 3. Television in politics—United States. I. Swerdlow, Joel L. II. League
of Women Voters (U.S.). Education Fund.
JK524.P675   1987   324.7   87-27171
ISBN 0-87187-446-6

To my sister, Jo Betty Swerdlow, with love and with admiration for what she represents.

Joby is a physician, a wife, a mother of two young daughters, and an active participant in the lives of family, friends, and neighbors. She loves nature, animals, and quiet walks in the country, and she is unrushed with the people who need her.

Once I asked how she found time to keep informed about elections. Joby responded, "How could I not find the time?" In her answer was much of what makes democracy possible.

CONTENTS

PART III.   DEBATE TRANSCRIPT HIGHLIGHTS

PART IV.   BROADCAST DEBATES AND GALLUP POLLS

A LETTER FROM THE LEAGUE
OF WOMEN VOTERS EDUCATION FUND

For more than thirty years, the League of Women Voters Education Fund has been involved in books designed to help the public understand a wide range of vital public policy issues. This book represents something different: coverage of an issue in which the League is—in part, at least—an interested party.

The League has been sponsoring issue-oriented and candidate debates since the early 1920s; in every presidential election since 1976, the League has sponsored prenomination and general-election presidential debates. Other organizations now argue that they, rather than the League, should sponsor debates between the presidential nominees. At the same time, many observers argue that the League's role should be preserved.

This disagreement, however, is only one among many crucial debate-related topics. Presidential debates are now perhaps *the* most important campaign events, and since 1976 the League has been committed to in-depth, scholarly analysis that encourages a better understanding of debates by researchers, students, journalists, political professionals, and the general public. Our commitment is stronger than ever as the 1988 campaign, with its promise of a record-setting number of debates, begins.

Following the 1984 debates, the League began to plan a book to fill the need for a comprehensive, timely resource on the status of presidential debates. By coincidence, just as we began to think about how to proceed, we were approached by Joel L. Swerdlow, a journalist, scholar, and writer on questions related to the media and presidential politics, who had a similar idea. This book resulted from our discussions.

Presidential Debates: 1988 and Beyond was conceived and edited by Joel Swerdlow, whose previous work includes the 1984 Twentieth Century Fund study, *Beyond Debate*. He is widely respected as knowledgeable and independent; this book reflects his work.

The League helped raise funds from the John and Mary R. Markle Foundation; suggested possible topics; assisted in recruiting contributors; coordinated the book's administrative aspects; and contributed the essay, "The League of Women Voters Should Sponsor Debates," one of six points of view on that issue.

We have resolved our potential conflict of interest by committing ourselves to supporting this important project while stepping away from control over its contents or conclusions. As the book neared completion, select members of our board and staff read the entire manuscript to assure themselves that it was fair and accurate.

We found the book to be far more; we are proud to be associated with this effort. We believe that readers will find the book stimulating, informative, and highly useful.

Nancy M. Neuman
Chair, League of Women Voters Education Fund

PREFACE

The contributors to this volume are distinguished men and women who have many opportunities to make their voices and opinions known. Thus, it is a special honor that they have chosen to be part of this book; their presence here indicates just how important debates have become in U.S. elections. Debates are now—and will continue to be—at the heart of the making of the president.

This book was conceived in response to two major gaps in what has been written about debates.

First, there was a need for an up-to-date, one-stop look at the various cultural, political, journalistic, and legal issues raised by debates. Discussion of debates from these perspectives could sometimes be found in scattered works and footnotes, but a comprehensive treatment was rare. The whole debate about debate sponsorship, moreover, has seldom been viewed objectively.

Second, retrieving the most basic information about debates required extraordinarily time-consuming research. To a large degree, I think this difficulty reflects our record-keeping customs, which remain wedded to the written word and are just beginning to take broadcast events seriously. For example, a researcher would have to invest an inordinate amount of time and energy to find out the context of Gerald Ford's gaffe about eastern Europe, a debate Frank Church appeared in, the names of the panelists in the third prenomination Democratic debate of 1984, the public's reaction to the 1960 debates, or the date of the first broadcast debate.

To meet this first need, the book brings together some of the best thinkers and practitioners of politics and the media. Included in this multidisciplinary group are a network anchor, a leading pollster, an academic expert on political advertising, an influential media critic, a legal scholar, a well-known writer and scholar on Congress, a key political strategist in the Reagan White House, a distinguished panelist from the 1960 Kennedy-Nixon debates, a prominent campaign consultant, and the head of the organization that has sponsored most of our presidential debates.

The contributors accepted responsibility for generating new analyses and crafting readable essays that would remain current and useful through the 1988 campaign and into the 1990s.

To meet the need for primary source material, *Presidential Debates: 1988 and Beyond* contains annotated highlights of debate transcripts, all existing data about each broadcast debate from 1948 to 1984, and selected Gallup Poll results from 1960 to 1987.

This book is written for the general public as well as for those with professional interest in presidential campaigns. It should be interesting and useful to political aficionados; journalists; and scholars and students in political science, journalism, history, communication, and other fields. It may be read in its entirety, or essays and transcript highlights of particular interest may be selected. The thorough subject index can help readers meet more specific needs.

Thus, this book should help those who want a basic understanding of broad issues—such as the relationship between television and presidential politics. Readers will also find here discussion of more focused concerns—such as how debate sponsorship relates to broadcast regulation. And finally, it should help those requiring an accessible reference source to fill in holes or answer specific questions.

As work on the book progressed, I decided to write an essay that examines the history of debates and related this history to the age of television. A series of strange conversations made the need for this essay clear.

When people would ask what I was working on and hear my response, they would ask the same question, "Are you for or against debates?" The question did not make sense to me. Debates are not something you are for or against. What do you do, for example, if you decide to be "against" debates? Boycott them by turning off your television set or canceling your newspaper subscription?

Frustration with these reactions led me to research into the history of debates and then try to use this history—presented in the essay that introduces the book—to suggest some realistic and constructive responses. In the process, I concluded that the prime purpose of debates may be their ritualistic aspects.

To view debates as rituals is a reminder that we who take a professional interest in campaigns must always remember not to take our research, techniques, and insights too seriously. The muscle and soul of democracy lie in the great mass of citizens for whom we work: the voters.

What we must do is to help keep these voters informed, interested, and legitimately convinced that here in America politics is indeed the business everyone.

That is why I have always found presidential debates so fascinating and full of potential. And that is why I hope this book can make a contribution.

Joel L. Swerdlow
Washington, D.C.
October 1987

A LETTER FROM THE LEAGUE
OF WOMEN VOTERS EDUCATION FUND

For more than thirty years, the League of Women Voters Education Fund has been involved in books designed to help the public understand a wide range of vital public policy issues. This book represents something different: coverage of an issue in which the League is—in part, at least—an interested party.

The League has been sponsoring issue-oriented and candidate debates since the early 1920s; in every presidential election since 1976, the League has sponsored prenomination and general-election presidential debates. Other organizations now argue that they, rather than the League, should sponsor debates between the presidential nominees. At the same time, many observers argue that the League's role should be preserved.

This disagreement, however, is only one among many crucial debate-related topics. Presidential debates are now perhaps *the* most important campaign events, and since 1976 the League has been committed to in-depth, scholarly analysis that encourages a better understanding of debates by researchers, students, journalists, political professionals, and the general public. Our commitment is stronger than ever as the 1988 campaign, with its promise of a record-setting number of debates, begins.

Following the 1984 debates, the League began to plan a book to fill the need for a comprehensive, timely resource on the status of presidential debates. By coincidence, just as we began to think about how to proceed, we were approached by Joel L. Swerdlow, a journalist, scholar, and writer on questions related to the media and presidential politics, who had a similar idea. This book resulted from our discussions.

Presidential Debates: 1988 and Beyond was conceived and edited by Joel Swerdlow, whose previous work includes the 1984 Twentieth Century Fund study, *Beyond Debate*. He is widely respected as knowledgeable and independent; this book reflects his work.

The League helped raise funds from the John and Mary R. Markle Foundation; suggested possible topics; assisted in recruiting contributors; coordinated the book's administrative aspects; and contributed the essay, "The League of Women Voters Should Sponsor Debates," one of six points of view on that issue.

We have resolved our potential conflict of interest by committing ourselves to supporting this important project while stepping away from control over its contents or conclusions. As the book neared completion, select members of our board and staff read the entire manuscript to assure themselves that it was fair and accurate.

We found the book to be far more; we are proud to be associated with this effort. We believe that readers will find the book stimulating, informative, and highly useful.

Nancy M. Neuman
Chair, League of Women Voters Education Fund

ACKNOWLEDGMENTS

The authors who contributed essays to this volume gave their time and talent generously. They did so because they want to make the election process work. Without these contributors this book would not have been possible.

Victoria Harian, presidential debates director at the League of Women Voters Education Fund, gave life to this book and then worked endlessly to guarantee its quality and integrity. Her judgment, skill, and knowledge of debates were invaluable.

The John and Mary R. Markle Foundation, along with its talented program officer Larry Slesinger, strongly endorsed the need for this book and provided financial support that made work on the project possible.

Marjorie L. Share of ML SHARE Associates made some unique contributions. She has the ability and confidence to ask the basic questions that those too close to a subject somehow overlook. Her creativity improved the book throughout, and her solutions to several key problems kept the project moving forward.

Also essential were the friendship and support of Yvonne Zecca, Beth Laverty, Gwen Murphy, Odell Dehart, Mary Hughes, Maurice Mitchell, and Robert Pepper of the Annenberg Washington Program on Communications Policy Studies of Northwestern University.

Pat Hersch, an extremely skilled writer, editor, and researcher, contributed her talent, energy, and insight to this book. One day Pat's talents as an author will be known to a wide audience.

Kara McCollum of the League's presidential debates staff deserves special thanks for her painstaking research of the who, what, when, where, and how of broadcast presidential debates dating back to 1948.

At Congressional Quarterly Books, David Tarr, John Moore, Amy Meyers, and Carolyn McGovern helped improve this book from beginning to end. A special bow, very deep, to Carolyn, who made it all better and made it all happen during the final three months.

Research assistance from the following key people helped answer the big questions and fill in the bothersome holes: Colleen McMurray of the Gallup Poll, Mark Maynard of the Roper Center for Public Opinion Research, Phil Levy of Bridge Street Books (perhaps Washington, D.C.'s best bookstore), and Joe Palaia.

Thanks also for research help to the *Des Moines Register, Nashua Telegraph,* Nielsen Media Research, Chicago Bar Association, ABC News, CBS News, the University of Southern California, Emmanuel College, the John F. Kennedy School of Government at Harvard University, Dartmouth College, and WCHS-TV in Charleston, West Virginia.

Many people at the League of Women Voters deserve a special salute: Dorothy S. Ridings, chair of the LWVEF when the book was conceived; Nancy M. Neuman, current LWVEF chair; Rosalind McGee, LWVEF communications committee chair; Monica Sullivan, publications director; Cynthia Hill, election services and litigation director; Maureen Thornton, legal counsel; Grant Thompson, executive director; Margaret Davis, LWVEF trustee; and Stephanie Drea, communications director.

My parents, Irving and Gertrude Swerdlow, read drafts of the portions of this book that I wrote. Their comments and suggestions had a toughness and credibility that perhaps only parents can convey. Both are college professors, and their experience in guiding students has been a great asset to me.

Others whose special touch was appreciated include Carolyn Sachs, Karen Menichelli, and Joyce Fitz of the Benton Foundation; Norman Sherman; Bill d'Alelio; Claretha Webster; Brian H. Fitzgerald; Nathan and Genevieve Share; Sheldon O. Burman; Emily Angelides; Frank Mankiewicz; F. F. Baboo; Aaron B. Swerdlow; Harry Sommer; Rosalyn Mazer; Laurie Share; Roger and Sandy Harrison; James David Barber; Deborah Goldman; Marie Tessier; Wallace Westfeldt; Joe McLaughlin; and Barbara Kaplan.

In addition to those who worked directly on this book, I am indebted to several people who have led the way.

Newton Minow and Lee Mitchell have been working to promote and improve presidential debates for more than a decade. Their guidance, support, and wisdom have been essential to my work in the field.

M. J. Rossant of the Twentieth Century Fund supported my work on a 1984 report, *Beyond Debate,* which is in many ways the foundation upon which this present book is based.

James Karayn (now of Karayn & Company, Philadelphia) has also made his influence felt on everyone who thinks seriously about debates. Many of the ideas in this book, in particular the concept of a federally chartered debate commission, originated with Jim. He has done much of the hard work and creative thinking that many people now take for granted.

Sidney Kraus, author of the recent *Televised Presidential Debates and Public Policy,* has been writing and editing major studies of presidential debates since the early 1960s. All who have followed him respect the reliability of his work.

Part I

ISSUES AND IMPLICATIONS
OF POLITICAL DEBATES

1. THE STRANGE—AND SOMETIMES SURPRISING—HISTORY OF PRESIDENTIAL DEBATES IN AMERICA

Joel L. Swerdlow

New eras in presidential politics are rare, and their arrival is frequently a time of opportunity.

Such an era is beginning now: the era of debates. There will be more presidential debates in 1988 than have occurred since the writing of the U.S. Constitution. And the 1990s promise to bring even more.

The story of presidential debates is characterized by contradictions and false starts. That such debates did not emerge much earlier is surprising, given the nature of our democracy, our politics, and our communications technology. At the same time, many of the factors contributing to the new era are only tangentially related to debates. The story of these surprises and of the strange causal factors is fascinating—and useful. Only through understanding the past can we have realistic expectations about, and take full advantage of, what the new era offers.

Issue Debates

From our earliest days, Americans have loved to argue and to listen to arguments about public policy. Colonists debated during town meetings. Revolutionary leaders debated the shape of their new Constitution. Congress recorded discussions in its official *Debates and Proceedings*. Often these arguments were as much entertainment as they were politics, and they had so pervaded our culture by the 1830s that Alexis de Tocqueville wrote in *Democracy in America,*

> To take a hand in the regulation of society and to discuss it is his [an American's] biggest concern and, so to speak, the only pleasure an American knows. This feeling pervades the most trifling habits of life; even the women frequently attend public meetings and listen to political harangues as a recreation from their household labors. Debating clubs are, to a certain extent, a substitute for theatrical entertainments.

Tocqueville visited America during what is now called the golden age of congressional oratory. Congress did not yet have an effective committee system, so issue argumentation occurred on the floor. Robert Y. Hayne, Daniel Webster, Henry Clay, John C. Calhoun, and other great speech makers used eloquent arguments to sway their immediate audience. They spoke largely to people within immediate earshot. At times, the most advanced technology of the day did bring key speeches to the nation; after the Hayne-Webster debate, one newspaper equipped a ship with "frames and cases and type and compositors" to work through the night as it carried Daniel Webster's words to New England printing presses.

These debates bear little resemblance to what a modern audience would tolerate. To speak for days was not unusual, and debate involved complex propositions aimed at an elite, well-informed audience. In a typical example, the 1830 Hayne-Webster encounter (called the "Great Debate" throughout the nineteenth century) centered on Hayne's assertion

> That this Assembly doth explicitly and preemptarily declare, that it views the powers of the federal government, as resulting from the compact to which the States are parties, as limited by the plain sense and intention of the instrument constituting that compact, as no farther valid than they are authorized by the grants enumerated in that compact; and that, in case of a deliberate, palpable, and dangerous exercise of other powers not granted by the said compact, the States who are parties thereto have the right, and are in duty bound, to interpose for arresting the progress of the evil, and for maintaining, within their respective limits, the authorities, rights, and liberties appertaining to them.

Great oratory died with the Civil War. Major contributors to its demise were the spread of the franchise, the growth of mass circulation newspapers, and the development of machine politics. Some historians assert that great constitutional issues also disappeared.

An idealized vision of past oratory took hold. "Oratory is the parent of liberty," declared an early twentieth-century citizens' handbook. "It is in the interest of tyrants to cripple and debilitate every species of eloquence. They have no other safety. It is, then, the duty of free states to foster oratory." Schoolchildren read, memorized, and recited speeches. Families saved pennies and nickels to buy collections of great American orations.

Idealization of past oratorical excellence contributed to the unique American belief that "truth" will always somehow emerge from an open, aggressive exchange of views. And yet, this belief had little impact on America's political campaigns. From Locke and Hume to Jefferson and Madison there was no mention of the notion that democracy needed—or was even well served by—debates between candidates for public office. In subsequent generations, the thinkers and organizers who gave us political parties argued with great force and persuasiveness that party competition was necessary to inform the public, curtail apathy, minimize corruption, and promote healthy dialogue—and yet none ever claimed that democracy benefited when candidates debated. As generations passed, electoral reforms included the secret ballot, direct primary, recall, referendum, control over campaign contributions, and intraparty democracy—and still, no mention of campaign debates.

"Debate" remained largely an issue-oriented notion and not a device for either mass persuasion or election campaigning. Thus, a 1940s dictionary of American politics defined the word as something occurring in a "legislative assembly."

Debates in Nonpresidential Campaigns

Even though electoral competition was essential to the American political process from the beginning, American politicians did little campaigning. *Candi-*

date is derived from the Latin word *candidatus*, meaning "clothed in white," someone pure, above seeking votes.

In the late eighteenth century, when a few candidates dared to campaign, they usually did so at the risk of censure. Many newspapers condemned anyone who traveled around, in the words of a typical editorial, "for the purpose of inducing people to vote for him." Candidates, historian Samuel Eliot Morison notes in *The Oxford History of the American People*, "were supposed to play coy, obeying a call to service from their country, saving their energies for the task of government. Electioneering was done by newspapers, pamphlets, and occasional public meetings." Surrogates would sometimes debate each other at such meetings, if debating means appearing before the same audience at the same time. These events were usually billed as discussions of the issues, not arguments about who should be elected.

"Vote-for-me" campaigns became accepted in local and statewide elections during and following the Jacksonian era, although as late as 1847 in Pennsylvania—one of the most politically sophisticated states—newspapers complained loudly when gubernatorial candidates first delivered stump speeches.

Active campaigning soon evolved into the speaking tour. Travel was by steamboat, canal, and railroad. In addition to partisan rallies, political club meetings, and parades, candidates appeared at nonpolitical gatherings such as festivals, carnivals, barbecues, Fourth of July picnics, and church meetings. Political opponents would often meet at such events, speaking in turn. Rejoinders might be given if the crowd was interested.

Most candidates debated at one time or another; many also toured together, presenting a series of debates. This was particularly popular in the West and South where debates served more than just a political function. They often provided the year's most stimulating entertainment, as well as an opportunity for friends and relatives to socialize. In the South, the ultimate political debate—a duel using revolvers—was uncommon, yet real.

Debates, however, played neither a definitive nor an important role in the evolution of vote-for-me practices. They are most noteworthy, in fact, for their lack of impact and for the historical quirks they produced.

During the nation's first congressional elections, for example, two future presidents debated. James Madison and James Monroe were running against each other for a congressional seat from Virginia. Madison later described to a friend what happened:

> We used to meet in days of considerable excitement and address the people on our respective sides; but there *never was an atom of ill-will* between us. On one occasion we met . . . at church. Service was performed, then they had music with two fiddles. They [the congregation members] are remarkably fond of music. When it was all over we addressed these people, and kept them standing in the snow listening to the discussion of constitutional subjects. They stood it out very patiently—seemed to consider it a sort of fight of which they were required to be spectators. I then had to ride in the night, twelve miles to quarters; and got my nose frost-bitten.

The frostbite made more of an impression on Madison than did the debate. Indeed, cold weather was the reason for the Madison-Monroe confrontations. Both men suffered terribly from the cold as they toured the district. As longstanding friends, they decided to travel together—not to better inform the public—but to keep one another warm in the coach.

Throughout U.S. history, from colonial times to the age of television, only one of these encounters is not forgotten: the series of senatorial debates between Abraham Lincoln and Stephen Douglas in 1858. Putting these debates in context shows just how limited the "debate" notion was.

Lincoln and Douglas had their first major conflict in 1854. Lincoln was a former one-term House member. Douglas, the incumbent senator, had recently introduced the Kansas-Nebraska bill, which repealed the 1820 Missouri Compromise, thus shaking the nation's sense that the slavery question might somehow be avoided. Douglas toured Illinois to sell his constituents on the virtues of this new measure, and Lincoln took to the stump in opposition. Because Douglas was by far the more popular and drew larger crowds, Lincoln, in what was an unusual move, began to follow him around the state. Douglas spoke in Springfield during state fair week, for example, and Lincoln appeared the next day. Two weeks later, they met by agreement in Peoria. Douglas spoke in the afternoon, Lincoln in the evening.

In 1858, when they were senatorial opponents, Lincoln once again followed Douglas. Beginning with the Chicago speech opening Douglas's campaign, Lincoln often stood in the crowd watching Douglas, sometimes shouting out that a rebuttal would be delivered later that same day or the next day.

Various newspapers, depending on their partisan preference, ridiculed or defended Lincoln. The papers also created their own minidebates by printing excerpts from each of the candidate's speeches side by side. Live debates, however, did not seem to have been on anyone's mind.

Then Lincoln suggested to Douglas "an arrangement for you and myself to divide time, and address the same audiences." He did not say "to debate great issues," "to point out the differences in our opinions," or "to ask each other questions." He wanted to get out of the audience and onto the platform with Douglas.

Douglas had been irritated by Lincoln's tactics, and he knew from Republican party announcements that Lincoln intended to keep following him. This, as well as confidence in his own debating experience and skill, prompted Douglas to accept. Lincoln then wrote, "I shall be at no more of your exclusive meetings."

The Lincoln-Douglas debates are remembered for many reasons. They are, as debate specialist Lee Mitchell has pointed out, the first debates in an election with national significance. The debates addressed an issue—slavery—that was threatening to tear the nation apart. Newspapers, utilizing telegraph wires that made instantaneous communication possible, gave the debates a huge national audience. Lincoln went on to become a larger-than-life myth (no one refers to the Douglas-Lincoln debates). What is forgotten, however, is why the debates occurred in the first place: because they met the logistical and strategic needs of the candidates. Also forgotten is that the Lincoln-Douglas encounters were popular mostly because they were excellent theater, and not because what was said was particularly wise or revealing.

Even though historians report that an idealized "spectacle of debates captured the imaginations of the country," the Lincoln-Douglas debates sparked no debate era, no demand from the people or the press for more debates. Among politicians, the benefit to Lincoln—who nearly won the senatorial contest and went on to become president only twenty-four months later—of sharing a platform with a more popular incumbent was clear, as was the practical lesson: if you're ahead, why debate?

"After the Civil War," political scientist M. Ostrogorski noted in *Democracy and the Organization of Political Parties*, "the face-to-face debate, which enabled the citizen to grasp then and there the arguments pro and con presented by public men, disappeared almost entirely." Some debates did occur. Usually sponsorship was by local parties, and the format was roughly Lincoln-Douglas style. But these debates are memorable mostly for their social aspects.

The 1896 Tennessee gubernatorial race, for example, featured forty-one debates between the two major candidates. Tennessee history buffs remember this election not because of the debates, but because the opposing candidates were brothers. The brothers played fiddles and told stories and jokes. "The campaign was characterized by little that dealt with real issues," one local historian noted later. "The debates were pleasing, entertaining, and marked with dignity but were not profound. Everywhere the joint campaign took the form of social ritual." Like other debaters throughout the nineteenth century, the two candidates sometimes slept in the same bed while traveling in the back country.

One reason debates disappeared was that they were no longer needed. Debates had been largely a logistical convenience: travel was difficult for candidates and voters alike, and it simply made sense for opponents to appear together. As America became urbanized, and as railroads grew, logistics became less compelling. The slow emergence of an "objective" press, which promised to supply nonpartisan descriptions of what each candidate said, also made actually listening to the candidates seem less important. Indeed, politicians, newspaper editorialists, and civic reformers made no effort to institutionalize debates at any level or to convince the public that candidate debates were desirable—even though America experienced a growth in mass democracy during the last part of the nineteenth century.

Debates did experience a renaissance in the 1920s. Leading the way was the League of Women Voters, which was dismayed that after so much struggle to receive the franchise so few women actually voted. The League's national convention in 1921 discussed "a new kind of political meeting . . . which is more popular than the old fashioned political rally" that would help inform and energize female voters. By 1922, the League had sponsored candidate debates, including much-praised events in the Ohio and Indiana senatorial races. The League's national president called these debates "the dawn of a new kind of campaigning."

Challenging a frontrunner to debate became a popular technique. Indeed, the challenge often generated more attention than the debate itself. Robert Caro described in *Path to Power* what happened in the late 1930s, for example, when Lyndon B. Johnson was running for Congress:

> Whenever, during the campaign, his path had crossed Johnson's, he [Emmett Shelton, Johnson's opponent] had attempted to shame Johnson into debating him. Arriving in a town to find Johnson's campaign car there, he would park his own right alongside, and would use his loudspeaker to challenge

Johnson to debate. Johnson, aware of his weakness in debating, had refused to do so. In one particularly painful incident, Shelton had parked directly outside a store in which Johnson was shaking hands and had stayed there, blaring, over and over, a challenge to Johnson to come out and debate, for quite some time—and Johnson had not come out, refusing to leave the safety of the store until Shelton had driven away. Now, however, their paths crossed again—in Smithville on a Wednesday on which hundreds of farmers had come into town for a prize-drawing set up by the merchants—and, this time, when Shelton repeated the challenge, Johnson at last turned on his tormentor.

Johnson, according to witnesses, won the subsequent debate, during which each candidate spoke for about five minutes.

Such debates, as with most debates in American history, were quickly forgotten, except when a debater later became nationally prominent. A California member of Congress named Jerry Voorhis debated in 1936 and also participated in a series of 1946 encounters. The press, politicians, and public saw nothing noteworthy about these debates, which are remembered only because Voorhis's 1946 opponent was Richard Nixon. Nixon's successful debate tactics foreshadowed his later political techniques and helped to begin his climb to the White House.

Presidential Elections in the Pre-broadcast Era

Until recently, debates played an even less important role in campaigns for the nation's highest office. Indeed, the pre-Jacksonian notion of the noncampaigning candidate endured into the twentieth century. Candidates, by custom, could work full time writing letters, conducting private meetings, and cajoling, but could do little publicly.

During the nation's first contested presidential election, in 1800, candidates openly consented to letting others, including hired speakers, campaign for them. No special value was seen, however, in having these surrogates debate. Thus, what was probably the first presidential campaign debate happened by chance.

New York's presidential electors were selected by the state assembly, and control of that assembly came down to perhaps a dozen contested seats in New York City. The leader of New York Republicans (the present-day Democrats) was Aaron Burr, the party's vice-presidential candidate. A close friend of Burr's later wrote:

> It was understood that General [Alexander] Hamilton [leading spokesman for the Federalists] would personally attend the several polls during the three day election; that he would counsel and advise his political friends, and that he would address the people. Here again all seemed to feel that Colonel Burr was the man, and perhaps the only man, to meet General Hamilton on such an occasion.

The Federalist *Daily Advertiser,* reflecting popular beliefs of the time, lamented that a "would-be Vice President could stoop so low as to visit every corner in search of voters." When Hamilton and Burr met by chance at polling places, they debated. Little record of these encounters exists.

Burr's activities did nothing to shake the anticampaigning tradition: would-be presidents had to remain decorously closelipped. This is one reason why none of America's famous orators ever became president. Men such as Webster, Calhoun, and Clay, whose eloquence permeates America's history books, could not speak on their own behalf when running for president. The great congressional orators had another disadvantage—one that is relevant to understanding the behavior of today's presidential debate participants. Because these orators had made their views known on important, controversial issues, they were unable to hide behind the vagueness necessary for success in national elections. Their lack of electoral success, of course, was part of a larger phenomenon. The great orators of this era were congressional leaders, and no one in the nineteenth century—and so far in the twentieth—moved directly from a position of congressional leadership to the presidency.

Few people argued that presidential candidates should speak out. Indeed, their silence was often considered a strategic necessity. In 1836, for example, a prominent political leader wrote of Whig nominee William Henry Harrison, a retired general with little experience in the public arena:

> [Let him] say not one single word about his principles or his creed, let him say nothing—promise nothing. Let no Committee, no Convention, no town meeting ever extract from him a single word about what he thinks now and will do hereafter. Let use of pen and ink be wholly forbidden as if he were a mad poet in Bedlam.

Harrison lost, but four years later did become the first presidential candidate to "take to the stump" and openly advocate his own election. His subsequent victory, however, was attributable not to these speeches but to a split among the Democrats.

Even though the nation was somewhat startled at the sight of Harrison asking for votes, the public began to expect that a presidential candidate would at least say something about his positions on key issues. In 1856, for example, Republican Thaddeus Stevens said about the soon-to-be-elected Democratic presidential nominee, "There is no such person running as James Buchanan. He is dead of Lockjaw."

The remainder of the century, however, saw only two major presidential vote-for-me efforts. In 1860 Stephen Douglas toured the country (the tours started under the guise of a trip to New England to visit his mother; Lincoln did not make one campaign speech in 1860). More than a quarter of a century later, in 1896, Democratic nominee William Jennings Bryan traveled 18,000 miles delivering speeches. Bryan's Republican opponent, William McKinley, rejected advice that he, too, go on a speaking tour. "I have to think when I speak," McKinley explained.

McKinley stayed home on his front porch, but what he did there was far more significant than a speaking tour would have been: he promoted the notion that even a stay-at-home candidate must actively engage in vote-for-me activities. McKinley delivered up to sixteen speeches a day to crowds estimated as large as 30,000. Margaret Leech's *In the Days of McKinley* described the scene:

> [E]xcursionists carried to all parts of the country enthusiastic reports of the Republican candidate. They had been right close to him, they had shaken his hand. They had seen him in his setting, and it was exactly right—the friendly town; the neat, unpretentious house and the porch hung with trumpet vines; and

the First Methodist Church where McKinley worshiped with his mother every Sunday. Many of the visitors saw the dear old mother, sitting beside her son or rocking on her own front porch. Many saw and stared at the invalid wife.

Bryan ran again in 1900, prompting historian Charles Francis Adams, Jr., to describe him as "a talking machine, he can set his mouth in action, and go away and leave it, sure that it will not stop until he returns." McKinley, now the incumbent, gave himself permission not to campaign; Vice President Theodore Roosevelt, feeling "as strong as a bull moose," traveled extensively.

McKinley's attitude—that the best strategy for an incumbent president is to remain presidential—has been followed by most of his successors even though many present-day commentators seem to believe that the presidential stay-at-home technique—often called the Rose Garden strategy—is something new. Television and Madison Avenue selling techniques have in many ways isolated incumbent presidents from the pressures and dangers of campaigning, but this is merely further development of stay-at-home tendencies that have always been present. Incumbent presidents have openly and aggressively campaigned mostly when in trouble (for example, Herbert Hoover in 1932, Harry S Truman in 1948, and Gerald R. Ford in 1976), or when they wanted to roll up a huge majority (for example, Lyndon Johnson in 1964). Otherwise, they follow a strategy of minimal exposure to voter and press scrutiny. When asked to respond to his opponent's criticisms in the late summer of 1940, for example, Franklin D. Roosevelt responded, "I don't know nothin' about politics."

It is logical to believe, however, that the American public would have welcomed debates as presidential candidates started campaigning. Bryan-McKinley confrontations, for example, could have drawn hundreds of thousands of people and could have clearly delineated the basic issues—such as which economic classes should be the principal beneficiaries of federal policies—that still define American politics. But when presidential candidates met or came close to meeting during campaigns, the country's press and opinion makers—in sharp contrast to their present-day attitudes—encouraged nonconfrontational gentlemanly demeanor. In 1896, for example, Bryan visited Canton, Ohio, site of McKinley's front porch. Bryan stayed away, even though a large group of his supporters left his rally to pay McKinley a courtesy call. In 1912 Theodore Roosevelt and William Howard Taft, locked in a bitter and emotional battle for Republican convention delegates, passed through the same town yet avoided each other. That fall, incumbent Taft and Democratic challenger Woodrow Wilson stayed, by chance, in the same Boston hotel at the same time. They met for a friendly, nonpolitical chat. During the 1936 presidential campaign, Franklin D. Roosevelt and his Republican opponent, Kansas governor Alf Landon, participated in a governors' conference in Iowa. They earned praise from the press for treating each other with great courtesy and for not mentioning their differences.

Presidential Elections: The Broadcast Era

Less than a decade after World War I, radio was broadcasting national political conventions, and paid and unpaid political speeches. Issue debates between civic leaders were also regularly scheduled, highly popular radio programs. Face-to-face encounters between presidential candidates would have been easy to stage, yet the history of radio yields only a few references to the possibility of such debates. During the 1936 presidential campaign, Republican senator Arthur Vandenberg of Michigan, who was not his party's presidential nominee, staged a fake radio debate with recordings of Franklin D. Roosevelt's speeches; and in 1940, Republican presidential nominee Wendell Willkie challenged FDR to a series of debates on "fundamental issues." FDR simply ignored the challenge at no political cost because the press—and presumably the public—regarded the proposed debates as a ploy by a far-behind underdog. One radio debate did occur. In 1948 Republicans Harold Stassen and Thomas E. Dewey debated during the Oregon primary in a radio broadcast that attracted between 40 and 80 million listeners. Yet there was no demand for—or serious suggestion of—a radio debate in the subsequent Dewey-Truman general election.

The absence of radio debates is especially noticeable because a simple rule has guided the relationship between the broadcast media (radio and, later, television) and presidential campaigns: once something becomes technically feasible, it is quickly done. This has held true for coverage of national conventions, campaign events, and election returns, and for the use of paid time for partisan messages. Debates are the only major exception.

Of course, a change of the "equal time" law or in Federal Communications Commission (FCC) regulations would have been needed for radio debates to take place, but there is no evidence of public desire for such a change. Few people took seriously the notion that a president or would-be president should perform live over the air under adversarial circumstances. And, as in the past, politicians found it in their interest to avoid delineation of issue positions. Issue fuzziness was the best way to build electoral coalitions. "Every one takes part," Henry Adams wrote a friend during the 1884 presidential campaign, describing a phenomenon that has remained valid. "We are all doing our best, and swearing at each other like demons. But the amusing thing is that no one talks about real interests. By common consent they agree to let these pass. We are afraid to discuss them."

Underdogs, however, have always wanted to share the airwaves with incumbents, much as Lincoln had wanted to join Douglas on the platform. Thus, in 1944, the Republican party bought time for a radio address directly following time purchased for FDR. It was not a presidential campaign debate, but voters could sit back and listen to supporters of two principal candidates for president provide back-to-back explanations of why their choice deserved votes.

Television debates, however, did arrive right on schedule. In early May 1952 most major Democratic and Republican contenders made a joint appearance—broadcast live to a national radio and television audience—in front of the League of Women Voters' annual convention. In 1956 Estes Kefauver and Adlai Stevenson met in a nationally broadcast debate during the Democratic primaries. At the 1960 Democratic convention, John F. Kennedy and Lyndon B. Johnson debated in front of a joint session of the Massachusetts and Texas delegations, and a national television audience. And in the fall of 1960—the first general election in which television was the dominant national medium—the Kennedy-Nixon debates occurred.

That presidential debates took place in 1960, however, had little to do with debates per se and much to do with unique circumstances. In 1960 each of the major candidates had reasons to want to use television's enormous audience for his own purposes. Broadcasters wanted to carry debates as part of a larger effort to demonstrate that they were civic-minded and did not need federal regulation. Many debate advocates, frustrated and angered by commercial dominance of America's airways, saw debates as one way—and far from the most attractive way—to elicit free air time from the networks. And many people, dissatisfied with how America conducted its presidential campaigns, saw face-to-face debates as part of a larger reform. Thus Stevenson, who as the 1956 Democratic nominee had thought debates were a gimmick, wrote in early 1960:

> I would like to propose that we transform our stumbling, fumbling, presidential campaign into a great debate, conducted in full view of all the people. Suppose that every Monday evening at peak viewing time, for an hour and a half, from Labor Day until election eve, the two candidates aired their views. They might on each evening take up a single issue. Each in turn might discuss it for a half hour, followed by rebuttal of one another for the third half hour. There are other possibilities, including face-to-face debate. But the central idea is that, in some manner, the principal figures, the candidates for president, appear together at the same prime time each week for a serious presentation of views on public questions. The time should cost them and their parties nothing.

The 1960 presidential debates generated high expectations. Debate planners, acutely aware of the Lincoln-Douglas glamour, wanted to initiate what they saw as "the TV debate era," when televised debates would be a fixture in presidential campaigns. To have presidential candidates meet face to face in front of the entire nation seemed—and was—nothing less than revolutionary. The optimism that accompanied this revolution was part of an idealism that surrounded television in general. In the early 1960s people still expected television to "ring with intelligence and leadership."

There was good reason to believe the debate era had indeed arrived. Throughout the 1960s television increasingly dominated all other aspects of the campaign. Partisan loyalties and political machines were dissolving, making the ever-nebulous "public opinion" an all-important determinant of electoral results. Democratization of the electorate—most notably, the addition of blacks and young people to voter rolls—greatly expanded the made-for-TV political audience. Intraparty democracy, in the form of more and increasingly contested primary elections, opened fertile ground for prenomination debates; indeed, Democratic would-be nominees met in 1968 and 1972.

Television itself, furthermore, encouraged a demand for debates by the very way it presented news and public affairs programs: every issue was depicted as always having two equal sides, covered one after the other, on roughly equal terms. One public official would say a tax increase was needed; another would say it would be a disaster. One person would advocate changes in the nation's civil rights laws; another would say that action should be left to each state. The implicit message, copied by major newspapers, which began to feature "issue debates" on their op-ed pages, was powerful: the way to learn about public affairs is to see both sides. Public affairs discussion is adversarial, with winners and losers.

Yet the presidential debate era failed to appear: no more general-election presidential debates occurred until the middle of the next decade.

This hiatus in debates from 1960 to 1976 is most directly attributable to the equal-time provisions of the Communications Act of 1934. But Congress was free at any time during those years to eliminate or suspend these provisions, just as the FCC was free to do what it eventually did in 1976: issue administrative rulings permitting broadcast presidential debates by sidestepping equal-time rules.

Public opinion polls continued to show strong public support for presidential debates. Yet this support never translated into an organized or vocal demand for presidential debates.

No general-election presidential debates took place for sixteen years for one simple reason: in 1964, 1968, and 1972, the frontrunner did not want to share an audience with his opponent.

The Age of Debates

The age of debates has evolved slowly over the past decade, but the evidence of its permanence is inescapable.

At the state and local level, more candidates have been debating much more often. Exact statistics have not been compiled, and much of the evidence is anecdotal, but it is impressive. A 1986 National Association of Broadcasters study found that "virtually all congressional candidates debated their opponents." In the 1986 Dallas mayoral election, candidates reportedly met more than sixty times. And on popular television entertainment programs, even judicial candidates debated.

Presidential debates have developed more slowly, just as presidential campaigning itself lagged behind. In 1976 a unique set of circumstances—an unelected incumbent; an unknown majority party challenger; a few key individuals such as Charles Benton, who funded early debate organizing efforts; and an organization, the League of Women Voters, which provided the necessary impartial organizational framework—helped produce presidential debates. Such debates recurred in 1980 and 1984. Debates, furthermore, now permeate the presidential nomination process. Joint candidate appearances begin more than six months before the first primary, and prospective nominees of the two major parties debate each other, as do would-be First Ladies.

Our idealized visions of a golden past—the great oratorical debates, the Lincoln-Douglas debates, and the aura of the 1960 Kennedy-Nixon encounters—obviously contributed to the current age of debates. But the causes of the age of debates have been complex.

• By the mid-1970s, the nation was entering a period of healing. Presidential debates had disappeared in the 1960s and early 1970s, precisely when America was fighting its most bitter, bloody, and divisive foreign war. By 1975 the Vietnam War was over, the Watergate scandals had been resolved by presidential resignation, and debates promised to be much less passionate—and less threatening to the established order—than they would have been in the 1960s.

• Technology has made possible—and encouraged—an increase in the debate-oriented approach to political campaigns. The *Congressional Quarterly Weekly Report* noted in late 1985, "The technology to produce commercials fast enough to stimulate a debate [has arrived]. One day's set of TV ads for one candidate was followed soon after by his opponent's set of counterads, and the process repeated several times in an intricate series of tactical moves."

Congressional Quarterly called this "instant response politics."

● New technology is also making a variety of debates less expensive and easier to distribute. In mid-1987, for example, some presidential candidates organized a debate in Iowa and then bought satellite time to bounce their confrontation directly to interested local broadcast stations and to a roomful of political journalists gathered in Washington, D.C. Total cost was $11,000. Satellite transmission of television and radio programs, in the meantime, has prompted a number of programs in which members of Congress debate an issue for about sixty seconds each. Such programs can now be seen or heard in virtually every media market. This builds upon television's "two equal sides" approach to news, further solidifying the public's expectation that debates are the way to hear public policy discussed.

● A growing deregulatory mood in America—feelings only indirectly related to debates—has prompted the weakening and dissolution of federal equal-time restraints on the broadcast of debates. Until 1975, no broadcast station could carry a debate unless every candidate for that office was included or received equal time; until 1983, no broadcast station could host a debate. Now broadcast stations are free to do what they want within narrowly defined confines of fairness.

● Television coverage of the U.S. House of Representatives and Senate has inspired and sharpened debate. Unlike Hayne, Webster, and other great congressional orators of the past, today's legislators can—and must—speak directly to the public at large. Dramatic statements and subtly staged confrontations have become common. The result: still another reason for voters, journalists, and public officials themselves to believe that political dialogue should be in the "debate" mode.

● To sponsor a debate is to receive extraordinary media attention, so a wide variety of organizations—from newspapers to universities—now try to sponsor presidential confrontations. Likewise, candidates know that talking about debates, issuing challenges to debate, and best of all, actually organizing a debate, are sure ways to augment campaign coverage.

● Intraparty reforms since the early 1970s, by spawning primaries and caucuses, have created fertile ground for debating—especially since the public now expects all would-be presidents to campaign for their party's nomination. The last time a major party convention selected someone who had not actively sought the nomination was 1952; since then, there has been at least one prenomination debate in every election except 1964.

● As presidential candidates increasingly opt for a "selling-of-the-president" strategy that keeps the president hidden behind controlled media exposure, and as the campaign press conference atrophies, debates have become the prime vehicle through which journalists can ask questions. Thus, the news media have become—perhaps somewhat subconsciously—proponents of debates. New corporate concerns about newsgathering costs are also pro-debate. It is much cheaper to cover a debate than to travel around with a candidate.

Given the present ascendancy of campaign debates, there is every reason to believe that they will continue to flourish. Presidential candidates, always concerned with what historian Arthur M. Schlesinger, Jr., in *The Coming to Power* calls "competition for visibility," will find it more and more difficult to reject the huge national audience that debates offer. Candidates will also increasingly use debates as an excuse to avoid something they invariably hate: frantic cross-country trips. Preparing for a debate and reaching voters via a debate are perfect excuses to stay home.

Television technology, in turn, will continue to encourage debates simply because it makes reaching so large an audience so easy. The ultimate proof of how technology drives debates is that other democracies with political and campaign traditions unlike our own are now turning to televised "American-style" presidential debates. In Great Britain, for example, the most recent parliamentary election began with a challenge that candidates for prime minister debate on television.

Debates will also flourish because the issue of whether broadcasters should be required to provide presidential candidates with free air time will remain very much alive. Considerable support for free air time currently exists in Congress and the nation as a whole. Reformers will press for dramatically enlarged debates, probably modeled after practices in other countries, where a candidate gets free time one evening and the opponent gets equal time to answer the next evening. The first candidate then gets additional time the third evening, and so on. Also attractive to reformers will be the notion that debates can be relied upon as an antidote to 30-second TV commercials.

At the same time, forces that will change presidential debates—and the debate process—are clearly at work. Debates are now the only major campaign device that invariably favors the underdog. This characteristic alone will prompt frontrunners to manipulate debates into minimal events that will satisfy the press and the public.

The increase in independent and cable channels, furthermore, will give viewers many choices other than debates. The potential impact of this on fall presidential debates is significant. One of the most extraordinary things about debates is that tens of millions of voters have watched them and then decided not to vote. No one knows how much of this consistently extraordinary debate audience has been the product of "roadblocking," or showing a debate on all three major broadcast networks.

Audience slippage—in 1980 millions of households switched to a movie on ABC rather than watch the Ronald Reagan-John Anderson debate—could force debates to become "better television." They could be made more compelling, more visually stimulating with computer graphics to highlight candidate arguments, and perhaps could even become more dangerous for the candidates.

On the other hand, debates may move in the opposite direction. Growing dissatisfaction with presidential campaigns, the feeling that reform has unnecessarily lengthened and complicated the nomination process, and the widespread belief that campaigns generate little useful information, may force debate planners to devise events that help convince citizens that rational choices do indeed exist. The solution here might be debate formats which permit more thoughtful, lengthy presentations of candidate positions.

No matter which way debates go, improvements are not hard to imagine. Adlai Stevenson's 1960 proposal—which had been developed in the mid-1950s by

Newton Minow and other Stevenson aides—remains sound, insightful, and well worth a try in 1988. Why shouldn't major party nominees meet at least once a week on television to "discuss the great issues of the day"?

Change is certain. Television simply does not respect its own traditions. Every major area of the television-politics relationship—commercials, political convention coverage, press conferences, reportage of election-night returns—has been altered significantly since the advent of TV. Only presidential debates, at least so far, have remained the same.

As the next phase of presidential debates evolves, the crucial question is not whether we are for or against debates. They are inevitable. But it is essential to have realistic expectations. Looking for too much from debates can cause unnecessary confusion and disappointment.

Throughout American history, great and compelling issues have only rarely been addressed—let alone clearly delineated—during presidential campaigns. Debates cannot breathe life into an idealized past that never existed.

To avoid use of the word *debate*, furthermore, is not useful. Some people still want to call these events "joint discussions," because they are not "true debates."

Again, an idealized past serves as a poor guide. We have never had "true debates" for major office in this country. Lincoln and Douglas had no mutual interrogations, no sharp give-and-take. They took turns giving long speeches to the same audience. We call these encounters debates, as did the public at the time, because the name "the Lincoln-Douglas joint discussions" has no zing.

Debates, if not overused, do offer great practical opportunities. They give lesser known candidates a chance to be heard. They create new opportunities for discussion of the issues. They generate free air time for the candidates. But most importantly, they can make a profound contribution to the health of our democracy.

Writing in the late nineteenth century, scholar James Bryce noted in *The American Commonwealth* that "for three months [during U.S. presidential campaigns] processions, usually with brass bands, flags, badges, crowds of cheering spectators, are the order of the day and night from end to end of the country." These civic rituals somehow went to the heart of America, a nation that uniquely defined—and defines—itself by its political institutions.

The processions Bryce described no longer exist. Politics, particularly presidential politics, has gone indoors. "Three people in front of a television is a political rally," one campaign professional recently noted. But this shift has not changed the need for periodic civic rituals, part serious, part emotional, and part fakery, but in their totality an unabashed bow—however theatrical—to democracy and the sovereign will of the people. That is, in their own way, what debates have become.

2. LEGAL ISSUES SURROUNDING TELEVISED PRESIDENTIAL DEBATES

Charles M. Firestone

Since the beginnings of broadcasting, two overriding and sometimes conflicting constitutional concerns have shaped the laws, regulations, court decisions, and academic commentary affecting presidential debates. The first is integrity of the electoral process: legally qualified candidates should be treated fairly and equally under the law. The second is the First Amendment. Any legal scheme that affects broadcasters' editorial discretion has serious implications for their freedom of speech and press.

The Laws Affecting Broadcasting

In the late 1980s we find ourselves enmeshed in an active reexamination of the treatment of broadcasters under the First Amendment. That amendment provides, of course, that Congress shall make no law abridging the freedoms of speech or press. If this certain-sounding language were absolute, however, we would be unable to enforce laws against extortion, blackmail, obscenity, or incitements to riot. Accordingly, courts often balance First Amendment rights against other societal interests, particularly when electronic media are involved.

Because relatively few frequencies are available for broadcast use, and because simultaneous use of the same or nearby frequencies in the same locality will cause electromagnetic interference, Congress has long regulated such use by means of a licensing scheme. This scheme is one of the nation's greatest restrictions on the freedom of the press.

Court decisions in 1923 and 1926 determined that the government lacked authority to restrict broadcasters to particular channels or hours. The ensuing havoc prompted broadcasters themselves to call for congressional regulation and resulted in an entirely new regulatory regime under the Radio Act of 1927.

Congress established a Federal Radio Commission that could limit the number of broadcast licenses in each locality so as to minimize electromagnetic interference. The commission also could select "licensees" for these few frequencies according to the "public interest, convenience, and necessity." Since not all those

The author wishes to acknowledge the help and research assistance of Neil Anapol, UCLA Law School class of 1988.

who wanted a frequency to disseminate their viewpoints or other speech could be granted a license, those selected would be considered public trustees. This contemplated a rather extensive regulatory regime for the broadcasters' operations.

Congress feared the monopolistic powers inherent in broadcast media and the potential for their discriminatory treatment of political candidates. Its solution was the equal opportunities rule. In final form, Section 18 of the Radio Act read,

> If any licensee shall permit any person who is a legally qualified candidate for any public office to use a broadcasting station, he shall afford equal opportunities to all other such candidates for that office in the use of such broadcasting station, and the licensing authority shall make rules and regulations to carry this provision into effect: *Provided,* that such licensee shall have no power of censorship over the material broadcast under the provisions of this paragraph. No obligation is hereby imposed upon any licensee to allow the use of its station by any such candidate.

Congress recodified this language as Section 315 of the enlarged Communications Act in 1934 and transferred the powers of the Federal Radio Commission to the newly created Federal Communications Commission (FCC). Section 315 applied to all broadcasting stations—radio and, later, television.

FCC Interpretation of Section 315: Is a Debate a "Use"?

In applying the congressional directive for "equal opportunities" in broadcast political campaigns, the FCC had to interpret various elements of the statutory language. Who is a "legally qualified candidate"? What are "equal opportunities"? Who is another candidate for that office? Most significantly for our purposes, what is a "use" of a broadcast facility?

Under Section 315 of the Communications Act, only a use triggers "equal opportunities." Thus, if a debate were a use, and if the debate were carried at no cost to the candidates, then the station would have to provide equal amounts of time to each opponent excluded from the debate. And if this were the case, obviously some broadcasters would be inhibited from carrying a debate among fewer than all legally qualified candidates for a particular office for fear of numerous requests for equal opportunities. These decisions, then, placed the constitutional interest in fair treatment of candidates in conflict with the broadcasters' freedom of the press.

It was important that the federal agency charged with enforcing this law avoid either a political slant or undue infringement on First Amendment rights, whether that of the candidate, broadcaster, or the public at large. Accordingly, early FCC interpretations were rather rigid. The FCC considered any candidate's appearance, in recognizable voice or picture, a use of a broadcast facility, triggering equal opportunities to all other candidates for the same office. The only exception was a 1957 decision involving incidental inclusion of a candidate in a newscast. But this was reversed in 1959 when a minor candidate for mayor of Chicago named Lar Daly was allowed equal opportunity to respond to 21 seconds of news coverage of incumbent mayor Richard Daley's meeting with the president of Argentina at Midway Airport.

Few, if any, FCC decisions generated the storm of congressional controversy that ensued after *Lar Daly*. Broadcasters claimed that an equal-opportunity application to news coverage of individual candidates would "chill" their editorial discretion. How could they interview a candidate on "Meet the Press"? What about coverage of the political nominating conventions? Fearing that *Lar Daly* would end broadcast political coverage during election years, Congress acted quickly to carve out news-type exemptions from Section 315 equal-opportunity obligations.

In its original form, the 1959 measure exempted newscasts, news interviews, news documentaries, on-the-spot coverage of news events, and panel discussions. Of the five exemptions, panel discussions engendered the most objections. One senator argued, for example, that it could have mischievous effects in states with de facto one-party government. Since the real race in such states occurs in the primary, and the primary often includes many viable candidates, discretion over whom to invite for a panel discussion would give broadcasters considerable influence over the election. Congress removed the panel-discussions exemption from the final measure and included a proviso to the news-documentary exemption that the candidate's appearance be incidental to the presentation of the subjects covered by the news documentary. Also, the words *bona fide* were added to each of the exemptions to further limit the categories of exempted broadcasts.

Left unanswered by the legislative history of the 1959 amendment, however, was the status of political debates. Panel discussions came the closest to debates, and that exemption was eliminated before passage.

The 1959 amendment to Section 315, then, was an attempt by Congress to balance the previously strict dictates for equal treatment of candidates, on the one hand, with First Amendment interests in unfettered broadcast news coverage on the other.

Due to the uncertain status of political debates under the 1959 amendment, however, the networks were unwilling to air major party presidential debates or other such limited coverage of the 1960 election if they had to provide equal time to perhaps fifteen to twenty other presidential candidates.

As a compromise from an earlier proposal in the Senate to force prime-time coverage of the candidates, and in response to the networks' pleas for a free hand to conduct responsible coverage of the election, Congress completely suspended the equal-opportunities provision of Section 315 for the 1960 presidential and vice-presidential campaigns after the party nominations. The Great Debates of 1960 resulted.

After the 1960 election, however, the FCC returned to enforcing Section 315. In a series of decisions over the next twelve years, beginning with two 1962 rulings, the commission consistently held that political debates were not exempt from equal-opportunities requirements.

A broadcaster could still conduct joint interviews or debates with only two candidates but was then required to offer other candidates equal time. This principle came to a head in the 1972 Democratic presidential primary election. All three television networks broadcast joint interviews of the major candidates, George McGovern and Hubert Humphrey, just before the crucial California primary, to the exclusion of less popular candidates Shirley Chisholm and Sam Yorty.

The FCC ruled that the programs came within the news-interview exemption to Section 315. The decision was released June 2, 1972, only four days before the primary. Representative Chisholm immediately appealed to the U.S. Court of Appeals in Washington, D.C. In a unique decision based on emergency arguments presented that same day, the D.C. Circuit granted Chisholm "interim relief," ordering a reluctant FCC to grant her relief under Section 315.

The *Chisholm* matter came before the commission not too long after the FCC had proposed to Congress that it modify Section 315 to apply equal opportunities only to major candidates in general elections. In *Chisholm*, FCC chairman Dean Burch issued a concurring statement, supported by a majority of the commission, indicating displeasure with the court's interim order. Burch suggested that the constitutional balance should begin to swing more to the side of journalistic discretion.

> Equal opportunities does not *get* free time for the Vegetarian or Socialist Workers or other "fringe" parties. As a practical matter, it just *inhibits* presentations of the major party candidates. . . . The only loser is the public. . . .
>
> And that, in the end, is what really is at issue: not the rights of any particular candidate but rather, the overriding right of the American electorate to be informed.

Burch's concurrence signaled a shift in FCC attitude toward the exemptions—a greater willingness to trust in broadcast journalists and a less literal reading of the legislative history.

In 1975 the Aspen Institute Program on Communications, represented by former FCC general counsel and Burch's former special assistant Henry Geller, sought FCC revision of its policies concerning joint appearances of political candidates. In particular, the institute wanted the FCC to declare that political debates came within the 1959 exemption for "on the spot coverage of bona fide news events."

In an unusual agency reversal, the 1975 FCC overturned its 1962 decisions, finding that those earlier decisions had erroneously interpreted the legislative history of the 1959 amendment to Section 315 and the 1960 suspension of Section 315.

The commission found that Congress had passed the 1959 amendment "to foster public consideration of major candidates while assuring minor candidates access to reasonable opportunities for air time." By departing from its prior opinions, the commission crowed, "we can aid the broadcaster in rendering a most unique public service—bringing a political debate 'live into the home of every interested voter.' "

On appeal, the D.C. Circuit affirmed the FCC by a 2-1 vote, but the renowned First Amendment jurist, J. Skelly Wright, dissented. He argued that the FCC was substituting its own judgment for that of Congress. In other words, while the commission had by then come to the conclusion that the balance of constitutional concerns lay in freeing broadcasters to cover political debates without the inhibitions of Section 315, Judge Wright asserted that Congress had not yet made that choice. But the commission prevailed and the Supreme Court declined to hear an appeal.

Interpreting the Debates Exemption

Under the *Aspen* ruling the new exemption required a debate by legally qualified candidates, appearing in a bona fide news event, initiated by nonbroadcast entities, and covered live and in its entirety. Since 1976 the FCC has issued a number of decisions interpreting these elements.

1. *A debate.* A debate, according to the commission, is "a regulated discussion of a proposition between two matched sides."

2. *Legally qualified candidates.* The debates pose no unique problem here. One must meet the minimum legal qualifications for the office, declare candidacy, secure a place on the ballot, or publicly commit to seek election by write-in and wage a substantial write-in campaign.

3. *Bona fide news event.* The commission defers to the broadcaster's reasonable, independent, good faith journalistic judgment that an event is newsworthy. Obviously, the broadcaster's intent must be unbiased.

4. *Initiated by nonbroadcast entities.* Initially the commission took the position that on-the-spot coverage of a bona fide news event could not include an event sponsored by the broadcaster itself, and until 1981 the agency even required that the debates not take place in a broadcaster's studio. But in 1983 the FCC loosened the rules and allowed broadcasters to sponsor debates, with the hope that this would increase the number of broadcast debates.

5. *Covered live and in its entirety.* Until 1983 the FCC held that a news event included an element of timeliness. Accordingly, a rebroadcast after more than a day, absent unusual circumstances, removed a debate from the exemption category. In 1983 the commission deleted the requirement of simultaneity altogether, reasoning that more voters could see the debates if the events could be replayed later. To qualify under the news *event* category, however, the debate still had to be carried in its entirety. Taped excerpts during a newscast would not come under the news event exemption but would fall within the bona fide newscast exemption. An edited version of the debate, however, would not qualify.

The Fairness Doctrine

Section 315 also contains a sentence that the four news-type exemptions do not relieve broadcasters from their obligations to provide contrasting viewpoints on issues of public import. This language alludes to the FCC's Fairness Doctrine, (whose fate is in litigation as of this writing), which required reasonable (not equal) opportunity for the presentation of contrasting viewpoints on controversial issues of public importance. This doctrine, then, could be viewed as a safety valve to assure the public that all responsible points of view are aired during an election.

The commission has ruled that, under the doctrine, excluded candidates may have contrasting viewpoints to offer on the issue of who should be elected, but candidates themselves are not controversial issues. This means, the commission explained, that broadcasters have great discretion as to how to present various viewpoints: "Since a broadcaster need present only *significant* contrasting views on any particular issue, he need only make a reasonable, good faith judgment on the significance of a particular candidate and, on this basis, decide how much coverage, *if any*, should be given to his or her candidacy and campaign activities." *John W. Spring* (1986).

This FCC argument is part of a broad deregulating effort. During the Reagan years, the FCC has been at the forefront of deregulatory activity. It proposed to Congress's deaf ears the abolition of all program-related regulation, including Section 315 and the Fairness Doctrine. In 1985 the commission opined that the Fairness Doctrine was unconstitutional due to its alleged chilling effect on broadcasters' rights of free press. In 1986 Judge Robert Bork, writing for a three-judge panel of the United States Court of Appeals, held that the Fairness Doctrine was not mandated under the Communications Act. In reaction, Congress tried to codify the doctrine in 1987, but President Reagan vetoed the bill. The FCC thereafter abolished the doctrine completely, engendering strong reactions in Congress, and appeals to the courts by disgruntled citizen groups.

Thus with this deregulatory philosophy, the commission of the 1980s has plodded in one direction: from requiring equal treatment of all legally qualified candidates to recognizing the value of deregulated, unrestrained broadcaster discretion—including the freedom to air bona fide candidate debates with no legal restraint.

Corporate Support of Debates

When the FCC's *Aspen Institute* case opened the doors for televised presidential debates in 1976, the League of Women Voters Education Fund sought to sponsor candidate debates in both the primary and general elections. These debates cost hundreds of thousands of dollars, however, and the Education Fund, a tax-exempt organization, needed to raise the money. Two sections of the Federal Election Campaign Act (FECA) affected League sponsorship: (1) the act prohibits certain expenditures by tax-exempt organizations for the purpose of "influencing a federal election" 2 U.S.C. § 431(e); and (2) corporations and labor organizations cannot make contributions or expenditures (directly or indirectly) "in connection with" federal elections. 2 U.S.C. § 441(b). When the League wanted to accept funds from corporations, labor unions, and foundations to defray the expenses of the debates, questions arose as to whether sponsoring a debate came within the concept of influencing an election, whether corporate and union contributions to the sponsoring organization were "in connection with" a federal campaign, and more broadly what rights or restrictions applied to media organizations, most of which are corporations, in sponsoring or airing presidential debates.

In response to a League inquiry, the general counsel of the Federal Election Commission (FEC) explained that the League violated none of the applicable statutes in sponsoring a series of candidate discussions at the primary level. Since the League invited all the candidates to debate, there was no question as to whether it was supporting a particular candidate or party. Thus corporate and union contributions to the League were allowed. The commission's general counsel, however, distinguished these primaries from the general election, when the League sought to sponsor only debates between President Gerald R. Ford and Governor Jimmy Carter, thereby excluding Eugene McCarthy (on the ballot in twenty-nine states) and several minor party candidates. In that situation, he stated, the debates were not partisan activities—that is, not contributions intended to influence a federal election—and thus the League could sponsor them. But the expenditures were nonetheless made "in connection with" a federal election. Therefore corporations and labor unions could not indirectly sponsor the debates by contributing funds to the League. Only contributions from individuals and unincorporated associations could be used for the projects.

Review of this FEC determination by the U.S. District Court for the District of Columbia resulted in a stipulation of dismissal and a commission promise to issue new regulations.

Over the next three years the FEC considered various proposals concerning sponsorship and format of candidate debates. Ultimately, it decided that nonprofit organizations [tax exempt under Internal Revenue Code § 501(c) (3) and (4)] that do not endorse, support, or oppose political candidates or parties may stage "nonpartisan candidate debates" and may use corporate or labor organization donations to defray their costs. FEC Reg. § 110.13(a). Under the new regulations, broadcasters, bona fide newspapers, magazines, and other periodicals could also use their own funds to stage nonpartisan candidate debates but could not accept donations from other corporations. FEC Reg. § 114.4(e). The structure of the debate would be left to the discretion of the staging organization, provided that the debate include at least two candidates in face-to-face confrontation and not promote or advance one candidate over the other. FEC Reg. § 110.13(b). *Letter to J. Curtis Herge*, AO 1986-37.

Unfortunately, these regulations failed to resolve many of the controversies that brought them into being in the first place. It is not clear whether the phrase "the debates do not promote or advance one candidate over the other" is meant to apply to all candidates in a particular election or just to the candidates participating in the debate in question. Under the former interpretation, candidates not invited to participate would usually have a claim that FEC rules were being violated and that they must be included lest the contributing organization be prosecuted for illegal campaign contributions. Under the latter interpretation, the excluded candidate would not have a claim.

In the 1980 Republican primary in New Hampshire, for example, the *Nashua Telegraph* sponsored a debate between presidential candidates George Bush and Ronald Reagan three days before the election. When three of the other candidates for the Republican nomination complained to the FEC, it advised that the *Telegraph*, a corporation, was illegally contributing to the Bush and Reagan candidacies. Reagan responded by sponsoring the event himself and inviting the other candidates to attend. This effectively mooted the emerging legal case. At the same time, the commission's decision—based on fairness and nonpartisanship rather than First Amendment consideration—may well have influenced the election itself. Reagan's response seemed to contribute significantly to his subsequent defeat of Bush.

The FEC has had a checkered and indecisive record in trying to reconcile the congressional mandate to safeguard the electoral process with the constitutional protections of speech and press. Just when the commission appears to settle on one approach, it moves in an opposite direction, as in the case of the debate exemptions and *Nashua Telegraph* enforcement. More recently, it advised that free contribution of television time to federal candidates would be considered illegal (AO 1986-35), but it later vacated this decision to reconsider it. The commission then could not agree on a new opinion and closed the matter.

Conclusion

The preceding summary documents a legal trend toward removing restrictions on broadcasters and debate sponsors. The legal seesaw is tipping in the direction of First Amendment rights of broadcasters over equal treatment of all legally qualified candidates. But the question remains: what is in the public interest?

Both constitutional principles are central to our governmental system. The electoral process must be fair. The press, including the broadcast media, must be free. What system best accommodates these sometimes competing interests?

Most First Amendment cases eventually come down to weighing the strength of governmental interests, and the narrowness of the means employed to achieve those interests, against the presumption in favor of the speaker whose rights are being affected. What are legitimate government interests here, and what are the best means to achieve those interests?

The most obvious government interest in incidentally restricting broadcasters' free press rights is ultimately to uphold the integrity of electoral processes. While this is crucial to our democracy, exactly equal treatment of all "legally qualified candidates" is not. At least, since enactment of the Federal Election Campaign Act in the early 1970s, the federal government has apportioned public financing of candidates on an unequal basis—that of prior showings of their parties at the polls, or in the case of new parties, their showing in the election itself. As former chief justice Warren Burger observed in upholding that approach, "Sometimes the grossest discrimination can be in treating things that are different as though they were exactly alike." The important point here is that a free and fair election is the goal; the appropriate treatment of the various candidates on the broadcast media is only a means to that end.

A second, equally important government interest relates more closely to the First Amendment. The public needs to hear the views and witness the demeanor of presidential candidates. The public's rights are paramount in broadcasting. The problem with the total deregulatory approach is that the public needs access to the views of all candidates, and sometimes substantial third party candidates are squeezed out. This brings us to the narrowly tailored means to achieve the legitimate government interests. As Burch argued in the *Chisholm* case, allowing debates, without the "chill" of equal time for the excluded candidates, will foster greater public access to the views of major candidates. But how do we ensure access to other views?

First, federal candidate access under Section 312(A)(7) of the 1934 Communications Act and equal opportunities under Section 315 should continue to apply to all presidential candidates. This is a safety valve to allow those candidates to speak to the voters and, more importantly, to allow the public an opportunity to hear from those outside the mainstream. Recent FCC activity to abolish these laws is not only misguided but potentially destructive of our constitutional system.

Second, debates should remain exempt from equal opportunities requirements under the following circumstances:

(A) All major candidates, including third party candidates who receive substantial public financing, should be treated equally.

(B) Major candidates who receive a certain amount of public financing should be required to participate in debates as a condition for receipt of those funds. The debates, however, should be sponsored by an independent, nonbroadcast organization to avoid favoritism in format, in placement of a sponsoring broadcaster's own panelists, and in other controversial details. The FEC should take into account First Amendment considerations and should be expansive in interpreting its rules to allow for contributions to independent sponsorship of debates, without a finding of contribution to a campaign.

(C) Broadcasters, as part of their "trusteeship" (or as part of a spectrum fee for their exclusive use of the frequency), should be required to devote a few hours every four years to carriage of presidential and vice presidential debates that meet the requirements of (A) and (B) above.

Whatever the scheme, it will be impossible to fulfill all the constitutional concerns and interests. But we need to promote televised presidential debates in the future, and blind deregulation of broadcasters is not the long-run solution. The solutions described here resolve the competing interests most fairly and efficiently, recognizing the First Amendment interests of the public as well as of the broadcaster.

FCC Case Annotation: Key Decisions Affecting Broadcasts of Presidential Debates

1952   *Hon. Mike Monroney,* 10 P. & F. Radio Reg. 451 (1952): Debate between Republican and Democratic candidates for the same office triggers "equal opportunities" under Section 315; other candidates must be provided time on the station carrying the debate.

1957   *Allen H. Blondy,* 14 P. & F. Radio Reg. 1199 (1957): Incidental news coverage of the swearing in of a candidate for local judge, where candidate's appearance is minimal and not of advantage to him, not a "use." Prior to 1959, this is the only ruling where an appearance of a candidate does not trigger "equal opportunities."

1959   *CBS (Lar Daly),* 26 F.C.C. 715 (1959): Extensive ruling that any appearance by a candidate is a "use" of a facility requiring equal opportunity. Here, minor opponent provided time in response to all news coverage of incumbent mayor Richard Daley. Decision led to 1959 amendments to Section 315.

1962   *The Goodwill Stations,* 40 F.C.C. 362 (1962): Debate between two gubernatorial candidates, sponsored by independent entity and broadcast live and in its entirety, not exempt from Section 315. Candidates not included in debate entitled to equal opportunity.

1962   *NBC (Wycoff),* 40 F.C.C. 370 (1962): Same conclusion as *Goodwill Stations*—debates not exempt.

1963   *Nicholas Zapple,* 24 P. & F. Radio Reg. 861 (1963): Joint interviews not exempt from equal opportunities; even candidates who refuse invitation to appear are entitled to response time.

1966   *Jefferson Standard Broadcasting Co.,* 8 P. & F. Radio Reg. 2d 595 (1966): Station may not impute blame to candidate who refuses to debate or waive his or her rights, nor may it threaten to publicly blame candidate to entice the candidate to debate.

1968   *William F. Ryan and Paul O'Dwyer,* 14 P. & F. Radio Reg. 2d 621 (1968): A station's offer of equal time, but not in the debate with the major candidates in the election, is not in violation of Section 315.

1973   *Hon. Sam Yorty, Hon. Shirley Chisholm,* 24 P. & F. Radio Reg. 2d 447 (1973): Joint interviews of Democratic primary candidates Humphrey and McGovern on network news interview shows come within news interview exemption to Section 315 despite networks' expansion to one hour and move to prime time. On appeal, D.C. Circuit requires inclusion of Representative Chisholm or equal opportunities. Yorty's appeal to the Ninth Circuit was not in time.

1975   *Aspen Institute,* 55 F.C.C. 2d 697 (1975), *aff'd Chisholm v. FCC,* 538 F.2d 349 (D.C. Cir.), *cert. denied,* 429 U.S. 890 (1976): Overrules *Goodwill Stations* and *NBC (Wycoff);* reinterprets legislative history of 1959 amendment to Section 315, and declares debates in the circumstances of *Goodwill Stations* to be exempt as on-the-spot coverage of bona fide news events.

1976   *American Independent Party,* 62 F.C.C. 2d 4 (1976): A degree of candidate input into format is accepted, but if sponsoring party loses control to the candidates it may lose exemption status.

1978   *M. Robert Rogers,* 42 P. & F. Radio Reg. 2d 1406 (1978): One candidate before a panel of questioners is not exempt as a debate; burden is on challenger to show that a meeting of candidates was not a debate.

1979   *New Jersey Broadcasting Authority,* 46 P. & F. Radio Reg. 2d 558 (1979): Rebroadcast of a taped debate in excess of one day no longer "on-the-spot" coverage, thus not exempt. Overruled in *Henry Geller,* 1983.

1981   *Socialist Workers Campaign,* 50 P. & F. Radio Reg. 2d 595 (1981): Relaxes rule that debates cannot be held in broadcaster's studio; allows such locale so long as nonbroadcaster sponsor maintains control over format, content, and participants.

1983   *Henry Geller,* 54 P. & F. Radio Reg. 2d 1246 (1983), *aff'd League of Women Voters Education Fund v. FCC* (D.C. Cir. No. 83-2194, March 8, 1984): Allows broadcaster sponsorship of debates and delays in rebroadcasting beyond one day, so long as the debate is rerun in its entirety.

1986   *John W. Spring,* 1 FCC Rcd 589 (1986): Broadcaster retains discretion as to how the issue of who should be elected should be treated under the Fairness Doctrine. Note: Fairness Doctrine rescinded by FCC August 6, 1987, Syracuse Peace Council 63 P. & F. Radio Reg. 2d 541 (1987).

3. TELEVISION, PRESIDENTIAL CAMPAIGNS, AND DEBATES

Kathleen Hall Jamieson

Since the advent of the broadcast media, the length of political messages has decreased steadily. Survival of the briefest increasingly has become a political imperative. The 30-minute speeches that reached the nation's Motorolas during the 1940s were standard fare by 1952, the year of America's first telecast presidential campaign. By 1956 the 5-minute speech and spot were edging out the longer speech. In 1964 the 5-minute ad gave way to the 60-second spot and then the 30-second spot. With time for little more than a slogan, an assurance, and a smile, such ads cost candidates more and delivered less than did their dimly remembered ancestor, the political speech.

Not only are we seeing less of candidates now, but when offered longer exposure we opt instead for entertainment. On September 22, 1964, Americans faced a revealing dilemma. Would they settle into their sofas to watch " Petticoat Junction"? Would they savor the sin and seduction of "Peyton Place"? Or would they watch past president Dwight D. Eisenhower discuss the future of the world with Republican presidential nominee Barry Goldwater? In overwhelming numbers, Americans confessed that in their hearts they preferred clinches and comedy to political conversation between a person who had been president and one who aspired to be.

This was not an aberration. On November 4, 1979, the movie *Jaws* faced off against Roger Mudd's documentary on presidential aspirant Edward Kennedy. *Jaws* swallowed "Teddy." That pattern is repeated each time the viewing public chooses prime-time drama over network documentaries and yellowing movies over convention coverage.

Our collective preference for sitcoms and sharks would not be alarming if we read the major newspapers, digested position papers, and mulled over books about issues. But we don't. Instead, in campaigns without debates, spot ads and news snippets provide most of our information about those who would lead the nation. In practical terms this means that we base voting decisions on bites of information averaging a quarter of a minute to a minute in length.

Speeches, of course, are not necessarily substantive, and spots are not necessarily sterile. It takes less than 30 seconds to say "I will go to Korea." Nothing guarantees that a half-hour speech will say more than that. Indeed, many say less.

Still, a snippet cannot disclose a mind at work. Nor can it explore the complexities of an issue. Great public figures from Demosthenes to Churchill took the time to trace the history of their ideas and in the process revealed something of how they saw the world. Today, history has little place in public discussion except when selectively marshaled to expose a "mistaken" policy. There was an age in which speakers spoke until audiences nodded either in agreement or in sleep. When ideas governed length of utterance, speakers assumed the burden of outlining and scrutinizing policy alternatives, demonstrating a command of the issues, and only then defending the preferred policy.

By contrast, most spots argue by hitting and running, slinging a telling statistic or anecdote under a questionable claim as if it constituted proof. In "ad McNuggets" candidates can do little more than assert the virtue of their positions and invite agreement.

Benefits of Debates

The voter looking for a sustained encounter with political ideas will find in broadcast news little more and sometimes less than in spot ads. Indeed, some academic analysts believe that there is more issue content in ads than in news coverage. In 1984 the typical spot ad was 30 seconds long and the typical network news slice of a presidential candidate's speech, a bare 15 seconds.

As messages running an hour or longer, debates offer a level of contact with candidates clearly unmatched in spot ads and news segments. Uninterrupted by advertising, uncontaminated by the devices programmers use to ensnare and hold prime-time audiences, the debates offer the most extensive and serious view of candidates available to the electorate. These sustained encounters have several advantages.

Debates Demand Serious Attention

By reducing the substance of campaigns to spot ads placed between programs, we have tacitly acknowledged that their audience is inadvertent. Viewers become unaccustomed to questioning the claims of ads for deodorants, discount records—or political candidates. Political commercials not only equate the presidency with escapist drama and disposable products but also invite viewers to see the claims of the candidates as unworthy of attention in their own right.

In sharp contrast, the audience that views debates has not been tricked into attention. As prolonged, ad-free encounters, debates invite serious judgment. Unlike ads, debates encourage a focused attention that makes politics a topic of conversation even among people who usually avoid such subjects. The social pressure on the typical voter to take a sustained look at both candidates creates a climate conducive to political learning.

Debates Reveal the Candidates'
Communicative Competence and Habits of Mind

Although candidates' relentless rehearsals mean that many of their answers are canned, the very fact of rehearsal provides valuable evidence. To the extent that those who prepare a candidate for a debate also shape the subsequent presidency, the patterns of thought, recurring lines of argument, and pervasive presuppositions in a candidate's answers prefigure a presidency.

And as the clock ticks on, the likelihood diminishes that a candidate is merely speaking someone else's words. Even if answers are prepackaged, they are processed through the candidate's own thought and linguistic reflexes. Candidates, furthermore, cannot foresee all possible questions or memorize all possible answers. This means that debates provide otherwise elusive clues about the person who would be president.

The extent to which the debates presage a president's communicative patterns is evident in our ability to identify the candidates who said the following:

> The present tax structure is a disgrace to this country; it's just a welfare program for the rich. As a matter of fact, 25 percent of the total tax deductions go for only 1 percent of the richest people in this country. And over 50 percent of the tax credits go for the 14 percent of the richest people in this country. When . . . first became president in August of . . . , the first thing he did, in October, was to ask for a $4.7 billion increase in taxes on our people in the midst of the heaviest recession since the Great Depression of the 1940s. In January of . . . he asked for a tax change, a $5.6 billion increase on low and middle income private individuals, a $6.5 billion decrease on the corporations and the special interests. And in December of . . . he vetoed the roughly $18 to $20 billion tax reduction bill that had been passed by the Congress, and then he came back later on in January of this year and he did advocate a $10 billion tax reduction, but it would be offset by a $6 billion increase, this coming January, in deductions for Social Security payments and for unemployment compensation.

> I wish he could have been with me when I sat with a group of teenagers who were black and who were telling me about their unemployment problems. And that it was the minimum wage that had done away with the jobs that they once could get. And indeed, every time it has increased you will find there is an increase in minority unemployment among young people. And therefore I have been in favor of a separate minimum for them.

These typical debate statements from 1976 and 1980, respectively, reveal Jimmy Carter's fondness for hyperbole and detail and Ronald Reagan's habitual move from a single illustration to a generalization. Such statements can also reveal the arguments toward which the person gravitates. For example, Carter's hyperbolic bent contrasts with John F. Kennedy's restraint. While Kennedy contended in 1960 that "our power and prestige in the last eight years has declined," Carter in 1976 argued that "our country is not strong anymore, we're not respected anymore."

In the debates we see habits of mind that foreshadow presidential strengths and weaknesses. Reagan's casual respect for facts and his rambling closing statement in the last 1984 debate are consistent with his failure to monitor the intrigues revealed in the Tower commission report. Carter's hyperbole haunted him when, after the hostage taking, newscasts replayed his extravagant praise of the Shah of Iran. Carter's obsession with detail prefigured a presidency without a guiding theme. In contrast, Reagan's self-effacing humor and his genial ability to disarm and to reassure account for his victory in the 1980 debate with Carter and for much of his personal popularity as president. Similarly, Kennedy's humor served him well both in the debates and in the White House.

Some of the evidence we gain from debates is nonverbal: Gerald R. Ford and Carter standing woodenly through twenty-seven minutes of silence as technicians rushed to repair a malfunctioning sound system; Reagan striding comfortably across stage to shake a startled incumbent president's hand; Geraldine Ferraro maintaining eye contact with her hastily jotted notes rather than with the camera.

Patterns of communication not readily seen in other formats are revealed by debates. The snippets of time allotted for TV news cannot showcase candidate incoherence. Only by hearing Ford's entire summation in his first debate and Reagan's in his last could viewers adequately evaluate the ability of these two presidents to develop their own ideas. Any editing of these statements by the networks, in fact, would have looked like sabotage. Because few news outlets can or will take four minutes of news time to demonstrate that candidates are lost in their own speeches, debates fill an important need for the voter.

Debates Increase Candidate Accountability

Debates heighten the candidate's responsibility to engage the issues considered central by the other side. In his 1960 ads and speeches, JFK answered the question, "Who can better get the country moving?" Nixon, in turn, phrased the campaign's primary question differently. Capitalizing on Kennedy's comparative lack of foreign policy experience, the vice president asked, "Who better understands what peace demands?" Debates ensured that each candidate had to address the other's question in an environment that permitted the electorate to compare their answers.

Debates Check Manipulative Tendencies of Candidates

Political commercials tend to show candidates as heroic figures. News coverage counteracts this tendency because political consultants know that ads will not "play" if they create an image strikingly dissimilar to that seen on the evening news. Debates are an even stronger reality check on the manipulation of candidates' images. To mute the image projected by the first debate of 1984, for example, Reagan could not rely on ads or news coverage. Instead he needed a credible performance in the second debate.

Debates also magnify the personal responsibility of the candidates for the tactics of their campaigns. This is especially important in a time when sophisticated ads disassociate the candidate from attacks on an opponent.

Debates Prepare Candidates for Office

Conscious of a national as well as an international audience, aware that every word will be scrutinized by press and opponents, candidates do their homework. The process is careful and intensive.

The debate preparation period is the only time in the campaign reserved for study and reflection. Even candidacies built on new ideas require a candidate to endure endless handshaking and to repeat stock phrases with an air of spontaneity. Campaigns most accurately test not presidential talents but the candidates' ability to survive bad food and constant travel on minimal sleep. But the stakes are too high for candidates to stay on the campaign trail. To prepare for debates the nominees have to take a break from these mindnumbing rituals. They have to ponder the complexities of the world and to confront the strengths of their opponent's positions and the weaknesses of their own.

Sheltered within the cocoon of the campaign, applauded by partisans and briefed to respond with stock answers to standard questions, candidates are not necessarily forced to assess the cogency of their own convictions or to defend them against plausible, well-argued alternatives. As candidates rehearse for debates with their staffs, they will not only hear the other side, but they will hear it phrased pointedly, argued forcefully, and documented relentlessly—in some cases more relentlessly than in the actual debate.

The prophylactic effect of debates is felt as well when candidates fashion public stands in anticipation of questioning before a national audience. Those who hint at secret plans to end wars and balance budgets are aware that the debate panel will press for details, attempt to unmask ruses, and challenge inconsistencies.

Debates Reduce the Cost of Reaching Voters

During the primary season, when the candidates' capacity to raise money is as crucial as their positions on the issues, frequent debates can sustain an important but cash-poor candidacy. Without the debates of the 1984 Democratic primaries, for example, the campaign of Jesse Jackson would have withered. Lacking the money to mount costly multistate ad campaigns, Jackson sustained his campaign on articulate performances in the debates and on a talent for capturing free news time.

Likewise, prenomination debates enable the electorate to hear those who will not be able to raise enough money and garner enough votes to survive the primaries. In 1984 Fritz Hollings, George McGovern, and Alan Cranston offered important alternatives worthy of national attention—attention they received only in the early primary debates.

Debates Tell Us About Ourselves

Because debates mirror campaign trends, journalists and historians can find in them evidence of how campaigns—and the country—are changing. Vietnam, Watergate, and other systematic deceptions have fostered an American electorate more concerned about the character of candidates than about their stands on issues. Accordingly, debates have increasingly focused on personal beliefs and straightforwardness. The questions posed in 1984, for example, included: "Would you describe your religious beliefs, noting particularly whether you consider yourself a born-again Christian, and explain how these beliefs affect your presidential decisions?" "I'm exploring for your personal views of abortion, and specifically how you would want them applied as public policy. First . . . do you consider abortion murder or a sin?" "Given that you have been in public office for so many years, what accounts for the failure of your message to get through?" The debates of 1960 offer few comparable questions.

In debates we also see evidence of how spot ads have replaced substantive speeches. In 1960 candidates related their answers to a world writ large in speeches, but in more recent debates they have synchronized their answers with a world writ small in commercials. In response to a question on nuclear weapons control, Nixon told the 1960 debate audience that a major speech he was to deliver the following week would elaborate his position. Also in the 1960 debates the candidates reminded viewers that elaborations of their briefly expressed debate positions could be found in their speeches on the government's role in strikes, on the power of labor unions, on the standing of the United States in the world community, and on the specifics of farm policy. Both Kennedy and Nixon predicated their answers on a careful reading of their opponent's policy speeches.

In the debates of the past decade and a half, candidates have taken issue with claims made in each other's ads. For example, when asked in 1976 what responsibility he accepted for the mean-spiritedness of the campaign, Carter pledged not that the substance of his speeches would change but that "during the next ten days the American people will not see the Carter campaign running television advertisements and newspaper advertisements based on a personal attack on President Ford's character." Similarly, in 1984 Reagan reduced Walter Mondale's claim to strong leadership to a Democratic ad showing the former vice president standing on the deck of the *U.S.S. Nimitz*. If Mondale had had his way, noted Reagan, there would have been no *Nimitz* because "he was against it."

Shortcomings of Debates

Despite their many virtues, debates do have drawbacks. They, too, have been cursed with a compulsion to compress. By the time of the general election in 1984, debate speeches had been squeezed to half their 1960 length. From their inception, furthermore, presidential debates have borne the imprint of television: ideas must be trimmed to fit preset time limits. In an all too typical example, Mondale in 1984 was given 150 seconds to answer these questions: "Do you accept the conventional wisdom that eastern Europe is a Soviet sphere of influence? And, if you do, what could a Mondale administration realistically do to help the people of eastern Europe achieve the human rights that were guaranteed to them as a result of the Helsinki Accords?"

Nor is a debate an especially desirable forum for communication. Their Darwinian instincts honed, candidates have developed the ability to evade questions and to repeat stock answers. Questions are asked that too often advance journalists' ideas of what constitutes news rather than the public's need to compare the candidates. Candidates themselves seem more disposed to show their command of the facts than to relate those facts to larger issues.

Debates do not necessarily reveal the inner person who will be president. Nor do they demonstrate or test many of the skills central to conduct in office: an ability to ask significant questions, a talent for securing sound advice, a disposition to act judiciously, and a capacity to compromise without violating conscience or basic social principles. In addition, debates foster habits that are not desirable in a presidency: a willingness to offer solutions instantaneously and a tendency to simplify complex problems. Debates can also lead presidential candidates to make promises that as president they neither can nor should keep. In 1976, for example, both Ford and Carter criticized secret presidential decision making—a practice that is sometimes necessary.

Finally, voters can be seriously misled by the nonverbal communication on which television dotes and toward which viewers involuntarily gravitate. In the first presidential debate of 1960, Nixon, pale from a hospital stay for an injured knee and perspiring under the hot studio lights, had a somewhat sinister look, heightened by the beard apparent under his poorly made-up translucent skin. Nixon glanced repeatedly at a clock just off stage, inviting the inappropriate inference that he was "shifty-eyed." In addition, the freshly painted set had dried to a color lighter than Nixon's consultants had anticipated. Consequently, the grey suit he wore blended into the background, blurring his image. Finally, he had lost weight during his hospital stay, and his suit was a bit large for him. As he leaned on the podium for support, the suit shifted forward on one shoulder. The different perspectives of radio listeners and TV viewers illustrate the power and peril of visual communication. Those who heard the first debate on radio thought Nixon was the winner, while television viewers gave the debate to Kennedy.

In sum, debates benefit the electorate by revealing candidates' communicative competence and habits of mind, by increasing the candidates' accountability, by acting as a check on manipulation by candidates, and by helping to prepare the candidates for office. In addition to providing free television exposure, the debates give the candidates the opportunity to hold opponents responsible for their campaign rhetoric.

Because they mirror changes in both campaign practices and individual campaigns, debates are a useful object of study for scholars and journalists. Debates do have shortcomings, but, in a world where sharks and sitcoms lure voters away from political substance and where spot ads and news snippets masquerade as significant political fare, debates are a blessing.

4. THE IMPACT OF PRESIDENTIAL DEBATES ON THE VOTE AND TURNOUT

George Gallup, Jr.

If, as a solid majority of the U.S. electorate wishes, televised presidential debates are held during the 1988 campaign, these contests could play a pivotal role in the election outcome. This possibility is heightened by the fact that, for the first time in twenty years, no incumbent will be on either ticket.

This conclusion is based on Gallup measurements of viewer reaction to the debates since 1960 as well as test elections taken before and after each debate. In three of the last four presidential campaigns in which these postnomination confrontations have taken place—in 1960, 1976, and 1980—debates appear to have played a decisive role in the November elections.

In the 1984 race the debates did not make a crucial difference in the election outcome because of the one-sided nature of the race between President Ronald Reagan and Senator Walter Mondale. In the 1980 contest between Reagan and President Jimmy Carter, however, the incumbent's momentum appeared to have been stalled by the October 28 debate, held just one week before the election.

In 1976 the second of four presidential debates, that on foreign policy, may have checked President Gerald R. Ford's remarkable effort in catching up with challenger Jimmy Carter in the closing weeks of the campaign.

The series of four debates in 1960 proved to be a decisive factor working in favor of John F. Kennedy over Richard Nixon, in one of the closest elections in history. The seesaw battle recorded prior to the debates shifted to a fairly consistent Kennedy lead after these televised contests.

Effects of Debates

Presidential debates in all years have tended to reinforce the convictions of voters who were already committed. They have caused few people to change their minds; their main impact appears to have been on undecided or wavering voters. Furthermore, the debates have not caused sudden swings in candidate support; rather, they have tended to stall the momentum of a candidate, to dampen the enthusiasm of his or her supporters, and to prompt second thoughts.

Assessing the impact of the debates on voter *turnout* in the November elections is more difficult. While turnout in the 1960 Kennedy-Nixon contest was higher than in any of the next three presidential elections (1964, 1968, and 1972), when debates were not held, turnout levels declined in the last three elections (in 1976, 1980 and 1984), when debates did occur. Of course, turnout might have been still lower had there been no debates.

A New Type of Campaign in 1960?

American voters think televised presidential debates should be a permanent part of the electoral process. In a Feburary 1987 survey, 72 percent said they would like to see presidential debates held in 1988, while 16 percent said they would not, and 12 percent did not express an opinion. These findings are consistent with earlier survey results showing solid support for continuing the debates.

The public had long been ready for televised debates when they first appeared in 1960. In Gallup surveys in the 1950s the public had strongly favored replacing the traditional barnstorming campaign with radio and TV appearances by candidates, a radical proposal at the time.

In the spring of 1960 the public by a 5-4 ratio said they favored having the opposing nominees campaign completely by radio and TV instead of the whistle-stopping speeches, handshaking marathons, and other traditional methods of electioneering. (See Table 1.)

Such a plan, advocated at the time by electoral reformers, would have allowed major party candidates free TV and radio time on all major networks on six occasions during the campaign. Supporters of the plan felt that it would allow each nominee to reach a larger audience, and that the electorate would be better informed in general.

People interviewed also thought the TV and radio campaign would save money as well as wear and tear on the candidates, who would not have to travel around the country as extensively. Still others cited the fact that granting the exact amount of free air time to each candidate would give both candidates an equal chance and voters an opportunity to hear both sides.

On the other hand, a substantial minority of Americans opposed the idea—chiefly on the grounds that it would remove the personal element and much of the color from the campaign. Other opponents of the plan argued that they would not like to have their favorite TV programs replaced. Some said that the plan would, in effect, leave viewers with no choice but to listen to candidates' speeches or turn off the radio or TV.

Table 1   Would You Favor a New Type of Campaign?[a]

	National	*Republicans*	*Democrats*	*Independents*
Yes	49%	47%	52%	48%
No	39	40	38	40
No opinion	12	13	10	12

[a] Here is the question asked in the 1960 survey:

It has been suggested that, instead of speech-making tours across the country, the Republican and Democratic nominees for president be given television and radio time to make six speeches of one half-hour each. When these speeches go on the air, all other programs would have to go off. Would you like to have this new type of political campaigning, or not?

Table 2　Which Man Did the Better Job in the 1960 TV Debates?

Kennedy	42%
Nixon	30
Even	23
Undecided	5

Public Reaction to Debates, 1960-1984

1960

Public interest in the first of the Great Debates during the summer of 1960 grew sharply with 55 percent of Americans in a late August Gallup Poll professing "a lot" of interest in watching the upcoming debates. Among persons with a college background the figure was 73 percent.

The first debate on September 26 came at a time when millions of Americans were trying to choose between the two candidates; for the previous six weeks neither Kennedy nor Nixon had been able to gain a decisive lead.

The four debates proved to be a definite plus for Kennedy. Gallup Poll evidence indicated that an estimated 85 million adults watched at least one of the four debates. Among those who had watched one or more, the overall sentiment was that Kennedy had done better. (See Table 2.)

Kennedy also won in the Gallup E.Q. (enthusiasm quotient) ratings. Prior to the debates, surveys on two occasions had shown Nixon and Kennedy receiving similar ratings. (The ratings are the percentage of persons who on a 10-point scale give either candidate a "highly favorable" rating.) In a survey taken after the last debate, Kennedy's rating remained about where it had been prior to the first, while Nixon's declined. (See Table 3.)

1976

After a long hiatus, the public was ready for debates when they came on the scene again in 1976. A July Gallup Poll found 68 percent saying they would like to have the presidential candidates participate that fall in nationally televised debates, with 23 percent opposed and 9 percent not sure.

Those who favored debates felt, as in the 1960 survey, that many more people could be reached, that the electorate in general would be better informed, and that a series of debates would save a lot of "wear and tear" on the candidates.

Table 3　Enthusiasm Quotient Ratings, 1960

	Nixon	*Kennedy*
After convention	43%	42%
Before first debate	42	43
After fourth debate	36	43

Proponents of a debate revival also argued that such confrontations were needed to stimulate interest and activity among the electorate. Turnout in the thirty state primaries in 1976 averaged only 25 to 30 percent, and voter participation in national elections had been steadily dropping for sixteen years. Gallup Poll registration figures at the time indicated that this downward trend might continue in the presidential election that fall. For example, only half of young voters at that time were registered to vote in the upcoming presidential election.

Specifically, those who favored debates offered the following reasons:
● They would provide many more people with information about the candidates and issues.
● They would allow the electorate to see the candidates together and help voters make comparisons.
● They would let the candidates speak for themselves and not have their views filtered through the media.
● They would show how the candidates stand up under pressure.

Those who opposed a revival of televised debates offered these reasons:

● They would not provide any better understanding of the campaign.
● They are a waste of money.
● They are dull viewing.
● They would disrupt regularly scheduled programming.
● They may be misleading because a better debater would not necessarily make a better president.

On the eve of the first 1976 debate expectations were running high that the debate would have an impact. A large number of Americans had not decided which candidate they would vote for or even whether they would vote.

Given the volatility and "softness" of voter support in the early weeks of the 1976 campaign, the televised debates in all likelihood helped shape the race. President Ford was coming on strong and closing a wide gap between himself and Carter. Following the first debate (on domestic issues), which the public by a 4-3 ratio thought Ford had won, the president increased his share of the expected vote in two successive surveys. In fact, on the eve of the second debate, Ford came from as far behind as 18 points to gain a virtual tie with Carter. However, the second debate (on foreign policy), which the public by a 5-3 ratio saw as a Carter victory, boosted Carter's standings. It also stalled Ford's momentum. On the eve of the final debate (on all issues), Carter led Ford 47 to 41 percent.

The public regarded this third debate as a draw, and it did not appreciably help either candidate. Ford picked up strength in the final weeks, but not enough to pull him into the lead.

A postelection Gallup Poll concluded that the debates that year, as in 1960, had proved to be a major factor in the election outcome. That the second debate may have irrevocably changed the momentum in Carter's favor repeated a pattern set in 1960. In that year, before the first televised debate, Nixon led Kennedy. However, Nixon lost the lead after the first debate and never regained it.

Each of the three 1976 presidential debates was watched by approximately seven in ten Americans. In contrast to viewership in 1960, there was little fall-off between the first and last debates in 1976. As in 1960, the effect of the debates was to reinforce the convictions of supporters of each candidate, although some change (2 to 3 percentage points) in the test elections was recorded following each of the three 1976 debates. Another effect of the debate was to increase voter interest, which had been seriously lagging in the first stages of the campaign.

In 1976, as in earlier presidential election years, the huge costs of campaign spending prompted much criticism. Some experts argued that if presidential debates could be built into the electoral process, spending could be sharply reduced. They pointed out, for example, that debates would reduce the tremendous sums spent on broadcast advertising.

After a national election, the last thing voters want to hear about is politics. But were people jaded about the idea of presidential debates? Not at all. In a nationwide Gallup survey taken within weeks of the election, 66 percent said they favored having televised presidential debates again in 1980.

The proportion of people favoring a repeat of presidential debates four years hence closely matched the proportion that in July 1976—prior to the decision to hold debates—said they would like to have the presidential candidates participate in nationally televised debates. That survey showed 68 percent in favor of reinstituting presidential debates.

Many voters, however, were sharply critical of certain features in the format of the 1976 debates. Three changes were most frequently mentioned.

1. *Have the debates be more like real debates, with more interaction between the candidates.* A twenty-nine-year-old Geneva, Ohio, executive commented, "It should be a debate between the candidates and not between the reporters and the candidates—not a press conference. The candidates should have a chance to argue their points back and forth."

2. *Make the debates less formal and less rehearsed.* One respondent said, "The whole setting was too stiff and forbidding. The candidates should be allowed to sit and have a chance to be more relaxed."

3. *Get the public into the act.* Many voters felt that the real concerns of the public were not always put forth by reporters, who were sometimes on their own "ego trip."

1980

In 1980, in a survey conducted just prior to the first presidential debate, at least four persons in ten said they were "very likely" to watch, and another three in ten said they were "fairly likely" to do so. The same survey showed that Americans, by a 2-1 margin, disapproved of Carter's decision not to participate in the first debate.

Another question in the same survey asked what issues the public would most like to see the candidates debate. (See Table 4 for a list of the principal topics cited.)

On the eve of the first debate, the Ronald Reagan-George Bush Republican ticket was the choice of 41 percent of likely voters, compared to 37 percent for Democrats Carter and Walter Mondale and 15 percent for Independents John Anderson and Patrick Lucey. The GOP team retained a slight edge in a mid-October survey conducted before the first debate, 45 percent to 42 percent and 8 percent for Anderson. But the Democrats edged ahead in an October 24-26 survey: 45 to 42 percent, with 9 percent for Anderson-Lucey.

The October 28 debate, however, stalled Carter's momentum. Immediately

Table 4   Debate Topics Preferred by Registered Voters, 1980

High cost of living, inflation	51%
Foreign affairs	17
Unemployment	15
Tax cut	12
Energy matters	10
Conservation and the environment	3
Race relations, minority rights	2
Abortion	2
Women's rights, ERA	2
All other	31
Don't know	22
	167%[a]

[a] Total is more than 100 percent because of multiple responses.

following the debate, the race narrowed to Reagan, 44 percent and Carter, 43 percent. In the final Gallup survey, conducted Friday, October 31, through Saturday afternoon, November 1, Reagan held an edge over Carter, 47 to 44 percent. In the election Reagan won 51 percent of the vote to 41 percent for Carter and 7 percent for Anderson.

President-elect Reagan's sweeping victory in 1980 reflected one of the most dramatic shifts ever recorded in voter preferences during the last week of a presidential campaign, as shown in Table 5.

Reagan gained support at an average rate of 1.2 percentage points per day from Monday, October 27, through Saturday, November 1, and at an average rate of 1.3 percentage points from Sunday, November 2, to Tuesday, November 4, election day.

Table 5   Trend in Last 11 Days of 1980 Campaign

Polls	Reagan	Carter	Anderson	Other	Undecided
Saturday and Sunday, October 25 and 26	42%	45%	9%	1%	3%
SECOND DEBATE: TUESDAY, OCTOBER 28					
Wednesday and Thursday, October 29 and 30	44	43	8	1	4
Thursday through Saturday, October 30 through November 1	47	44	8	1	[a]
ELECTION DAY: TUESDAY, NOVEMBER 4					
Election results	51	41	7	1	[a]

[a] Undecided vote has been allocated among major candidates.

As in 1960 and 1976, the debates had in effect stalled a candidate's momentum. But the impact of the second debate on Carter's momentum also reflected some unique circumstances.

Dramatic developments in the Iran hostage situation over the weekend before the election clearly worked in Reagan's favor. Public discouragement and frustration rose after it became clear that the Iranian captors' new conditions for release of the hostages would be difficult to meet. In addition, at least a third of voters in an earlier Gallup survey conducted for *Newsweek* felt that, at least to some extent, the president was attempting to use the hostage situation to improve his political standing.

1984

Six in ten registered voters (61 percent) in a poll conducted in early September said they thought Reagan was likely to do a "better job" in the debates than Mondale, the choice of 22 percent. The balance thought the contests would be a standoff (7 percent) or did not express an opinion (10 percent).

Not surprisingly, the public's assessment of who would "win" the debates was closely related to their choice for president. In a test election conducted in the same survey, Reagan enjoyed a 55 percent to 40 percent lead over Mondale, with 5 percent undecided. Among his partisans in the test election, Reagan was the overwhelming (83 percent) choice to outperform Mondale in the debates. However, only a 45 percent plurality of Mondale's test election supporters thought he would beat the president in the debates.

The public expressed considerable interest in the debates, with 7 in 10 saying they were "very likely" (38 percent) or "fairly likely" (31 percent) to watch them.

Unemployment, the topic the public was most interested in hearing discussed in that year's debates, was mentioned by 18 percent of all respondents (and 26 percent of Democrats). Cited next most often was the economy in general (16 percent), followed by the federal deficit (13 percent) and foreign affairs (13 percent). Taxes were mentioned by 11 percent and the threat of war by 10 percent. Other frequently mentioned issues included the arms race (7 percent), the high cost of living (6 percent), the problems of the elderly (6 percent), national defense (5 percent), and education (4 percent).

Although the public had overwhelmingly expected that President Reagan would outperform Walter Mondale, the Democratic challenger's strong showing in the first debate at least temporarily confounded that expectation. A *Newsweek* poll conducted by Gallup after the first debate indicated that viewers felt that Mondale had done a better job, by a margin of 54 to 35 percent—very close to a reversal of the two candidates' relative standings in the latest presidential test elections. (The Gallup Poll's September 28-30 reading showed Reagan leading Mondale, 56 to 39 percent.)

Mondale's strong performance was ascribed to his greater "confidence and self-assurance." Mondale also outscored Reagan 45 to 37 percent on appearing "thoughtful and well-informed." President Reagan, on the other hand, succeeded in convincing debate viewers that he was "more capable of dealing with the problems facing this country" and that he "presented better ideas for keeping the country prosperous." He also "came closer to reflecting [the audience's] point of view on the issues" and "came across as more likeable." Ironically, Mondale appeared in the debate to have beaten President Reagan at his own game, by bet-ter displaying the qualities of presentation so closely identified with Reagan.

A major portion of the debate focused on the federal deficit and Mondale's plan for tax increases to reduce it. In a late September Gallup Poll, 41 percent of those aware of the Mondale tax plan favored it while 48 percent were opposed to the plan. Public opinion closely followed party lines.

Perhaps the strongest evidence of the debate's power as a campaign device is that among viewers who had not firmly decided on their presidential choice—including moderate supporters of either man and undecideds—63 percent said they were more likely to vote for Mondale because of the first debate, compared to 29 percent who expressed greater support for Reagan.

Neither candidate scored a decisive victory in the second debate; however, Reagan's performance represented a marked improvement over his showing in the first. In a survey conducted after the Kansas City debate, 43 percent of viewers said Reagan had done a better job, while 40 percent thought Mondale was the winner. A major factor in Reagan's improved showing was that viewers gave him a 44 percent to 38 percent edge over Mondale for seeming "thoughtful and well-informed." Similarly, the President succeeded in reversing the public's earlier judgment that Mondale was more "confident and self-assured." By a vote of 46 to 36 percent, Reagan was judged superior to Mondale in this respect after the second debate.

Reagan was also perceived by many debate viewers as having the edge on foreign policy issues—as he had had on domestic issues in the first debate. Reagan was seen as "coming closer to [the individual viewer's] point of view on foreign policy issues," 57 percent to Mondale's 38 percent; as "more capable of handling relations with the Soviet Union," 55 to 38 percent; as "having the best judgment on needed defense expenditures," 53 to 39 percent; and as "more likely to keep the U.S. out of war," 49 to 39 percent.

After the second debate, Reagan improved his performance overall and on perceived characteristics—confidence, thoughtfulness, and self-assurance. The second debate survey showed no increase in the proportion who said they were concerned that Reagan "may not be able to meet the demands of a second term"—45 percent after the first debate to 42 percent after the second.

Only slightly fewer voters felt they were likely to watch the vice-presidential candidates debate than expected to watch the Reagan-Mondale debates, with 61 to 69 percent, respectively, saying they were at least fairly likely to do so.

The public was evenly divided on the probable victor of the vice-presidential debate, with Democrat Geraldine Ferraro the choice of 38 percent of registered voters to 36 percent for GOP incumbent George Bush. The difference of 2 percentage points was within the statistical margin of error for polls of this size and design. Backers of the Mondale-Ferraro ticket were on much firmer ground with regard to the likely "winner" of the Bush-Ferraro debate, with a 64 percent majority picking their party's nominee and only 15 percent choosing Bush.

And, although a slim 52 percent majority of Reagan-Bush supporters favored Bush as the likely winner of his debate with Ferraro, she was chosen by 22 percent of those who said they would vote for the GOP ticket if the election were being held immediately.

The postelection survey in 1984 on campaign changes suggested that one of the principal reasons for the low level of voter participation in the election of November 6—nearly half of eligible voters failed to show up at the polls—may have been disenchantment with the electoral process. In the survey 53 percent of Americans called for changes in the way political campaigns are conducted.

Among the top complaints were the length of the campaign, the high cost of financing election races, mudslinging, and an inefficient nomination and election process. Again the public in a postelection survey was found to favor nationally televised debates, presumably in part as an antidote to some of the abuses they found in traditional forms of campaigning.

5. MEDIA COVERAGE OF PRESIDENTIAL DEBATES

Edwin Diamond and Kathleen Friery

Media coverage of presidential debates has been consistent through three decades and four campaigns. Media interest may begin even before the event is fixed. A debate about whether there will be debates, for example, signals to the audience that something important is happening. In the days leading up to the first debate, the media do run-up stories that serve to alert the less attentive public to the event. The debate itself receives page-one attention and top-of-the-newscast coverage. Television networks carry the debate and immediately analyze it. Even casual consumers of the news know something major is underway. For example, the day after the 1980 Ronald Reagan-Jimmy Carter debate each network dedicated a significant portion of its evening news to debate-related stories. Out of 22 minutes of news materials, ABC devoted 11 minutes and 55 seconds to the debate, CBS 9 minutes and 15 seconds, and NBC 6 minutes and 10 seconds.

Although the debates have consistently attracted a huge quantity of news coverage, the quality of that coverage has been inconsistent. Obviously, coverage of a big event, such as the presidential debates, does not occur in a vacuum: it follows certain familiar journalistic patterns. And just as the candidates in the course of a debate reveal parts of their overall persona, the media play out aspects of their natures. As with most news coverage, the media serve the news makers; candidates seeking votes, for example, benefit from the large audiences collected to hear their messages. The needs of news organizations are also served; putting their best competitive efforts forward, they may win "votes" in the form of audience patronage. Different media also have a chance to demonstrate what they do best—for example, the immediacy conveyed by television, the record-keeping role of print journalism.

But if the interests of the principals and the press were paramount, then the debates would have merely the status of other big-event entertainments such as the Superbowl or the Academy Awards. The interests of the citizen-public rather than those of the candidates or the press are most important in assessing the debates and most concern us in this essay.

Additional research was done by Maggie Soares and Kelly Sutherland. Diamond is director of the News Study Group at New York University. Friery, Soares, and Sutherland are research associates of the group.

As we started to look at coverage of the past four presidential debates, we assumed that the Kennedy-Nixon debates would stand apart. The times, after all, have changed since 1960. Television has assumed a central position in the life of the country. We expected to find not consistency of coverage but change, if for no other reason than the passage of sixteen years and its effects on both the press and political processes.

In fact, the 1960 coverage serves as a model for what we observed in 1976, 1980, and 1984. From the start, the media treated the debates as highly newsworthy. In its issue on sale September 21, 1960, *Newsweek* declared, "Many minds will be made up and some will be changed, after the series of historic Nixon-Kennedy television debates that begin on Sept. 26." Three weeks later *Time*, in its October 17 issue, decided that the debates were not only historic but one of a kind as well: "The election will be decided by an electorate that to an extent unique in history were able to look at the candidates and their programs in a cool and objective light, free of the usual hoopla, pennants and brass bands." Each 1960 debate became a page-one story in newspapers around the country. In addition, a new journalistic specialist, the television reporter, began to review the debates as a critic would theater or a television program.

In 1960, too, both print and television became fixated on the results of public opinion samplings. For example, the day after the first debate, a *New York Times* headline declared: "TV Debate Switched Few Votes, Nationwide Survey Shows." In the *Times* account of the first Kennedy-Nixon debate, a young reporter named Russell Baker stayed close to a factual accounting of what happened on the screen. After the second debate, however, he was offering two reportorial themes that would become dominant in all subsequent news coverage, print and broadcast, through 1984: what the polls were saying and how the debaters looked. At the same time television and press accounts commented on another subject that would later become familiar: worries that the public would be "bored" by too much political discussion. "Television ratings," declared a *Times* story after the third Kennedy-Nixon debate, "indicated that public interest was gradually falling off, although public opinion polls show that the debates were getting hotter." James Reston's news analysis after the fourth debate noted that the debates were over, and the general feeling was that it was "none too soon." Reston did not specify—the analyst's prerogative—whose "general feelings" he had sampled. Those of his fellow journalists? Those of the respective campaign staffs? Or those of the waitress in the coffee shop on his way to work?

Five media themes, we concluded, were sounded in 1960 and repeated in debate coverage through subsequent campaigns. The themes involve signaling the big event, picking the winners and losers, assessing the candidate's appearance, viewing the debates as theater, and avoiding the "boring" facts. These five topics constitute a framework for us to analyze media coverage of debates.

Signaling the Big Event

On one level, media attention to the presidential debates reflects journalism doing its job. Debates are fast-developing, many-sided news stories, and the media fascination with debates encourages public attention. The debates are hyped as the single most significant factor in the election process. Thus: "the outcome might well be decisive in this year's race for the White House" (*Newsweek*, September 27, 1976); "the 90 minute debate that could determine the outcome of [Carter's] battle for re-election" (*Washington Post*, October 29, 1980); the 1984 debates "put on competitive footing . . . an election that seemed to be a runaway" (*New York Times*, October 4, 1984).

On another level, television news has a greater stake than print in concentrating public attention on the debates. "Look at them" can dissolve into "look at us," and the signaling function begins to resemble self-promotion. For example, anchorman Frank Reynolds announced on ABC's "World News Tonight" for October 8, 1980, immediately before the first Reagan-Carter debate, "The country, the candidates and certainly Cleveland are ready now for what may well be the most important ninety minutes of the campaign. In Cleveland's beautiful old public hall over there, no stranger to political history, the podiums are in place. The stage is set for tonight's debate between Jimmy Carter and Ronald Reagan." Later, Reynolds introduced Sam Donaldson with the Carter entourage for more buildup. Donaldson: "Late today the president and his wife walked over to the hall to look over the stage, check the lighting and microphones, and, as history tells us, perhaps of most importance, check his make-up." Over half of the "World News Tonight" broadcast that evening was devoted to the debate and the campaign. The newscasts of CBS and NBC had similar coverage.

The media often attempt to focus public attention on key points. Coverage may create certain standards of performance, or a kind of expectations game. In 1980 the media alert informed the public that Carter needed to stress his "experience" in the Oval Office, "reach out" to traditional Democrats, and make Reagan appear to be a trigger-happy cold warrior. Reagan, on the other hand, had to appear "presidential," "informed," and "not dangerous."

When the Reagan-Carter debate in Cleveland was over, polls seemed to show that Reagan had "won." But his winning was attributed, to some extent, to how relaxed, dignified, and in control he appeared—in effect, he had met the media expectations of success, in part by being alert to these expectations and preparing for them. Thus, Walter Cronkite reported on CBS immediately following the debate that Reagan had succeeded in allaying suspicions that he was "dangerous."

The fact that the public had been prepped to look in a certain direction—at style—raises questions about what substantive aspects of the debate may have been ignored. Did the audience, for example, forget to listen carefully to what was said? Reagan's chief poll taker, Richard Wirthlin, later declared that from watching the debate he was convinced that Reagan had won. But when he read the transcript of the debate the next day he thought, "Thank God it was on television." Reagan did not score well on substance. Similarly, in 1960, the "inexperienced" and "callow" Kennedy—as he was pictured in the many news accounts—exceeded the expectations of much of the television *viewing* audience by looking "good" but did worse with the radio *listening* audience, which concentrated on what was being said.

Picking the Winners and Losers

Inevitably, the two-candidate debate format leads to media concentration on who won and who lost. It is an accepted and easily understood model of news to stress competition and resolution. By 1984 journalists were able to characterize the outcome of the debates by giving the "score." Thus, Peter Jennings's opening report on ABC's "World News Tonight" for October 8, 1984: "So what do you do after a debate? You debate who won." Mondale, he said, had "by varying degrees won." Jennings then introduced correspondent Brit Hume, who said that Mondale had flown to New York that day for a Columbus Day parade and that "the way he was feeling, he didn't need a plane." Hume reported on a "tumultuous rally" in a New York hotel, where running mate Geraldine Ferraro introduced Mondale as the "heavyweight debater of the world." Next, Sam Donaldson reported that President Reagan's motorcade drove "slowly and painfully" out of Louisville where the "heavyweight debating champ had stubbed his toe on Mondale last night." Donaldson added: "Reagan struck a plaintive note in refusing to claim victory."

Opinion surveys are often used to reinforce the winner and loser images. After the first Reagan-Mondale debate, for example, a *Newsweek* poll showed that 54 percent thought Mondale had won, while 35 percent gave the win to Reagan. A *USA Today* poll gave a different breakdown: 39 percent named Mondale the winner, and 34 percent named Reagan the winner. On ABC, Barry Serafin at least had the good sense to point out that whatever the won-lost count, 61 percent of those sampled favored Reagan before the debate and 59 percent still favored Reagan after the debate. This last point is critical. Many news organizations have shown an awareness that, as Warren Mitofsky, director of the elections and surveys unit at CBS News, told the *New York Times* during the 1976 campaign, "The word 'win' is a media term." Polling "victories" are without meaning—the chief purpose of the debates is to get more votes on election day.

The media focus on the winner-loser story, however, cannot be extirpated. It spreads despite journalists' own awareness of its negative effects. When two academic researchers, Steven H. Chaffee of the University of Wisconsin and David O. Sears of the University of California at Los Angeles, looked at the 1976 debate coverage they found that 17 percent of newspaper space and 10 percent of TV news time dealt with the question of which candidate had won the debate. Our own sampling suggested that these percentages increased in 1980 and 1984. To put this substantial amount of coverage in perspective, it helps to know to what extent "winning" a debate or series of debates translates into winning votes on election day. According to a study of the 1984 election by the political scientist Gerald Pomper, among those voters who relied on the candidates' debates to decide their vote, Mondale gained three out of four votes. Mondale's problem, Pomper added, "was that less than a tenth of the electorate used the debates to determine their choice." In fairness, though, it ought to be pointed out that, in a very close election, such relatively small shifts can mean victory on election day— thus justifying much of the media attention.

Assessing the Candidate's Appearance

Sears and Chaffee also found that the greatest amount of coverage in 1976— more than four in every ten newspaper and broadcast stories—had been "given over to statements about the performances of the candidates, the personalities and competence levels they projected, and the impact the debate would have on their campaigns." Our own analysis of newspaper and magazine stories and network television coverage in each of the debate years reaffirms that media discussion of the images projected and dissections of the candidates' physical appearance and gestures constitute a major part of the coverage following a debate.

Television, of course, is a visual medium, and debates are live events, so reporters naturally try to describe how the candidates "appear." Just as obviously, the viewers have witnessed the same sequence of images and know what just happened. Yet reporters are supposed to report—even on what everyone has just seen a few moments before, whether it is a telecast of the Superbowl game or of a presidential news conference. After the first 1984 debate, most reports of Reagan's performance concluded that he was "defensive" and "tentative." The Great Communicator for the first time had "failed to turn the medium to his advantage," Howell Raines wrote in the *New York Times*. Raines's statement held a double message: the media have certain expectations for Reagan, and he did not measure up to these presumptive standards.

When people talk about their perceptions of events, Democratic voters see the virtues of their candidates, Republicans of theirs. Journalists rendering "professional" opinions supposedly transcend such selective perceptions. But when the topic is "personality," which is subject to so many different interpretations, objective verdicts become impossible. For example, CBS presented a special late news report following the 1980 Carter-Reagan debate; each correspondent had something to say about how the candidates appeared. Bruce Morton: "Reagan was the only one who seemed to have any fun with it. I thought Mr. Carter looked stale ... not ill at ease, but formal and no warmth, no sense of humor to him." Walter Cronkite agreed with Morton's assessment: "I think that as far as the warmth of the individual goes, Reagan clearly was a little more at home tonight with the audience than President Carter was ... it seemed to me he [Carter] was a little tight tonight." If viewers had turned off their sets at that point, they would have thought Reagan's "style" had been judged clearly superior to Carter's. Viewers who stayed tuned learned that Dan Rather, reporting from the Cleveland Convention Center, viewed the "warmth" issue differently: "Both men scored, if you must score, perhaps evenly in that department." Leslie Stahl and Bill Plante, also at the convention center, agreed with Rather's assessment. Stahl said, "I don't think Carter looked that uncomfortable; in fact, I was surprised that he was as relaxed and as composed as he was."

As demeanor and image become touchstones of success, we enter not only a subjective area of judgment, but also one full of nuance. In a society of television viewers, naturally, some of the coverage is bound to treat the debates as television peformances, rather than strictly political events. The resident TV critics on newspapers have grown in stature and gained credibility. They are not trained as political reporters or necessarily interested in politics. They write about the candidates as performers, sometimes in a way that calls as much attention to the critics as to the debates. Thus, Tom Shales, writing for the *Washington Post* after the first Reagan-Mondale debate, noted that Reagan looked handsomely presidential, his eyes glistening, while "Mondale's fried-egg eyes didn't look so sunken as usual, but they didn't particularly glisten either."

Viewing the Debates as Theater

Such "glisten factor" coverage pushes presidential debates further into the realm of theater, and away from substantive matters of policy. Stories concentrate not just on the way the candidates individually perform, but also on the visual dynamics of the evening as a whole. News is presented as dramatic confrontation within the confines of the 21-inch screen. When the debates do not provide "excitement," they are pronounced "dull," the deadliest media sin. "The debate failed to inject into the tepid campaign the excitement and voter involvement many predicted it would," reported the *New York Times's* R. W. Apple (also playing the expectation game), after the first debate between Gerald R. Ford and Jimmy Carter. Similarly, Susan Fraker wrote in *Newsweek:* "Hardly anyone would claim that the 1976 debates lived up to their great expectations. They bored some people, confused others." The *Times* in 1980 used almost the same language about the first Reagan-Carter meeting: "A flat encounter, hardly the dramatic confrontation that so many politicians had said would have the decisive impact on the nip-and-tuck election."

Journalism too often looks to theater rather than to the seminar, to memorable moments rather than to information-filled exchanges. According to the *Washington Post*, the "sharpest moment" in the first 1984 Reagan-Mondale debate came when Mondale accused Reagan of having a secret plan for tax increases. Reagan responded with a line he had used in the 1980 debate with Carter. Here is the *Post* account: " 'You know I wasn't going to say this at all but I can't help it, there you go again. I don't have a plan to raise taxes. . . .' 'Remember the last time you said that?' the Democratic challenger asked the president, resting an elbow on the lectern and turning to face Mr. Reagan. The television cameras framed the two of them, eye to eye, for the most dramatic moment of the debate." All three networks included this "moment" near the top of the following night's newscasts. Re-reading the exchange years later, we realize how empty of meaning it was, the camera-pleasing theatrics aside.

The media, star-struck and entertainment-minded, use frames of reference from theater or sports—everything is a metaphor for politics, except politics. James Reston in the *Times* began it back in 1960: "[Senator Kennedy] started out, like the Pittsburgh Pirates, as the underdog who wasn't supposed to be able to stay the course with the champ." David Broder of the *Washington Post* continued the locker room tradition on October 29, 1980, under the page-one headline "Carter on Points, But No KO": "Jimmy Carter accomplished almost every objective except the most important one: the destruction of Ronald Reagan's credibility as a potential president." On October 8, 1984, Donaldson on ABC's "World News Tonight" pulled out the Reagan-Mondale "fight" image once again: "the challenger looked good, but that doesn't matter. . . . [There was] no knockout and nothing will change." Donaldson's one-line verdict encapsulated an entire season of media coverage of political campaigns: the stress on appearance, on the score, and on touting the outcome.

Avoiding the Facts

As we have seen, it is normal for the media to report on both public and press impressions of the debate performances. One problem with this is that, while most people who watch a debate have some personal reactions, they may not know enough of the facts of the debate. A woman interviewed on ABC after the first Ford-Carter debate in 1976 raised this "issue about the issues" when she asked: "Who do you believe? They rebut each other and being an ordinary citizen, I feel like I'm not in a position to know which one is telling the truth."

Television is an information-poor medium: facts, statistics, charges, and countercharges fly past the viewer, often too rapidly to be digested. But because television is at the same time an emotion-rich medium, qualities of appearance such as "competence" and "trustworthiness" are easier to pick out. The media, by steering away from the facts, reinforce this process. The problem with relying on personal impressions of "trustworthiness" and "ability" is that what the audience sees is not always what the audience gets. After the first presidential debate of 1976, according to a study by the political scientist Thomas Patterson, the network newscasts spent 50 percent of their debate coverage on "winning" and "performance," while only 34 percent of the coverage dealt with "issues" and "policies."

One difficulty for journalists is that they have heard all the facts—repeatedly. Any journalist who has covered a campaign knows how repetitive candidates can be. The journalist's audience, however, has not had that•exposure. When journalists talk about public boredom they may actually be referring to their own.

A related problem is the power of the media to "make" a fact. This was demonstrated in the second 1976 Ford-Carter debate in San Francisco. Ford sought to praise eastern Europeans—and win some Polish-American votes. Instead, in responding to a question, he stated that eastern Europe was free of Soviet domination. Immediately following the debate, polls showed Ford with a slight edge over Carter. Then the television coverage jumped on the mistake. Donaldson reported on ABC that Ford's statement was "shocking and insensitive," and Ford's standing in the "who won" polls quickly dropped. By the next day, ABC reported that 50 percent of those polled thought Carter had won, and only 27 percent considered Ford the winner. Or, to take another example, in 1980 the CBS postdebate analysis of the Carter-Reagan encounter in Cleveland did review briefly the major points that each candidate had made, but the program did not cover any of the contradictions or mistakes made. CBS reviewed what the audience had just seen without offering much illumination of the issues or potentially confusing statements. Immediate television analysis focused—again—more on impressions than on substance. The network evening news over the next couple of nights also failed to highlight any mistakes. The messy matters of content were left to print. The *New York Times* did a front-page analysis two days after the debate and the *Washington Post* a story the day following the debate (though not on the front page). Both papers reported Reagan's denial of having said that the control of nuclear weapons "is none of our business." Reagan's statement had been made in response to Carter's allegation that he had said this and that it was a "dangerous" attitude. In fact, earlier in the year, in response to a question about nuclear arms in Pakistan, Reagan had replied that he would be sorry to see that country develop nuclear arms, and he had added: "Aren't we interfering with someone else's business by saying no to them? I just don't think it's any of our business." Television had let that go by, or at least left it for print to tidy up.

Looking back at the five themes we observed in the news coverage of the presidential debates, it is clear to us that the *alerting functions* of media should be distinguished from the *analytical functions.* Alerting news tells the media consumer an event should be attended to. Analytical news separates the ephemeral aspects of the event from its core and explains why the latter is important. There is no question about the alerting value of the press. Media coverage of the debates can influence not only how the audience perceives the candidates, but also how the candidates see themselves and how they act as well. After being told that they were "dull," Ford and Carter in 1976 "came out swinging," according to news accounts. Following Ford's eastern European "gaffe," we in the audience knew—as did Ford and his strategists—that he could not afford to make a mistake in his next and last debate.

The media cannot create news out of thin air, despite the popular mythology about the power of the press. Some new information must come to light before the audience can be alerted to it. Thus, the "senility factor" in 1984. The *Wall Street Journal* had reported in a page-one story after the first Reagan-Mondale debate, "Until Sunday's debate age had not been much of an issue in the election campaign. . . . The president's rambling responses and occasional apparent confusion injected an unpredictable new element into the race." The audience and not just the experts had observed an apparently befuddled Reagan. In visual terms, the press reminded viewers of what a lot of them had seen. Donaldson noted on the morning of the second debate, "People will be watching tonight because of Louisville to see whether the President stands up, makes sentences that make sense from the standpoint of not stammering and stuttering, and doesn't drool."

After the debate Reagan was reported as having been "measurably sharper" by Tom Shales and "more composed than the first time" by Howell Raines. Worries about Reagan's age, partly built by the media, had been deconstructed by the media—rising and disappearing in the period of a few days. It was, though, still the same Reagan and the same electorate. Perhaps dismayed by the implications of the senility construct, but certainly not swayed, the voters swallowed once and pulled the lever for Reagan on election day.

Our major concern here is about the second media function, the analytical values of the coverage. We see several reasons for this concern. First of all, when the media report who "won," they generally do not advance anyone's knowledge of what was said in the debate and what it means. Debating who won takes us one step further away from the debate itself; for example, the evening of the 1980 Reagan-Carter debate ABC conducted an instant phone-in poll to determine who had won. The ABC poll had many flaws—for one, the callers were a self-selected sample. But ABC went ahead anyway and announced its final tally—Reagan 2 to 1 over Carter. Ted Koppel kept reminding "Nightline" viewers that the "poll" was "unscientific," but he also termed Reagan's victory "enormous" and "much bigger than expected." The following evening, "Nightline" discussed what had been wrong with the ABC poll the night before, the media discussing the media.

As a result, viewers watching "Nightline" that evening were twice removed from the debate.

Second, we are concerned about media coverage that sometimes serves to separate—rather than connect—the viewer/voter from the central enlightening purpose of the debates. Coverage of the debates could be improved if the media concentrated less on the winner and loser and were more careful not to exclude substance when commenting on style.

Third, we should let television be television and print be print. We like drama as much as the next viewer; conflict and personality are factors in every campaign and ought to be covered. Television naturally focuses on images more than do the print media. Voters looking for the text of a debate should go to the newspapers of record. Together the two media can provide us with a more complete file, words and pictures of each candidate. Finally, the media—and especially television—must focus on what the debate can do for the public and not on what it can do for any specific medium. Journalists can show a concern for their own "image" and "appearance," by resisting the temptation to take center stage themselves during the debates.

6. NONPRESIDENTIAL DEBATES IN AMERICA

Norman Ornstein

From an early time in America's history, the speech on the hustings was a favored form of political campaigning. The tradition developed early and persisted long. Almost inevitably, the practice of rival candidates offering themselves up for direct comparison by making speeches to potential voters took hold; equally inevitably, the rival speeches frequently became direct interchanges, or debates. Thus, the practice of debating as a form of political campaigning has deep roots in American political tradition.

The Evolution of Political Debates

The tradition almost certainly is southern in origin, and probably began in Virginia. A Yankee newcomer to the state noted in 1811 that "people in these parts get into office by 'stump oratory,' praising and electioneering by themselves"; a native Virginian added that the "science of spouting" was practiced by every politically ambitious young Virginian, since "eloquence is almost the only road to fame and influence in the state."

The practice, begun before the Republic, took hold for several reasons. Most politicians of the early nineteenth century were trained according to a classical curriculum, which put a heavy emphasis on oratory and rhetoric; for example, courses on rhetoric were required at the College of William and Mary. The legal training and background of most political figures added to the value of public speaking. Holiday celebrations and political meetings generated by the revolutionary movement and by the development of the first party system provided many opportunities for stirring public speeches; public speaking also took on new power with the tremendous evangelical movement and its accompanying revival meetings. Moreover, stump speaking provided an opportunity for freeholders in the society, who rarely ran for office themselves, to assess those members of the gentry who dominated the political process—in a fashion that stressed the freeholders' power over the office seekers. Historian Daniel P. Jordan in *Political Leadership in Jefferson's Virginia* has offered another compelling reason for the widespread practice: "it must be remembered that rural isolation characterized Virginia in the Dynasty era. The typical citizen rarely saw the inside of a theater or a school and did not subscribe to the *National Intelligencer,* the *Richmond Inquirer,* or other newspapers of the period. Hustings speeches provided a substitute means of being educated, edified, and entertained."

As campaigning became a series of charges and countercharges, stump speaking became a form of debating, directly or indirectly. Good orators had to be prepared to take on rivals, hecklers, or hostile crowds. In a debate in Virginia in the 1830s between challenger George W. Bolling and incumbent U.S. House member George C. Dromgoole, Bolling went on the attack, taking advantage of the well-known fact that Dromgoole often bolstered his confidence on the campaign trail by consuming a quart of toddy—three-fourths whiskey and one-fourth water. Bolling asked the audience if Dromgoole, whose presence in Congress had been inconsistent, was preferable to a man like himself who would faithfully attend congressional sessions. Dromgoole quickly responded, "Fellow citizens, had you rather have to represent you, me, who will often be absent, but who will support your interest by my speech and vote when I am present, or Colonel Bolling, who will always be present, but who will always speak and vote against you?" Dromgoole was returned to Congress.

In another instance early in the Republic, in Kanawha County, Virginia, after several candidates for Congress and the General Assembly had spoken at great length, the final candidate among them rose, required to speak by tradition, even though his views were well known. The hour was late and the crowd restless, so, according to one witness, he said simply, "If you choose to elect me, I will serve you to the best of my abilities; if you don't, you may go to _____." He left the platform to loud cheers and was overwhelmingly elected.

The term *stump speaking* probably came from the practice of felling a tree to create a raised platform for the speaker. In areas where newspapers were scarce, public speaking became almost essential to communicating with voters. One authority on nineteenth-century Illinois noted, "Unless a candidate at all accustomed to public speaking—and few others were selected—was able and willing to meet his opponent on the stump, his prospect of success was slim."

A New York reporter, describing Illinois politics in 1858, was surprised by the open and tumultuous air that surrounded stump politicking:

> It is astonishing how deep an interest in politics this people take. Over long dreary miles of hot and dusty prairie, the processions of eager partisans come— on foot, on horseback, in wagons drawn by horses or mules; men, women and children, old and young; the half sick just out of the last "shake"; children in arms, infants at the maternal front, pushing on in clouds of dust and beneath a blazing sun; settling down at the town where the meeting is, with hardly a chance for sitting, and even less opportunity for eating, waiting in anxious groups for hours at the places of speaking, talking, discussing, litigious, vociferous, while the roar of artillery, the music of bands, the waving of banners, the buzzes of the crowds, as delegation after delegation appears; the cry of pedlars, vending all sorts of wares, from an infallible cure for "Agur" to a monster watermelon in slices to suit purchasers—combine to render the occasion one scene of confusion and commotion.

Changing History: The Lincoln-Douglas Debates

The *New York Post* reporter was in Illinois in 1858 to witness the debates between Senator Stephen A. Douglas and his challenger, Abraham Lincoln, which attracted national attention at the time. The Illinois Senate race was perhaps the epitome of stump speaking; both Douglas and Lincoln covered the state on extensive speaking schedules, in addition to their debate encounters. By one account, Douglas traveled over 5,000 miles and made 59 speeches, two to three hours in length, in fifty-seven counties; gave 17 additional addresses of from 25 to 45 minutes, and made 37 replies to addresses of welcome. All but 2 of his public speeches were outdoors, with 7 delivered during rainstorms. Lincoln, by his own account, gave 63 full speeches and 130 addresses in all.

With all this talking, it is not surprising that a series of joint encounters was proposed; also not surprisingly, the challenge came from Lincoln, who was the decided underdog in the race. (This was the era before direct election of senators; the campaign was for candidates for the state legislature, who would in turn select the state's U.S. senator.)

Douglas, who certainly could hold his own with anybody in a debate, recognized the political pitfalls of refusing the challenge; he also realized that debates would attract national attention that could further his presidential ambitions. He accepted the challenge.

Douglas and Lincoln agreed to seven debates to be held in towns in the seven congressional districts in which they had not yet appeared. Each debate was to be three hours in length with the first speaker given an hour and the second, an hour-and-a-half. The first speaker would return for the final half hour.

News of the debates quickly captured attention, including national attention. Historians believe that the Senate debates subsequently shaped presidential politics. The focus on states' rights deeply damaged Douglas's chances, while vaulting the obscure Lincoln to national prominence.

Our rosy—but hazy—images of history suggest that the seven debates were the epitome of sparkling dialogue, sharp wit, and deep intellect, keeping the large audiences spellbound for each three-hour clash. Although the debates were compelling, reality was less striking. As Walt Anderson has described them in *Campaigns: Cases in Political Conflict*, "The Lincoln-Douglas debates may not have been great distillations of political wisdom. The two candidates occasionally rose to eloquence, but more often their speeches were windy, repetitive, and full of distortions of one another's previous remarks."

Despite the attention they attracted and their enormous significance, the Lincoln-Douglas debates did not trigger an institutionalization of debates in American politics. Debates continued to appear in elections in the South and the Midwest. For example, a series of debates in 1888 propelled the political movement of Ben Tillman (later known as Pitchfork Ben), and another series in 1890 helped to elect him governor of South Carolina. Tillman then provided an impetus for the end of Reconstruction and the resurgence of white supremacy in the South.

But the Tillman case was more the exception than the rule. In general, as the nineteenth century ended, debating had declined as a campaign art form in the South—no doubt in major part because of the decline of two-party politics. Reuben Davis, a veteran member of Congress from Mississippi, lamented the condition in 1889:

> Forty years ago, constant practice had made our public speakers so skilful in debate that every question was made clear even to men otherwise uneducated. For the last twenty years this practical union between politicians and people has not existed. Only one party is allowed to speak, and the leaders of that party no

longer debate, they simply declaim and denounce. Upon this crude and windy diet, the once robust and sturdy political convictions of our people have dwindled into leanness and decay. In my judgement, this state of affairs is fatally injurious to our institutions, and dangerous to our liberties. The people follow with confidence the misleading and uncontradicted assertions of their leaders, and act upon false impressions, to their own prejudice and the injury of the common good. The evil of mischievous assertion is greatly lessened when free discussion is allowed, and error exposed and combated by the unsparing vigor of an opposing party. Free government becomes an absurdity when all shades of opinion are not allowed the fullest expression.

Another reason for the passing of face-to-face debates was the changing nature of the electorate and of party competition. Democratization raised the need for more mass mobilization; this in turn led to the development and expansion of mass political rallies organized by the parties. In 1902 political scientist M. Ostrogorski in *Democracy and the Organization of Political Parties* commented sadly on the replacement of debates by speeches at partisan rallies. Debates, he noted, allowed citizens "to grasp then and there the arguments pro and con presented by public men," while rallies had as their goal "not so much to instruct and convert as to edify the audience, to strengthen them in the party creed."

The Twentieth Century

While debates clearly diminished in American politics around the turn of the century, they did not die out entirely. Debates still were held—for example, in some southern races where genuine primary contests took place. More common, perhaps, was the time-honored strategy of an outsider or insurgent challenging a frontrunner or incumbent to debate, with the latter refusing. In 1926, for example, in a three-way Democratic party primary for the Senate, underdog John Van Valzah challenged incumbent senator Duncan U. Fletcher to debate jointly at every county seat in the state. Fletcher replied tartly, "If you are finding it impossible to interest the people in your candidacy, it is not my purpose to accept your self defense challenge and neglect official duties going all over the state to promote your campaign."

Debates began to pick up steam in other parts of the country, especially in areas of strong two-party competition. And many of them, in retrospect, influenced the course of American politics and history. High on that list was the series of five debates in 1946 between incumbent Democratic congressman Jerry Voorhis and his Republican challenger, Richard M. Nixon. The first debate was organized by Independent Voters of South Pasadena, a liberal, New Deal-oriented political action group trying to play a role in conservative southern California politics. Its goal was actually to arrange a debate between two candidates for the California Assembly. The strategy to "smoke out" the reluctant incumbent assemblyman was to organize a forum with candidates for various offices debating issues on the same platform. Included in the invitations were the area's candidates for the U.S. House—incumbent Voorhis and his challenger, Nixon.

Before agreeing to debate, Nixon insisted on several conditions—he would be allowed to arrive late because of a previous commitment, he would speak last, and there would be no set topic. Apparently without much thought, Voorhis's managers readily accepted.

The first debate was held on a balmy evening in the junior high auditorium in South Pasadena. Almost 1,000 people attended, exceeding everyone's expectations. Voorhis had neither prepared nor been briefed for the debate; he apparently assumed that he would simply slaughter his inexperienced opponent.

It turned out very differently. Nixon, with impeccable timing, arrived onstage just as Voorhis finished speaking. Nixon's prepared talk attacked bureaucracy, red tape, and the mess in Washington and called for strong action to stop the labor disputes and strikes that had gripped the nation after the war. But the real impact of the debate came in the question-and-answer period. Nixon had created a major campaign issue out of an alleged endorsement of Voorhis made by a communist-dominated group called the CIO-PAC. In fact, the group had condemned the anticommunist Voorhis, calling him in an editorial a "false liberal." For much of the campaign up to the debate, Voorhis, following the typical incumbent's strategy, had simply ignored the Nixon charge. But two days before the debate, in a paid ad in community newspapers and in a press release, Voorhis denied the charge flatly.

During the question period in the debate, the issue came up again, as recounted by Voorhis backer Paul Bullock:

> Voorhis was now ready to challenge Nixon on the PAC issue. He knew, beyond question, that the CIO-PAC had refused to endorse him, and now was the time to call Nixon's bluff. What he did not know (and what those of us who *did* know had completely forgotten to tell him) was that a political committee of the Southern California chapter of the *National Citizen's* PAC had reluctantly recommended an endorsement of Voorhis, in a mimeographed bulletin circulated internally within the organization. A copy of that document had come into Nixon's possession, and he was ready when Voorhis demanded the promised "proof" of the PAC charge. Walking up to Voorhis . . . Nixon shoved the piece of paper at his opponent and identified it as documentary evidence of the truth of his allegations.
>
> Voorhis was completely taken by surprise. Unprepared for this move and confused by it, he mumbled that this seemed to be a different organization. Nixon then read to the audience the names of those people who served on boards or committees in both organizations, omitting the numerous others who did not fit in that category.

The problem worsened through the rest of the question-and-answer period. There was a three-minute limit on answers to questions, and Voorhis, unable to deal with the intricacies of complex issues in three minutes, was constantly on the defensive, seeming fuzzy or uncertain; Nixon, on the other hand, always came up with a rapid, brief, simple, and adequate response.

Nixon clearly won a major victory in the debate, and he knew it. Within days he challenged Voorhis to more debates, and four more were held throughout the district. Nixon stepped up his attacks on Voorhis's alleged endorsements, claiming in ads that Voorhis had admitted the truth of Nixon's charges. New allegations about Voorhis's voting record were made in subsequent debates. Voorhis remained almost constantly on the defensive, accepting Nixon's allegations and charges as the terms of discussion during the following debates—a set of actions which, as he himself later conceded, were mistakes. Many of Nixon's charges were fabricated or at best distorted—but they were never effectively rebutted or challenged.

In the end, bolstered by his stunning debate successes, Nixon won a sizable victory against a popular and entrenched incumbent. Admittedly, 1946 was a good year for conservative Republicans, but Nixon's victory was one of the most stunning upsets and ensured the newly elected congressman a good deal of attention—and good committee assignments in Congress as well—all of which were useful in Nixon's subsequent career.

Sixteen years later, yet another critical debate occurred in a congressional campaign with national significance. After John F. Kennedy became president, his Massachusetts Senate seat became vacant; the 1962 contest to fill it quickly came down to a Democratic party primary battle between Kennedy's brother, Edward Moore Kennedy, a young political novice, and Edward McCormack, the Massachusetts attorney general and nephew of Speaker of the House of Representatives John McCormack. The high-profile campaign involved an all-out effort by Kennedy and the vaunted Kennedy organization. As Murray B. Levin, in *Kennedy Campaigning: The System and the Style as Practiced by Senator Edward Kennedy*, noted, "If Edward Kennedy overwhelmed McCormack in September and demolished the Republican candidate in November, not only was he likely to be re elected to the Senate again and again but a truly dra matic win would enhance the mystique of Kennedy invincibility. The prestige of the President and the legitimacy of Edward Kennedy's candidacy were also at stake. [While Kennedy had enormous sums of money and a major organization at his disposal, he] almost made a calamitous error of judgment during the campaign when he accepted McCormack's invitation to debate the issues on television, with results that were quite unpredictable."

The Kennedy team recognized that McCormack was likely to be on the attack throughout the debate, and Kennedy decided to act the part of a United States senator: dignified and cool, ignoring all attacks. While McCormack had planned on attacking to force Kennedy to blow his cool—and thus the election—neither he nor his advisers had apparently considered the possibility that Kennedy would ignore the attack.

The first debate, held on August 27, covered subjects from tax cuts and shoe tariffs to nuclear stockpiles and the United Nations. Both candidates followed their game plans. The most dramatic moment of the debate and of the campaign came with McCormack's closing statement: "If his name was Edward Moore, with his qualifications, with your qualifications, Teddy, if it was Edward Moore, your candidacy would be a joke, but nobody's laughing because his name is not Edward Moore. It's Edward Moore Kennedy."

Kennedy appeared stunned and ashen-faced at this attack; the debate ended with McCormack's supporters bursting into wild applause. Afterwards, many Kennedy people were morose, while the McCormack camp was enthusiastic. But by the next morning, both sides began to change their views. It soon became clear that McCormack had gone too far—that he had enraged (and energized) Kennedy supporters and alienated many other Democrats. Yet Kennedy's restraint and decorum had served him well. Kennedy's image shifted from that of the frontrunner at the head of an immense machine, running against a valiant underdog, to that of a nice young man under vicious attack.

The second debate, held on September 5, two weeks before the primary, proved dull and relatively meaningless. McCormack was less aggressive and avoided personal attacks, while Kennedy repeated his bland recitation of issue positions, facts, and figures. On election day Kennedy outpolled McCormack by better than 2-1; in November, Kennedy outdistanced his Republican opponent 56 percent to 44 percent.

In the years since the Kennedy-McCormack encounters, debates have affected many important campaigns. One of the most common features of these debates has been that overconfident candidates have discovered that image and appearance can outweigh substance. In 1964 Democratic Senate candidate Pierre Salinger confidently approached a debate with his Republican opponent, Hollywood actor George Murphy. As Dan Nimmo noted in *The Political Persuaders,* "Salinger hoped to demonstrate to 3.5 million Californians that Murphy did not know enough to be a senator. Murphy, however, was more interested in appearances—in looking like a senator rather than talking like one. Salinger looked pudgy, self-indulgent, irritable, and shady, but Murphy smiled, radiated, and portrayed an image of sincerity and courtliness. Instead of responding to Salinger's arguments, Murphy (like Kennedy in 1960) reiterated the points he had made throughout the campaign. Salinger (Kennedy's press secretary in 1960) complained, 'I guess this just shows the futility of trying to come to grips with anyone as slippery as my opponent.' "

That same year the New York Senate race between Republican incumbent Kenneth Keating and Democratic challenger Robert F. Kennedy was affected by a debate that was *not* held. Keating, former Kennedy aide Jeff Greenfield later wrote in *Playing to Win: An Insider's Guide to Politics,* "challenged Robert Kennedy to debate, buying broadcast time just before the election and presenting an empty chair just to 'prove' that Kennedy would not debate. The only problem was that Kennedy was in the same broadcast complex, and decided to accept the 'invitation.' Keating's aides barred the door, and after the broadcast Keating fled Kennedy and the press."

By the 1980s, after televised presidential debates had become a staple in presidential primary and general elections, candidates, journalists, and other political actors made candidate debates a basic feature in elections at all other levels. These days, debates are the norm, not the exception, in congressional, mayoral, and gubernatorial politics; when debates do not occur, usually because of a frontrunner's reluctance to take chances, failure to debate often becomes a principal issue.

The impact of debates is heightened because they are frequently televised on both commercial and public channels. A recent survey by the National Association of Broadcasters of 303 television stations found that over half offered free time on their stations to political candidates for broadcast debates, up from 45 percent in 1984. Nearly 50 percent of the stations actually aired political debates.

Many of those debates were sponsored by the television stations themselves, although an outside sponsor was also often involved. State and local chapters of the League of Women Voters have been particularly active in congressional debates. In 1986, for example, twenty-eight of the thirty-four Senate contests saw debates; in twenty-one of these races, some or all of the debates were sponsored by a state League. Local Leagues also sponsored upwards of fifty debates in 1986 House races.

Not surprisingly, debates have often proved critical to the victory or defeat of candidates. The tactics surrounding debates—the obligatory debate challenge from underdogs, the reluctance of incumbents to debate, the "empty chair" tactic—have remained an integral part of the campaign scene.

In many key 1986 races the challenger's bid to debate and the incumbent's reluctance to accept became an integral theme. Even where it did not affect the outcome of the race, this pattern had a significant impact on the images of the candidates. In the Ohio gubernatorial contest the refusal by challenger and former governor James Rhodes to debate incumbent Richard Celeste clearly hurt Rhodes in his ultimately unsuccessful comeback effort. Rhodes's refusal enabled Celeste to be the aggressor in the campaign, thus blunting the charges that he had been tied indirectly to a major savings-and-loan scandal.

In Florida incumbent senator Paula Hawkins refused for months to debate her challenger, Florida governor Bob Graham. When she finally agreed to a debate, her earlier refusal became a major issue during the discussion, and many observers viewed her excuses as weak. In Alabama freshman GOP senator Jeremiah Denton refused to debate his opponent, Democratic representative Richard Shelby, and found hardhitting television ads making an issue of it late in the campaign. A round of commercials beginning October 22, 1986, had the theme, "Is Jeremiah Denton in Touch with Alabama?" A narrator said Denton "comes home rarely . . . tells us he's too busy to see us . . . gets angry when we ask him why. . . ." Then a filmclip showed Denton ranting, "I can't be down there patting babies on the butt and get that done in Washington." The screen turned black with white letters: "Denton Refuses to Debate." "What," asked the voiceover, "could Senator Denton be hiding from? A copy of the *Congressional Record* was then slammed down as the narrator asked, "Do you think it's his record?"

In several instances incumbents set so many unrealistic conditions for a debate that they incurred the wrath and ridicule of political analysts and journalists. A refusal to debate his Republican opponent on television, followed by an insistence that the one debate contain every minor party candidate and appear on a UHF public television station instead of a network affiliate put Washington, D.C., mayor Marion Barry on the defensive and attracted a scathing editorial in the *Washington Post,* but it had no material impact on the election.

Probably more injurious were the tactics employed by New York governor Mario Cuomo to avoid debating his Republican adversary, Andrew O'Rourke. Cuomo, who on the strength of his stunning debate performances four years earlier had come from behind to win the Democratic nomination against New York mayor Edward Koch and the governorship over Republican Lewis Lehrman, insisted for months that he would not debate O'Rourke until the Republican made a full financial disclosure. When that issue disappeared, Cuomo insisted that the television debate include Lenora Fulani, the candidate of the extremist National Alliance Party and a follower of Louis Farrakhan. All other candidates withdrew from the television debate under that condition. One debate ultimately was held, though not on television, and it was inconclusive and anticlimactic. The reaction to Cuomo's strategy, however, was not inconclusive. Columnist Mary McGrory wrote that Cuomo "choked on the debate question— with disastrous results." The *New York Times* editorialized, "The conciliatory, mediating tactics that brought peace to Forest Hills surely helped Mr. Cuomo achieve his favorable legislative results. Why, then, in his campaign has he struck so authoritarian a posture? . . . Was it necessary to dodge television debates even into the closing hours of the campaign just to try adding a few more percentage points to his total?" (Cuomo had first come to prominence when as an attorney he had mediated the Forest Hills public housing disputes.)

In keeping with tradition, clever and offbeat tactics by challengers occasionally "smoked out" incumbents. In New Hampshire, for example, Senate Democratic challenger Endicott Peabody went around the state debating a chicken (actually an aide dressed up in a chicken outfit) to dramatize the failure of his opponent to debate. The ploy got so much attention that incumbent Warren Rudman finally agreed to debate.

For all these campaign ploys, the overwhelming share of Senate and gubernatorial campaigns in 1986 featured one or more debates, and many, if not most, of these were televised. The debates tended to reinforce themes that the candidates had adopted in their stump speeches and television advertising. This meant that the negative, attacking style that characterized many elections in 1986 also dominated many debates. Both incumbents and challengers went on the offensive. Sometimes their tactics took particular advantage of television's visual impact.

In North Dakota Republican Senate incumbent Mark Andrews, facing a stiff challenge from Kent Conrad, ran an ad featuring the *Village Voice*, which had endorsed Conrad along with several other Democratic congressional candidates. In a debate in Fargo on October 19, Andrews waved a copy of the *Voice* at the television cameras and noted that Conrad's picture was right next to Bella Abzug's. Andrews charged that Conrad was out of step with North Dakota. "Let's not give New York or Massachusetts another senator." Andrews lost.

Not all 1986 debates focused on personalities and tactics. For example, debates between Republican Constance Morella and Democrat Stewart Bainum in the congressional district of Montgomery County, Maryland, focused on a range of important policy issues, from arms control to medicare. Even in debates that featured personal attacks, serious discussion of issues was important as well. Throughout these debates many of the patterns now evident in presidential campaigns also held true: "winning" a debate does not mean ultimately getting more votes, and style can be far more significant than substance. In Washington state, for example, in a very close Senate race, incumbent Republican Slade Gorton won the debates on points but lost support on style. A panel of undecided voters selected by the television station that broadcast the debate gave the debate "victory" to Gorton, but said that after the debate they were *more*, not less, inclined to vote for Democratic challenger Brock Adams. A leading Republican described Gorton's demeanor as "too cold, too tight, too forced." The debates may have made the difference in Gorton's narrow defeat.

Like presidential debates, the nonpresidential debates have high visibility within the affected communities and states, but they remain distinct in many respects from presidential debates. Most congressional, gubernatorial, and mayoral debates tend to look more at issues, voting records, and positions of candidates; concrete issues and genuine differences are emphasized more. The thrust of public expectations is also different. As political scientist Nelson Polsby wrote in 1984, "modern [presidential] debates are the political version of the Indianapolis Speedway. What we're all there for—the journalists, the political pundits, the public—is to see somebody crack up in flames." With some exceptions, that is much less true in nonpresidential debates, in part because the stakes are lower.

Yet presidential debates and most other political debates tend to have similar formats: a panel of journalists asks questions of the candidates, with time allowed for response and rebuttal. Most modern-day political debates are not close equivalents to the Lincoln-Douglas contest—or by extension, to stump speaking, where candidates openly presented themselves and their cases to gatherings of voters. But of course, even if the format and the audiences have changed, the prevalence and importance of debates today can be linked directly to stump speaking and the era of campaign oratory. In part because they draw so directly on this democratic tradition in American politics, debates in all likelihood will continue to expand in their presence and importance.

Part II

THE DEBATE
ABOUT DEBATE SPONSORSHIP

7. SPONSORSHIP OF PRESIDENTIAL DEBATES: WHO DOES IT? WHO CARES?

Frank J. Donatelli and Leslie C. Francis

Clearly, presidential debates are in the public interest. It must be remembered, however, that no matter how much these contests contribute to a better informed electorate, they may or may not be in the strategic interests of the candidates themselves. And *it is the candidates and their managers who will ultimately determine whether or not debates are held—and what form they will take.*

A candidate enters a presidential race because he or she wants to be president of the United States, to possess and wield the power unique to that office. Presumably, every serious candidate will view the presidency as a means to further the public interest, yet the foremost concern during the course of the campaign will be winning.

All candidates develop strategies and organizations which they hope will propel them into the Oval Office. Every campaign speech, rally, media advertisement, and press release must be tailored to fit that strategy. The decision whether to debate, whom to debate, how often to debate and in what format will depend primarily upon the role a debate plays in the overall strategy, and whether or not participation in a debate advances that strategy. Presidential debates have been held *only* when the major candidates have found it politically prudent to participate.

In 1960 the three major networks sponsored, in rotation, four debates between Richard Nixon and John F. Kennedy. In a series of twelve preliminary meetings, network representatives negotiated directly with the candidates such basic questions as debate format, number and timing, composition of the panel, and the details of set design. Major questions were not settled until both candidates and the sponsor were satisfied. This was the high-water mark for sponsor control over presidential debates. Since the Kennedy-Nixon encounters, presidential debates have been marked by the passing of control from the sponsors to the candidates, who have made the major decisions.

Debates took place in 1960 because both Kennedy and Nixon perceived that they were consistent with basic strategic considerations. Kennedy was uniquely skilled at utilizing television, and he believed that a series of debates might negate questions about his readiness for the job. Nixon also had confidence in his media abilities, as well as in his knowledge of the issues. Also, he did not want to be viewed as ducking Kennedy by not debating.

In 1964 Lyndon B. Johnson refused to debate Barry Goldwater primarily because he did not see any advantage in giving his underdog opponent free exposure. Nor was Johnson particularly comfortable with television or adept at using it.

Because of his experience in 1960, Nixon managed to avoid debating in 1968 and 1972. He saw no reason to take a major risk by giving additional exposure to his Democratic challengers, Hubert Humphrey and George McGovern, respectively.

Presidential debates resurfaced in 1976 because the major candidates believed such contests would be in their self-interest. Gerald R. Ford was an unknown commodity in national electoral politics. A series of nationally televised debates appeared to offer him the opportunity to prove himself and to overcome a large deficit in public opinion polls. Democratic challenger Jimmy Carter, also not widely known, felt that debates would boost his recognition and enhance his presidential credentials. Moreover, Carter had been actively campaigning for greater openness in government, and a debate with President Ford clearly reinforced that message.

Four years later the situation was much more complex and uncertain, yet it illustrates better than any recent presidential election the political considerations which dominate the issue of debates at that level. By not campaigning actively for renomination during the Iranian hostage crisis, President Carter ended up not debating his principal Democratic challenger, Senator Edward Kennedy. That fact came to haunt him. Because his "Rose Garden strategy" of the spring was still fresh in the minds of the voters and the media, the Carter campaign felt pressured to debate in the fall. The League of Women Voters then sought to sponsor a debate among the three major candidates—President Carter, GOP challenger Ronald Reagan, and independent John Anderson.

Carter's staff believed that Anderson, a former Republican representative who unsuccessfully sought his party's presidential nomination, would draw more votes away from Carter than from Reagan. For Carter to participate in a three-way debate and thereby increase Anderson's stature would be a strategic mistake. Meanwhile, the League of Women Voters insisted that Anderson was a viable candidate and therefore had to be included in any debate that it sponsored. The three campaigns and the League then spent weeks engaged in the political equivalent of a mating dance, until Reagan and Anderson agreed to meet in a debate without Carter's involvement.

Campaign chronicler Theodore H. White described the event in *America in Search of Itself: The Making of the President 1956-1980*: "The debate in Baltimore, on September 21, went on as scheduled, Carter absent. . . . For a full hour and a half, Reagan let Anderson carry the attack on Carter while he showed himself not as a demon, but rather as a quizzical, cheerful man." In hindsight, the Carter strategy turned out to be wrong. White explained, "Three days later, the polling apparatus of the nation began to report the results. Though Anderson had scored best, as one-on-one over Reagan, the big loser was not Reagan but Carter. The image the Carter campaign had painted of Reagan the killer had simply not shown on the screen."

The night of the Reagan-Anderson debate turned out to be the high point of the latter's 1980 campaign. Just days after the Baltimore encounter, the League offered a new formulation—a two-way debate between Carter and Reagan, followed by a three-way contest including Anderson. Carter's campaign accepted immediately, but Reagan demurred, claiming such an arrangement would be "unfair" to Anderson.

By the middle of October, polls showed the race between Reagan and Carter tightening, with Anderson dropping fast (to substantially below 15 percent, the level used by the League of Women Voters to classify him a viable candidate).

Jimmy Carter's chief political strategist, Hamilton Jordan, described in *Crisis: The Last Year of the Carter Presidency* what happened next. "Reagan . . . decided to debate without John Anderson. To me, this was a clear sign that Reagan and company realized that we were closing in on them. . . . [W]e had everything to lose and very little to gain in a debate. . . . But now, it couldn't be avoided."

Jordan, of course, was correct. The Reagan camp had concluded that only a Reagan-Carter debate would provide the opportunity to move undecided voters toward Reagan. Although the polls were one factor in the decision, Reagan and his advisers also felt that he could beat Carter in a one-on-one situation. Negotiations were held and a deal was struck: the two major party nominees would meet in a single debate, a week before the election.

On October 28, 1980, Carter and Reagan squared off in their only face-to-face contest of the year. While many observers thought Carter won the contest "on points," Reagan turned out to be the real winner in the eyes of most viewers. He did not seem dangerous or unpredictable but rather at ease and pleasant. Many voters felt comfortable with him as a potential president.

Days later and hours before the polls opened on Tuesday, November 4, the effects of the prolonged Iranian hostage crisis and the results of the debate crystallized for millions of American voters who had been, to that point, undecided. The result was a tremendous shift toward Reagan and an electoral vote landslide.

In 1984 the decision of an incumbent president well ahead in the polls to debate his opponent did much to institutionalize these fall contests. Reagan, who had participated in debates in the 1980 primaries and as a challenger in 1980, felt he should do so again as an incumbent. Meanwhile, former vice president Walter Mondale, having lagged behind all summer, was eager to debate the president, knowing that such an event might be his only chance to pull off an upset.

Just as the decision on whether to debate is determined by the candidates' perceptions of their own self-interest, the format of presidential debates is dictated more by the candidates' strategies than by considerations of a broader public interest or the preferences of the sponsors or television networks. While an outside sponsor may push for a format which includes several debates and allows the candidates to cross-examine one another, ultimately the key choices are the candidates' to make.

In negotiations over debate format, the candidate who stands to gain least from a debate, the frontrunner, will be at a decided advantage. Because he or she does not need a debate, the frontrunner's threat to withdraw will be the most credible. The other major candidate, whose only political hope may ride on a series of successful debates, often will have little choice but to accede to the frontrunner's demands. In 1984 that was clearly the case.

Three main factors explain the shift in control from sponsor to candidate since 1960. First, the candidates are aware of their leverage. There can be no debates without them, and they will not agree to anything contrary to their self-interest. Second, the candidates now have a historical perspective of the importance of fall debates and are more careful to ensure that all of the particulars negotiated are consistent with their overall campaign strategies. Third, the proliferation of potential sponsors has reduced sponsor leverage.

In 1960 Congress suspended for one year the equal-time regulations that had prohibited coverage of debates unless all candidates were included. Anxious for Congress to make the suspension permanent, the networks moved quickly and aggressively to secure acceptances from the two major candidates. The potential for other groups to offer competing bids was limited.

The success of debates in 1976, 1980, and 1984 under the sponsorship of the League of Women Voters has enticed other groups to express interest in sponsoring the 1988 debates. Having so many willing suitors is bound to strengthen the candidates' bargaining position, no matter who is finally selected to host the debates.

All of the potential sponsors have their advocates, and each can make a strong case. Our main purpose here is not to knock down their respective arguments or to support any particular category of sponsor. Instead, we propose that *any* sponsor should be asked to answer several key questions.

How does a prospective debate sponsor propose to deal with the reality of candidate control, while also seeking to maximize candidate accountability to the voting public? What steps will be taken to ensure that candidates will not be able to hide behind real or contrived disagreements with the sponsor? And does a prospective sponsor both fully understand and share the high stakes involved in the events?

Such political accountability is the best way to guarantee that the wide range of important issues—from how major independent and third party candidates are treated to whether presidential debates are institutionalized—are resolved in ways which best serve the public interest.

In 1980, for example, had the major party candidates been forced to justify to the public their reasons for including or excluding third party candidates, and had the League of Women Voters possessed a more acute understanding of the political dimensions of its approach and decisions, chances are that Carter and Reagan would have debated more than once. The real lesson is that such key strategic decisions should be made by the candidates who, in return, should be forced to accept the political consequences of their decisions.

Regardless of who sponsors debates in 1988—and beyond—the press, the public, and the sponsors themselves must understand that it will be the candidates who will drive every major decision surrounding the events themselves. That is the way it is, and—frankly—that is the way it should be. As usual, however, the voters will have the final say.

8. POLITICAL PARTIES SHOULD SPONSOR DEBATES

Newton N. Minow and Clifford M. Sloan

Who should sponsor presidential debates? To answer this question, we must consider both the history of debates and the goal of institutionalizing them.

Some observers have suggested legislation requiring presidential debates; others recommend a governmental commission to administer debates. This cure might well be worse than the disease. As it is, we live in an overly legislated and regulated age, and any move to impose legislation in new areas of human affairs should bear a heavy burden of justification. Despite the value of presidential debates and the public interest in them, it seems unwise for the government to intrude on this aspect of campaign decision making. In addition, legislation requiring debates might well pose constitutional problems.

Excluding a governmental body, there are at least three potential sponsors: the media, as in 1960; an independent organization such as the League of Women Voters, as in 1976, 1980, and 1984; or the major political parties. There are currently no legal obstacles to any of these groups' sponsoring debates. In considering the possible sponsors, the most important question should be which sponsor is most likely to bring about the institutionalization of debates.

The networks took great pride in their sponsorship of the Great Debates in 1960. But as television producer Don Hewitt noted at the time, network involvement confuses the role of the media. The networks have no more of a function in planning presidential debates than they do in planning nominating conventions. To be sure, networks have sponsored debates in the presidential primaries, and local media frequently sponsor local debates. The networks also regularly interview candidates on shows such as "Meet the Press," "Nightline," and "Nightwatch." Nevertheless, in the general election the central role of the media should be to *cover* the campaign. When the networks participate, as they did in 1960, in planning and sponsoring the debates, that role becomes blurred. Most important, designating the networks as sponsors does not advance the goal of institutionalizing the debates. Since the networks quite properly have no official role vis-à-vis the candidates, the commitment of the networks to sponsor the debates does not ensure that candidates will participate and debates will occur.

Sponsorship by an independent organization such as the League of Women Voters eliminates the problem of the confusion of journalistic roles. But like the networks, an independent organization lacks a formal relationship with the candidates. Without such a relationship, arrangements about the debates must, as

Adapted with permission from "For Great Debates, A New Plan for Future Presidential TV Debates," by Newton N. Minow and Clifford M. Sloan, a Twentieth Century Fund Paper, 1987.

in previous presidential debates, be left to the brief period *after* the nomination conventions when the general election campaigns are in full swing. Significantly, the absence of a relationship between an independent organization and the candidates means that relying on such an organization does not help to institutionalize presidential debates.

In contrast, sponsorship by the political parties offers several advantages. Although candidate participation is not absolutely assured, political parties are the most likely vehicle for institutionalizing debates. Because of their close relationship to the candidates, political parties can accomplish much of the debate planning well in advance of the actual campaign—and, to a great extent, commit the candidates to the planning of details.

In fact, the Democratic and Republican parties have agreed in principle to sponsor the 1988 presidential debates. This agreement is an important step toward institutionalizing the debates as a central element of presidential campaigns. To further this goal, in February 1987 the Democratic and Republican parties established a not-for-profit, tax-exempt, bipartisan presidential debates organization to plan and administer a series of debates.

The parties have also set up a broadly based committee of citizens to advise on the planning and conduct of the debates. The presidential debates organization and its advisory committee should have the authority necessary to resolve the disputes and questions that inevitably arise.

Before the presidential campaign, the bipartisan organization should determine the date, place, and number of debates. Specifically, it should agree, as early as possible, to a series of at least four debates—three between presidential nominees and one between vice-presidential nominees—to take place between Labor Day and the last week in October. In July 1987 the parties announced the dates of four 1988 debates, one of which is likely to be a vice-presidential debate, and all of which are scheduled for this period. A series of debates allows greater focus on a particular subject; it also gives voters the opportunity to evaluate candidates over a period of time and in a number of appearances. A vice-presidential debate is also essential. Amid the novelty of the Great Debates in 1960, few observers noted that the nation, viewing four debates between John F. Kennedy and Richard Nixon, saw no debate between Lyndon B. Johnson and Henry Cabot Lodge. Yet, by the time of the next presidential election, it was Johnson who occupied the White House.

To be sure, parties are not frequently in the business of compelling their candidates to take actions against their wills. Candidates who receive the presidential nomination possess significant power over their party's machinery. It is possible, moreover, that a reluctant candidate could try to avoid debates by using the party as a shield to deflect criticism.

But even if these points are conceded, political party sponsorship remains the best vehicle for institutionalizing debates. The parties already have an ongoing role in establishing and administering procedural rules in such areas as delegate selection. If the political parties similarly establish debate arrangements many months before the nomination, and if the parties determine the dates and locations of a series of debates well in advance of the selection of the nominees, party sponsorship will create a powerful momentum in support of debates, a dynamic that cannot be achieved by groups with no relationship to the candidates.

An objection that has been raised to party sponsorship is that the parties are, by their nature, partisan, and that an independent broker is necessary to represent the public interest. Moreover, it is argued, the parties cannot be expected to be fair in their treatment of independent and third party candidates.

The suggestion that, in the absence of party sponsors, the debates are outside the control of the partisans and the candidates rests more on myth than reality. As the League itself has explained, and as many studies of the debates have shown, candidates and their aides have exercised extremely close control over all aspects of debate preparations. Placing responsibility in the hands of the political parties is really a truth-in-advertising measure, with the added benefit of accountability. If the debates do not take place, then it will be the fault of the political parties. If severe problems develop with the debates, then that too will be the responsibility of the parties. And if the debates are established and institutionalized, as they should be, then that should be the parties' accomplishment.

Establishing the parties as sponsors of the debates has still another advantage: it provides the parties with a meaningful role in the age of television. Television has played a significant part in the decline of political parties. "By giving candidates and office holders direct access to voters," an American Assembly conference at Columbia University in 1982 concluded, "television has replaced the political party as the principal network of political communication." Yet political parties continue to serve an important function as a mediating institution in the American polity. As political analyst Nelson Polsby observed in *Consequences of Party Reform,*

> Given the formidable needs for coordinated political activity required in the face of the constitutional separation of powers; of the federal structure of the nation; of its geographic reach; of the heterogeneity of section, race, ethnicity, occupation, and economic condition that characterizes the American population, it is fair to say that parties still have work to do and were they not to exist, something like them would have to be invented.

Instead of pitting television against political parties, presidential debates can provide an opportunity for parties to participate in using television for vitally important events in the political life of the nation. Indeed, sponsorship of presidential debates represents an encouraging commitment by the parties to campaigns centered on substantive discussion of issues.

Political party sponsorship could end much of the artifice that has surrounded presidential debates. Other steps should also be taken to accomplish this goal. The panel of journalists, for example, could be eliminated. The resulting face-to-face encounters should come closer to actual debates rather than parallel press conferences. Even if the panel is retained, there are ways to bring the public more directly into the debate process. A massive canvass of the American people could be conducted to determine the questions that they would most like answered. The League of Women Voters, with its debate experience and voter-education mission, is well suited to undertake such a project. The results should be publicized before each debate, with the moderator asking the designated questions if the candidates have not answered them.

Of course, third parties and independent candidates pose an extremely difficult problem, especially if the major parties are sponsors of the debates.

In analyzing this problem, it is helpful to keep in mind certain characteristics of the American political system. First, the two-party system has been durable. The two current major parties have been contending for the presidency since 1856. Second, third party campaigns have sometimes profoundly affected the dynamic of the presidential campaign. On the other hand, there also have been numerous fringe candidates who have received almost no public attention or votes. If all of these candidates were included in every presidential debate, dozens of people with no serious chance of representing a substantial national voice would be heard from. (The problem is not new. In 1858 Abraham Lincoln and Stephen Douglas explicitly excluded all other senatorial candidates from their two-man debates.)

Various attempts have been made to arrive at precise criteria for distinguishing "serious" third party candidates from other candidates. One version of a Senate bill in the late 1960s attempted to use the 1912, 1924, 1948, and 1968 third party candidates as the basis of comparison, but a key participant in this effort concluded that "developing a formula creates more problems than it cures." In 1979 a Twentieth Century Fund task force reported, after examining the "many precedents for determining what qualifications make a 'significant' candidate," that "criteria of selecting such participants cannot be fixed in advance." The League of Women Voters attempted to establish unbiased criteria with their 1980 conditions of legal eligibility, ballot eligibility, and standing in the polls. This, however, added to the artifice of presidential debates because it gave a patina of science and objectivity to an inherently subjective and political judgment.

In the end, devising a strict set of criteria for the participation of third parties and independent candidates seems impossible. One point, however, is clear. This problem should not undermine presidential debates, as it has done in the past. Through a bipartisan presidential debates organization, the major political parties should continue to commit themselves to debates between the Democratic and Republican party candidates. At the least, the public would be guaranteed, as it was not in 1980, a series of debates between the major contenders—and third party candidates would not threaten the goal of institutionalizing debates.

This is not to say that debates with third party candidates cannot occur if party sponsorship is established. Other organizations would be free to sponsor debates that include third party candidates. A suspension of Section 315 for presidential campaigns would provide other avenues for public evaluation of the excluded candidates, such as lengthy interviews, conversations with experts, and provision of free time to candidates.

9. NETWORKS SHOULD SPONSOR DEBATES

Tom Brokaw

When asked whether the networks should sponsor presidential debates, former White House press secretary Jody Powell was appalled. "Could you imagine what would happen if the networks got hold of it?" he asked. "I can just hear it now: Walter Mondale! Come on down!"

That is an amusing but altogether misleading scenario, especially from someone who has been an active participant on programs such as "Nightline" and "Sunday Morning with David Brinkley," discussing important issues with dignity and understanding. These same networks nightly produce news programs that treat seriously and cover extensively the presidential election campaigns from prenomination through the election. In addition, they provide special coverage of the key primaries, reporting the results, interviewing the candidates, and analyzing the vote. The record of the network news divisions as serious, thoughtful components of the election process is, I believe, exemplary. To be sure, there have been critics of election-night vote projections, and there is a continuing debate about the picture-versus-issue emphasis of day-to-day television campaign coverage. But overall the role of networks in campaign activities is worthy and should be expanded to include regular sponsorship of the presidential debates.

The merits of the case are obvious, beginning with the important role that networks have played in covering the national political conventions for the past thirty-five years. During that time they have been at once sensitive to the desires of the political parties and faithful to the viewers' need for fair and accurate analysis of what is happening behind the scenes as well as at the podium or on the floor. The networks have fulfilled a journalistic obligation that is essential to the ability of voters to have a clear picture of their choices.

That same journalistic function must be preserved for the presidential debates. Debates could become self-serving organs of the political parties or, in the hands of other well-meaning organizations, exercises in frustration for all concerned.

Clearing away the legal obstacles to network sponsorship of debates has been a first step. The Federal Communications Commission has interpreted the Communications Act of 1934 more broadly since the early 1980s, so that in sponsoring a debate broadcasters need no longer provide equal time for all candidates. The more compelling question now is why networks are the most appropriate sponsors. This is a more complicated and controversial issue.

First, the network news divisions that would be in charge of these arrangements are modern extensions of the vigorous, independent free press of the eighteenth century that the Founding Fathers sought to protect and encourage by adopting the First Amendment. Indeed, the First Amendment was adopted even though the press of that time was wildly partisan and outrageously critical of political figures. To their credit, modern network news divisions have no ideological drum to beat. While they have been accused of political bias, those accusations have come from all directions—the left, the right, and the middle. Network news divisions and print journalists in the modern political environment serve the same role as baseball umpires. The players and fans may not always like the judgment or the individual responsible for it, but they know the contest would be impossible without them.

To that end, I would not oppose joint sponsorship of the presidential debates by the networks and the American Society of Newspaper Editors or by individual networks and individual newspapers. Arrangements for such cooperation are already in place for national surveys at all three networks. CBS is associated with the *New York Times*, ABC with the *Washington Post*, and NBC with the *Wall Street Journal*.

The important issue is to place sponsorship of these debates in the hands of journalists. In our political system journalism is the common forum for making choices and what more appropriate forum than the presidential debates?

There is more to this than historic and philosophic considerations, of course. There is also the matter of form: which medium is best suited to deal with the message? By now there can be no serious argument against television as the most appropriate medium for the debates. It is the most "mass" of the mass media. It brings the discussion of the issues of the day into almost every living room in America. If television is the medium of choice, why shouldn't the people who know it best be in charge of arrangements for the debates?

As for the worries of Jody Powell and others that the networks would somehow cheapen the moment by adopting glitzy, detracting production techniques and by treating candidates as if they were contestants on "The Dating Game" ("Candidate number one, what would you do if Donna Rice wound up on your doorstep?"), such a suggestion would seem to be a deliberate attempt to make the networks suspect before their arguments can be heard.

The record speaks for itself. In 1984 Dan Rather and I moderated separate prenomination debates among the Democratic presidential candidates for our respective networks. The CBS program, conducted within the stately confines of the Low Law Library at Columbia University, aired just prior to the New York primary. The NBC debate was produced in a television studio in Burbank just before the California and New Jersey primaries. The formats were similar: all of the candidates sat around a single table and responded to questions from Mr. Rather or me. In both settings audiences were a mixture of partisans and the merely curious.

These dignified but lively debates went well. The single moderator format facilitated a coherent, continuous line of questioning. The candidates were easily encouraged to comment on or respond directly to statements by one of the other candidates. A great many issues were covered in some detail. All of the candidates and their managers expressed admiration for the format and gratitude for the opportunity.

The format and the production techniques were successful because they were designed and carried out by television professionals rather than by committees. They enhanced a spirited discussion among the candidates. The debate closely resembled the kind of dinner table conversation every host or hostess hopes to generate: informative, sometimes heated, occasionally witty, and always engaging. In the course of the hour voters could take the measure of the candidates' mental agility, positions on a wide array of issues, and general personal demeanor.

That is not to suggest that the round-table, single moderator format is the only choice. In fact, a variety of formats could be used in the course of a single campaign. Furthermore, the debates could use some production aids. If, for example, there is a spirited discussion about the Persian Gulf, why shouldn't it be accompanied by a visually appealing map of the area, showing the locations of the Gulf countries and their stake in the struggle for control? Obviously these visual aids should not overwhelm the participants or the issues, but if they help the voter/viewer follow the discourse, they should be included.

Still another argument for network sponsorship of the presidential debates is, frankly, the power of the networks. They won't be pushed around by the candidates or their campaign managers. If a candidate cannot agree to the common terms of the debate, then the network should choose to broadcast a discussion with his or her opponent. It's worth noting that in the 1984 Democratic primary debate on NBC the negotiations were relatively painless. The only objection came from the Gary Hart camp when I indicated I would ask about the personal experience of running for president, the effect on family relationships, and so on. Senator Hart's advisers were not eager for that subject to come up even then. Former Federal Communications Commission chairman Newton Minow and debate specialist Lee Mitchell published in *The Annals of the American Academy of Political Science* an analysis of television's role in presidential elections in which they argued that television debates should be the centerpiece of the next campaign. Their primary reason was simply but forcefully stated.

> Television broadcasting is a unique communications medium. It can bring together audiences far greater than could assemble in any, or even all, of our public stadiums and auditoriums. It can and does reach into more homes than any of our newspapers and magazines. In some respects television has become the national culture, cutting through age, economic and geographic barriers to bring simultaneously to all of us experiences such as the first walk on the moon, the struggle for civil rights at Southern lunch counters, the agony of the Viet Nam conflict, a government out of control in the Watergate hearings, "The Tonight Show" with Johnny Carson and "Good Morning America." It also has become the place where most people look for information upon which they may base their political viewpoints and voting choices.

If television can do all of that, why should the networks be denied the opportunity to produce what these thoughtful gentlemen call "the centerpiece" of the next election?

The parties should agree to make their presidential candidates available for a minimum of three debates on national television. Newspapers should endorse the concept as an opportunity for voters everywhere to judge for themselves the merits of the candidates. And the major networks should assure all concerned that the debates will be placed in the best possible time periods. Then the networks should be charged with the responsibility of producing the debates.

If there are other opportunities for debate—in newspapers, on radio, on cable systems, before special constituencies—all the better. But the three major debates should be produced by the networks for the American people. Network television news has earned that opportunity and the American public deserves to have the networks assume that responsibility. The time has come.

10. THE LEAGUE OF WOMEN VOTERS SHOULD SPONSOR DEBATES

Nancy M. Neuman and Victoria Harian

In September and October of 1988, when more than one hundred million Americans watch the presidential debates, they will see the culmination of a planning process the League of Women Voters Education Fund began just weeks after the 1984 debates concluded. As League planners lay the groundwork for the upcoming debates, we will keep an eye out for 1992, when one party will probably have an incumbent president seeking a second term—political dynamics that will differ significantly from those of 1988.

These changed circumstances highlight the important and distinct assets of the League of Women Voters as debate sponsor. We offer persistent pursuit of the public interest under *all* political circumstances. Thus, the League can best guarantee that debates that serve the public will endure in 1988 and beyond.

In assessing the likely health and well-being of future debates, a look at recent history and the League's experiences as debate sponsor provides some guidance.

In the presidential election of 1920, the year the League was founded, both the Warren G. Harding-Calvin Coolidge and James M. Cox-Franklin D. Roosevelt tickets vigorously courted the women's vote. Leagues of Women Voters around the country staged state and local candidate debates, described by one observer as a "new kind of political meeting . . . which is more popular than the old fashioned political rally. All candidates of all parties appear on the same platform and submit to questions."

During the ten months preceding the 1928 presidential election, the League sponsored a nationwide weekly broadcast on NBC radio in which editors, reporters, and representatives of the political parties debated major issues. In 1952 the League sponsored its first televised presidential primary debate. And with the 1976, 1980, and 1984 presidential debates the League of Women Voters became the only organization to have sponsored debates in three consecutive presidential primary and general elections.

Since 1976 televised presidential debates have become an American political institution and a success with the American public. A 1984 poll conducted by Frank N. Magid Associates showed that nine out of ten Americans have watched a televised debate. Nielsen figures from 1984 debates indicate that average viewership was approximately 130 million people per debate.

At the same time that debates have become firmly established as an expected—and demanded—element of the presidential election process, a "debate over debates" has been simmering, a debate in which the public's interest has been lost amid the various self-interests of the competing sponsors. If there have been any winners of this quadrennial debate sponsorship free-for-all, it has been the candidates, for whom the proliferation of would-be sponsors offers an opportunity to shop around for the best possible—in other words, the safest— debates.

The real focus for the serious issues at stake should be the public's agenda for debates and the sponsor that can best serve that agenda. The League of Women Voters has no vested interest in debates other than that they meet our institutional goal, to promote an informed electorate. We believe voters have the right to see significant candidates for the presidency and vice presidency in face-to-face encounters in an impartial, unbiased setting not under their own control, and where fair, nonpartisan rules are enforced and public education is the goal.

The League, free of any stake in the election's outcome, is chartered as a nonpartisan organization and has never endorsed a political party or candidate; its chief objective is to help citizens cast informed votes. In pursuit of this purpose, the League has viewed its debate sponsorship role as being the honest, independent broker in each of the presidential debates since 1976, ensuring that all candidates are treated fairly, that the inevitable disputes over ground rules and arrangements are resolved, and that debates take place.

Debate sponsorship has by no means been easy or routine. Each election has posed a new set of circumstances requiring the League to make difficult, often controversial decisions. Negotiations have at times been tough, but democracy itself is never tidy, and in the end the League has delivered the nonpartisan forum it sought.

One contender for the debate sponsorship "franchise" has been the broadcast industry. Since 1983 when the Federal Communications Commission reversed its longstanding policy and allowed broadcasters to sponsor their own political debates without affording equal time to all candidates for the same office, the three major television networks have attempted to build a case that they are the most appropriate general-election debate sponsor.

Network sponsorship of debates would leave American voters even more vulnerable to the already far-reaching influence of the broadcast media on presidential campaigns and elections. This influence has been exerted through the media's selection of which candidates and political events to cover as news, constant "handicapping" of candidates' election prospects, decisions on the sale of political advertising time, reporting and commentary on their own commissoned public opinon surveys, and, in many cases, outright endorsement of candidates. Expanding the already tremendous power of the broadcast media seems dangerous and unwise.

Simply put, those who cover the news should not make the news. Broadcasters are profit-making corporations operating in a highly competitive setting, one in which ratings assume the utmost importance. The environment in which they do business could leave them far more responsive to the demands of candidates than to the public interest. In the past three election years in which the League has sponsored presidential debates, the television networks have covered the debates as news events, fulfilling their appropriate role as disseminators of the news. This has allowed a healthy separation between the decisions the League has made as sponsoring organization and the decisions broadcasters have made in covering the debates. This separation serves the public interest and should be preserved.

In addition, twenty-eight years have passed since the networks sponsored presidential debates. Since 1984 their only experience has been through their sporadic sponsorship of prenomination debates, yet there are indications that they may have misread this experience in assessing their ability to handle general-election debates. The League knows firsthand about the vast differences between preconvention and postconvention debates. We have found no direct correlation between the tenor of negotiations with multiple campaigns in the primary and caucus season and the conduct of general-election debate negotiations with the final contenders.

The most recent entrant in the debate sponsorship competition—the Democratic and Republican national committees—may well provide the candidates with the safest, most risk-free debates option yet. If the political parties have their way, the presidential debates could be little more than political pillow fights, with no referee—no honest broker—representing the public.

Proponents of party-sponsored debates argue that such a plan would help "institutionalize" debates because the parties have the most leverage over the candidates and thus can guarantee that candidates will agree to debate. But history and common sense suggest otherwise. After the nominating conventions, the party hierarchy is headed by that party's nominee. The party chairs would have little if any authority over a reluctant candidate who decides that participating in a debate or agreeing to a particular format or ground rule would not be in his or her best interest.

Any debate sponsorship plan that does not incorporate the constant and steady pressure of an honest broker's willingness to go public is fatally flawed and vulnerable to exploitation by a skilled politician who does not want to debate.

Walter Mondale, the only person who has participated in televised debates both as a vice-presidential and presidential nominee, pinpointed this flaw in explaining why he believes party-sponsored debates would fail. During a 1986 seminar on presidential debates at Harvard University's Institute of Politics, Mondale described a plausible scenario involving a party's nominee and the party chair: as election day approaches, the nominee has second thoughts about his earlier commitment to the chairman that he would debate his opponent. The nominee, who now fears that a debate might deny him the presidency, calls the party chairman and mentions that he is thinking about cabinet appointments and is very much attracted to the idea of the chairman serving as attorney general of the United States. By the way, the nominee adds, "I don't want to debate." The party chairman hangs up the phone, intent on quietly scuttling the debate.

Mondale then asked what would happen if that candidate tried to cut such a deal with the president of the League. He answered his own question: it would be a matter of public record within minutes.

This awareness by the candidates that the League can and will apply public pressure has enabled the League to get the candidates to debate in every presidential election since 1976. The party-sponsorship plan provides for no such leverage, and the plan's proponents obscure this shortcoming with hollow phrases about the parties' clout over candidates.

The parties have also claimed that sponsoring debates would help them fulfill their goal of educating voters. But the principal goal of the parties is to elect their candidates—an appropriate, time-honored function. How can the voters expect party professionals to stage a fair and educational forum that puts the candidates at risk and under pressure? It is no secret that debates create more anxiety for party chairs and campaign managers than does any other preelection event. To the campaigns and the political parties, it makes sense to want to control the debates—currently the only campaign tool not already in the parties' kit—to shield their candidates and to package the events as best they can.

Understandably, candidates asked to take part in debates try to extract rules and formats most favorable to their own candidacy, frequently holding their participation hostage. In the heat of the campaign, with the stakes so high, it is unlikely that the parties will be able to agree on every aspect of the debates. Without a sponsor that is independent of a stake in either candidate to resolve disputes, it is likely that either negotiations will break down entirely or behind-the-scenes manipulations will result in debates that resemble canned, side-by-side campaign speeches.

Proponents of party sponsorship have argued that the bipartisan nature of joint party debates would provide the internal checks and balances necessary to preclude either scenario. But the League's experience with the campaigns in negotiating panelist selection for the 1984 debates is convincing evidence that backstage manipulations of debate ground rules do occur and that the public's interest is best served by a sponsor willing to blow the whistle on such abuses.

In 1984 the League agreed to a "good faith" process for selecting the press panelists—one that had been used with no difficulty in 1976 and was quite similar to that used in 1980. This process gives each candidate the right to raise objections to any panelist the League proposes; this right of challenge has been considered a means of ensuring that candidates are not distracted by the belief—however irrational—that a panel is stacked against them. In 1984 both campaigns abused the process by together rejecting some eighty-three names before we called a halt to their right of challenge. The League went public with details of the campaigns' abuses at a press conference in Louisville, Kentucky, the day before the first debate was to take place. Despite immediate threats from the campaigns that the League's action would jeopardize their candidates' participation in the second debate, our public announcement generated sufficient external pressure from the press and the public to convince both sides that further abuse of the selection process was not in either candidate's interest. By the time of the Kansas City debate, a greater degree of cooperation existed among debate negotiators.

This controversy provided a clear lesson that good faith agreements among the sponsor and the candidates do not prevent behind-the-scenes abuses. If future debates have formats involving a press panel, the ground rules must include a strict, well-publicized limit on the candidates' right of challenge. But this is only one rule among many over which there are constant tensions and disputes. The political parties' assurance that internal pressure will be enough to guarantee that neither side manipulates the process is simplistic and unrealistic and deserves the voter's skepticism.

Perhaps the most difficult—and certainly the most controversial—issue a debate sponsor must address is how to determine whether a third party or independent candidate has significant enough voter interest and support to warrant participation in a debate involving the major party nominees. The League faced this issue in 1980 when John Anderson challenged Jimmy Carter and Ronald Reagan as an independent candidate. Indeed, in almost any election year, it is not unrealistic to think of one or two candidates who, if not nominated, might seriously consider mounting an independent campaign with substantial grass-roots support.

Yet at their February 17, 1987, press conference announcing plans to jointly sponsor presidential debates, in response to reporters' questions about how they would deal with non-major-party candidates, party chairs Paul Kirk and Frank Fahrenkopf answered that party-sponsored debates would involve only the nominees of the two major parties.

The League knows from experience just how inadequate and short-sighted this response is. There is a clear public interest in seeing a serious independent candidate debate. While there is no simple formula to determine when such a candidate is sufficiently important to be included in debates, the League has addressed this question by establishing criteria for issuing debate invitations.

In 1980, after weighing the workability and legality of several options, the League decided on a criterion that required that a candidate who received a level of voter support in leading public opinion polls of 15 percent—or a level at least equal to that of a major party candidate—would be invited to debate. This objective criterion proved to be difficult to apply and unacceptably inflexible.

Following the 1980 election, the League reexamined its criteria and concluded that a wide range of objective and subjective measures should be used to determine which candidates the voters would want to see debate.

The new criteria used in the 1984 election, besides including the basic requirements that a candidate be constitutionally eligible for the presidency and be on the ballot in a sufficient number of states to have a mathematical possibility of winning an electoral college victory, specified that the League would exercise its "good faith editorial judgment" in assessing a number of factors, including substantial recognition by the national media; the extent of a candidate's campaign activity, organization, appearances, and fund raising; and national voter poll results. The League's approach has been upheld in the courts and by the Federal Election Commission as reasonable and consistent with the law.

A strong, two-party system is a cornerstone of American democracy, and the League agrees wholeheartedly that strengthening the parties' role in the presidential election process is a legitimate item for the public agenda. That the parties have lost both clout and function in recent years is undeniable. But it should not be the task of debates to help the parties regain lost ground; that burden is too heavy to fall on something as critical as presidential debates and poses unacceptably high risks to their existence.

In a contest in which the stakes are so high, it is vitally important for voters to have unbiased information. Debates that earn the public's trust as fair, nonpartisan educational forums suit that need. And there is no better match for that need than the League's sponsorship of presidential debates in 1988 and beyond.

11. THE U.S. CONGRESS
SHOULD SPONSOR DEBATES

Joel L. Swerdlow

The idea of televised presidential debates is appealing, but the reality has often been disappointing. Presidential debates have been too rehearsed, too shallow, and too lacking in useful information. But worst of all debates have sparked a debate about debates that consistently diverts public, press, and candidate attention away from real issues. "Sure, I'll debate," each candidate in effect says. Then begins a process of many months of posturing, maneuvering, and charade in which the public interest, if not lost, is certainly misplaced.

In a democracy where candidates are free to act any way they want—or can get away with—this certainly comes as no surprise. But what is surprising is that those whose profession it is to worry about the health of our democratic processes have not seriously considered the best and easiest way to maximize the good in debates and minimize the bad: have Congress sponsor debates and hold them in the House chamber in front of a joint session.

This idea does seem somewhat unorthodox, although presidential campaign historian Theodore H. White—certainly no radical regarding presidential elections—once suggested it.

For more than four years I have been testing the Congress-as-debate-sponsor concept among colleagues and political activists. I have elicited four major objections, none of which is convincing:

● *It offends separation of powers.* This is incorrect. The very people who wrote, ratified, and implemented the U.S. Constitution nominated presidential candidates via congressional caucuses. Separation of powers is an important, immutable principle; yet in practice this principle has meant constant change. U.S. senators, for example, used to argue cases before the Supreme Court. Now such an appearance would be unthinkable.

Obviously, American chief executives do not routinely stand in front of legislators and answer questions. But presidents do appear on Capitol Hill to deliver State of the Union messages and special addresses—appearances that were once considered outrageous. More and more voters now realize, furthermore, that one of the most important skills required of a president is the ability to work well with Congress. By addressing members directly and perhaps answering their questions before a live national audience, candidates could demonstrate practical skills necessary to govern effectively—at absolutely no cost to their independence.

Such candidate appearances, if handled properly, could also teach the nation—including the tens of millions of children who watch debates—powerful civic lessons about the need for White House-Capitol Hill cooperation.

● *Most members of Congress would oppose the idea because they would be out in their districts campaigning.* They might be campaigning, but they would fly back to Washington for a chance to be seen on national television. The allure would be irresistible, especially with new technology that permits increasing numbers of local stations to broadcast live from the nation's capital.

In fact, members of Congress are now very much involved in debates. Before and especially after debates we see senators and representatives being questioned on local and national television on issues such as who won. Congressional sponsorship would let such interviewees base their views on a close-up, real-life view of the debate, not on television images.

● *Members would applaud in a partisan way.* Maybe, and, if they do, what harm would be done? Live congressional reaction would make the whole extravaganza more compelling.

● *Politicians do not like to speak in front of an audience of other politicians.* Fair enough. But no one has heard a president of the United States complain about speaking to a joint session of Congress. The audience would be there as elected tribunes of the people, not as politicians.

As a debate sponsor, Congress offers considerable assets: dignity, prestige, influence, power, and direct ties to the American people. Alone among all potential sponsors, furthermore, Congress could make it extremely difficult—if not impossible—for candidates to play self-serving games about when and under what circumstances they would consent to a debate.

The debate format could be determined through nonconfrontational negotiations with the candidates. Indeed, Congress could best guarantee the most unbiased debate arrangements. Debates involve numerous variables, such as number and timing, that can affect election outcome. Any sponsor must achieve a delicate balance between resisting and responding to candidate pressure. Since candidates would have members of their own party among the debate hosts, fairness—or at least loud demands for fairness—would be guaranteed.

Either or both legislative bodies could invite major nominees to address them jointly. Less formal arrangements would also work well. In any event, an ad hoc congressional debate caucus—comprised of equal numbers of members from both parties and from either or both chambers—could handle arrangements.

Any number of formats is possible. The debates could be Lincoln-Douglas style: one candidate speaking and then turning the podium over to his or her opponent. If the candidates so desire, congressional leaders could then ask questions. Questions could also come from the floor. The parties could designate special questioners—perhaps their rising young stars—for a moment in the spotlight. Or formal propositions taken from the major party platforms could be debated. Any of these possibilities would propel debates past their current joint-press-conference atmosphere.

Debates are not complicated. Congress has all the necessary expertise, especially since both chambers are now comfortable with the presence of television cameras. Television networks and other media would unquestionably provide coverage, and the public could participate by sending their representatives questions they would like to have asked.

Everyone would benefit. The two major political parties organize Congress, so having Congress sponsor debates would strengthen the two-party system. Congress as an institution, as well as its members as individuals, would gain in stature. Candidates would enjoy the televised pomp and ceremony that now accompany presidential addresses to joint sessions of Congress. Candidates could also benefit from the opportunity to demonstrate their ability to gracefully face members of Congress representing the opposing party.

The League of Women Voters would lose a prestigious job assignment. This is undesirable yet unavoidable. But congressional sponsorship of debates would not prevent the League from remaining what it is today—the nation's grass-roots debate organization. In 1986, for example, League-sponsored debates occurred in a majority of all races for the U.S. Senate. Most gubernatorial and major city mayoral debates now feature League-sponsored debates.

Any presidential debate sponsor faces one major challenge: to organize debates in the public interest, which means avoiding a debate about debates. In the absence of third party candidates, this task is straightforward. Most of the actual control lies with the candidates. In such instances Congress is the sponsor best suited to push the candidates beyond their own parochial interests. Congress can do this because, of all potential sponsors, it has the most political clout.

A destructive debate about debates is most likely in the presence of a significant third party (or independent) candidacy. All potential sponsors face this serious problem. Despite the durability and desirability of the two-party system, third party candidates have been at least potentially important in the presidential contests of 1968, 1976, and 1980.

A serious third party candidacy has participated in presidential debates only once, and disaster resulted. In 1980, when Jimmy Carter, Ronald Reagan, and John Anderson each had strong support, the debate about who would debate whom and when received more press attention than did most issues. The fault lay with just about everybody: the candidates for manipulating debates to maximize strategic advantage, the news media for playing up what was arguably a nonstory, and the League of Women Voters for attempting to convince themselves and the country that an objective measure of candidate "significance" actually existed.

Scholarly literature and practical understanding still have not answered two basic questions about modern-day third party presidential candidacies: first, to what degree does the spread of *intraparty* democracy make special protections for third party candidacies less necessary, and second, to what degree do media events such as debates actually generate third party candidacies that would otherwise never exist? Answers to these questions would help us define when and why a candidate merits equal treatment with major party nominees. In the meantime, Congress may be the institution most able to handle third parties. Elected representatives, unlike political party officials and officers of the League, are fully exposed to public displeasure if they slight a candidate who deserves to be invited.

To keep its integrity, a debate sponsor must handle worst-case scenarios. Imagine a situation something like that in 1968. The nation is waist-deep in a bloody, undeclared war. Hundreds of thousands of antiwar demonstrators are in the streets. The president is prowar and wins renomination from his party. The opposition party, its primary vote split among many antiwar candidates, also nominates a prowar candidate. A strong antiwar leader, defeated in the primaries, gets on the ballot in all fifty states; polls show he has strong bipartisan support and could get 30 percent of the popular vote. Will such a candidate receive fair treatment in the debates? Pressure on Congress from his supporters either to get him invited or to get Section 315 of the Communications Act of 1934 suspended so he can receive compensatory attention, coupled with vast media attention that would accompany any unfair lockout from the halls of Congress, is certainly far from the worst outcome. Indeed, exclusion from a debate could be big news that would help this independent candidate more than would actually being invited. None of this may be pretty or tidy, but very little about presidential elections ever is.

Traditions must begin somewhere. Many of the political traditions we take for granted today were once considered radical. Presidential candidates aggressively delivering stump speeches on their own behalf? It just was not done until Stephen Douglas's 1860 campaign. A candidate addressing his party's national convention? This was quite improper until Franklin D. Roosevelt did it in 1932.

When a new approach is tried, and it works, we keep it; that is one of the beauties of American democracy. Congressional sponsorship of debates would fall into this category. It will work so well, so easily, and so quickly we will be amazed it has not been done all along.

House and Senate leaders need only pick up their telephones and set in motion a plan that would improve the 1988 and all future presidential elections. Nothing is stopping them but one of Washington's more formidable barriers: it has never been done.

12. A PRESIDENTIAL DEBATES COMMISSION

Douglass Cater

A curious dilemma besets our nation as we celebrate the two-hundredth birthday of our Constitution. The issue is not whether to hold but who should sponsor televised debates. Inaugurated in 1960 when candidates John F. Kennedy and Richard Nixon faced each other on four occasions, and renewed in varying numbers in 1976, 1980, and 1984, these debates are threatened by a divisive struggle over sponsorship overshadowing more substantial issues related to number, timing, format, and, not least, which candidates should be allowed to participate.

There are at least five possible presidential debate sponsors.

Some candidates and their managers insist they should have unfettered freedom to choose the sponsors and, indeed, to debate or not debate as each one calculates campaign advantages. Their arguments go far to demolish any notion of institutionalizing the debates with established times, frequency, formats, and procedures. It is the candidates who are at risk, they argue, and who therefore should be answerable only to the voters for how well or badly they handle their campaign strategies.

Television network spokesmen maintain that the networks can offer the most competent sponsorship because they are accustomed to both programming and technological requirements for such national events. Some broadcasters would not oppose joint sponsorship with the American Society of Newspaper Editors or, alternatively, would allow individual networks to collaborate with individual newspapers, following the tradition of their joint sponsorship of public opinion polling.

Still others claim that the logical sponsors are the two major political party organizations since they are, in fact, sponsors of the larger election contest. Control over the debates could strengthen the party system in an era when television tempts the candidates to conduct their campaigns as independent entrepreneurs with minimal ties to party organization.

A new argument has also been advanced that Congress should be the debate sponsor, with its members constituting the live audience and posing questions to the debaters. Without violating constitutional separations between the legislative and executive branches of government, such sponsorship could enhance the sense of joint responsibility for the conduct of government which must soon be shared by the newly elected president and the Congress.

Finally, the League of Women Voters puts forth a strong plea to be allowed to continue to be the nonpartisan sponsor as an outstanding voluntary association dedicated to citizenship education. League experience in arranging and sponsoring multicandidate primary debates, as well as the formal campaign debates of 1976, 1980, and 1984, demonstrates its capacity to make the tough decisions that will ensure the debates actually take place.

Counter arguments can be cited against each of these potential sponsors. Exclusive control by the candidates would leave an important instrument of voter education to the sometimes cynical manipulations of campaign managers, with the lead candidate holding particularly unfair advantage in setting the terms and, indeed, deciding whether to debate or not. Sponsorship by the networks would confuse their role as reporters rather than managers of political events and would create incentives to exploit the debates for maximum entertainment value. Political parties would not dare negotiate the debates in good faith until the major party nominees had been selected and had staked out their personal strategies. The Congress has neither sought such sponsorship nor is likely to go against the strategies of the two major candidates. (Besides, its members are not in session and are otherwise electorally engaged during the campaign season.) The League of Women Voters, despite its years of experience, lacks the enduring authority to assert primacy over all the other competing claimants.

So the competing arguments and counter arguments threaten to cancel out one another and to weaken the prospects for future debates. This would border on the tragic, for we, the voters, have glimpsed the possibility that these debates can perform a regular and highly significant role in the election process. Some critics will argue that they encourage excessive rhetoric and hyperbolic claims during the campaign's final stages. But they offer to the widest citizen viewership a chance to observe how our prospective presidents conduct themselves in comparatively unrehearsed circumstances. Granted that debating technique is not the primary requisite for the nation's chief executive, still there is abundant evidence that voters, watching in the quiet of their living rooms, see beyond techniques and measure the credibility and the overall competence of the candidates. So far, in the age of electronics, we have not developed a better means for voters to observe and compare and choose.

The League of Women Voters makes the best case and has demonstrated the most valid experience in managing very difficult negotiations. The League has been the honest broker when others have sought to gain special favor or else to scuttle the debates. Still I am troubled by the contention that candidates will turn to less diligent sponsors if the League should displease them.

The sponsor cannot ignore the difficult choice that must be made if the presidential debates are to become a permanent institution in America: who decides, and by what procedures, whether a third contestant should be allowed to join the debates? John Anderson's claim in 1980, as an independent and not a third party candidate, led to a prolonged squabble.

While I personally favor keeping the entry barriers high for third party candidates—and even higher for independents like Anderson—there can be no doubt that the time will come again when a tough choice must be made. Television itself has increased the likelihood that our nation is not forever wedded to the present two-party system.

This leads me to a sixth alternative: why not institutionalize a presidential debates commission with its membership designated by act of Congress? This could follow the tradition of the Smithsonian Board of Regents. Members could be appointed by bipartisan congressional leadership for fixed terms and be drawn from senior statesmen in the communications media, the political parties, the Congress, the League of Women Voters, and perhaps the living ex-presidents. This presidential debates commission would hire the professionals needed to implement its policies.

Why not designate that this major event will take place every four years in Philadelphia's Constitution Hall as a continuing reminder that we are pledged to a government of laws, not of men? No candidate would be compelled to participate. Yet to dignify the ceremony in such a fashion would represent a giant step toward making our presidential elections worthy of the awesome challenge and choice they pose for America's sovereign citizens.

Part III

DEBATE TRANSCRIPT HIGHLIGHTS

INTRODUCTION

Presidential debates are a unique and invaluable part of our nation's collective memory. They are an accurate reflector of their time and, taken together, reveal much about issues, political uses of television, workings of the news media, and changes in American life and politics.

Debates also offer access to the world behind the "selling of the president" strategies that now protect candidates so effectively. Examination of debate transcripts makes it possible to see through candidate rehearsals and evasiveness, to study provocative or headline-grabbing statements in full context, to test media-certified "truths" left behind in the flow of images that characterize modern presidential campaigns, and perhaps most importantly to see things—such as patterns of thought or implicit beliefs—that the candidates themselves often do not recognize.

Debates, of course, are broadcast events, and these transcripts are written. But history is recorded, studied, and remembered via the written word, and the problem of transferring political speech from one medium to another is not limited to debates. Most of those who saw Abraham Lincoln deliver what became known as the Gettysburg Address were not particularly impressed. Yet in written form the speech is brilliant. Likewise, Franklin D. Roosevelt's fireside chats—aural events that the public never actually saw—do not make compelling reading despite their enormous impact and appeal at the time.

Videotapes of the debates, furthermore, do not necessarily provide a more accurate record. *Any* after-the-fact analysis, even referring to audiotapes or videotapes, introduces distortion. Tapes of Richard Nixon and John F. Kennedy in 1960, for example, simply cannot recreate what it was like to view their debate performances over a quarter-century ago. Among other things, today's audience has had different generational experiences, which include strong preconceptions about both men. What has been said must always be considered in the context of life at the time it was said.

Perhaps the biggest failing of transcripts is that they fail to convey the wonderful, terrible feeling of live TV—a sense that anything can happen. Nor can they communicate the candidates' personalities. Someone who knows John F. Kennedy or Ronald Reagan only from reading debate transcripts, for example, would have little idea of why each captured the imaginations of so many Americans.

A note on transcript methodology: We have gathered the transcripts from several sources, principally from debate sponsors and newspaper accounts, but no definitive version of any debate transcript exists. Working from the live event and from videotapes, transcribers invariably arrive at minor, yet noticeable, differences. In the transcripts included here, the following have been deleted: (1) repeated phrases or false starts; (2) pauses and nonwords such as *ah* and *uh*; (3) polite salutations; (4) name of the questioner when it is included in the answer; (5) introductions and minor interruptions by the moderator or a panelist; (6) the infrequent audience reaction such as applause or laughter; and (7) parts of a question or answer that were irrelevant to the issue at hand. Candidates are listed in alphabetical order without titles. Panelists are identified only by last names. For more complete information about broadcast debates, including affiliation of panelists and titles of candidates, see Part IV.

OPENING AND CLOSING STATEMENTS

Candidates have total control over only one segment of a debate: the opening and closing statements. In these statements, candidates outline priorities, explain beliefs, and define their self-images. Thus, they are in many ways the most revealing part of debates. Note that these statements have grown steadily shorter over the years.

Statements from the opening of the first debate between John F. Kennedy and Richard Nixon on September 26, 1960, and the closing of the fourth and last debate on October 21, 1960, reveal, among other things, how each candidate's strategy had evolved. By the final debate, Nixon no longer agreed with Kennedy so much, and Kennedy had become defensive.

~

Kennedy-Nixon
September 26, 1960

KENNEDY. In the election of 1860 Abraham Lincoln said the question was whether this nation could exist half slave or half free. In the election of 1960, and with the world around us, the question is whether the world will exist half slave or half free, whether it will move in the direction of freedom, in the direction of the road that we are taking, or whether it will move in the direction of slavery.

I think it will depend in great measure upon what we do here in the United States, on the kind of society that we build, on the kind of strength that we maintain.

We discuss tonight domestic issues, but I would not want any implication to be given that this does not involve directly our struggle with Mr. Khrushchev for survival. Mr. Khrushchev is in New York, and he maintains the Communist offensive throughout the world because of the productive power of the Soviet Union itself.

The Chinese Communists have always had a large population, but they are important and dangerous now because they are mounting a major effort within their own country; the kind of country we have here, the kind of society we have, the kind of strength we build in the United States will be the defense of freedom.

If we do well here, if we meet our obligations, if we are moving ahead, then I think freedom will be secure around the world. If we fail, then freedom fails.

Therefore, I think the question before the American people is, Are we doing as much as we can do? Are we as strong as we should be? Are we as strong as we must be if we are going to maintain our independence, and if we're going to maintain and hold out the hand of friendship to those who look to us for assistance, to those who look to us for survival? I should make it very clear that I do not think we're doing enough, that I am not satisfied as an American with the progress that we are making.

This is a great country, but I think it could be a greater country, and this is a powerful country, but I think it could be a more powerful country.

I'm not satisfied to have 50 percent of our steel mill capacity unused. I'm not satisfied when the United States had last year the lowest rate of economic growth of any major industrialized society in the world—because economic growth means strength and vitality. It means we're able to sustain our defense. It means we're able to meet our commitments abroad.

I'm not satisfied when we have over $9 billion worth of food, some of it rotting even though there is a hungry world and even though 4 million Americans wait every month for a food package from the government, which averages 5 cents a day per individual. I saw cases in West Virginia, here in the United States, where children took home part of their school lunch in order to feed their families, because I don't think we are meeting our obligations toward these Americans.

I'm not satisfied when the Soviet Union is turning out twice as many scientists and engineers as we are.

I'm not satisfied when many of our teachers are inadequately paid or when our children go to school in part-time shifts. I think we should have an educational system second to none.

I'm not satisfied when I see men like Jimmy Hoffa, in charge of the largest union in the United States, still free.

I'm not satisfied when we are failing to develop the natural resources of the United States to the fullest. Here in the United States, which developed the Tennessee Valley and which built the Grand Coulee and the other dams in the northwest United States, at the present rate of hydropower production—and that is the hallmark of an industrialized society—the Soviet Union by 1975 will be producing more power than we are.

These are all the things I think in this country that can make our society strong or can mean that it stands still.

I'm not satisfied until every American enjoys his full constitutional rights. If a Negro baby is born, and this is true also of Puerto Ricans and Mexicans in some of our cities, he has about one-half as much chance to get through high school as a white baby. He has one-third as much chance to get through college as a white student. He has about a third as much chance to be a professional man, and about half as much chance to own a house. He has about four times as much chance that he'll be out of work in his life as the white baby. I think we can do better. I don't want the talents of any American to go to waste.

I know that there are those who say that we want to turn everything over to the government. I don't at all. I want the individuals to meet their responsibilities and I want the states to meet their responsibilities. But I think there is also a national responsibility.

The argument has been used against every piece of social legislation in the last twenty-five years. The people of the United States individually could not have developed the Tennessee Valley. Collectively, they could have.

A cotton farmer in Georgia or a peanut farmer or a dairy farmer in Wisconsin or Minnesota—he cannot protect himself against the forces of supply and demand in the marketplace, but working together in effective governmental programs, he can do so.

Seventeen million Americans who live over sixty-five on an average social security check of about $78 a month—they're not able to sustain themselves individually, but they can sustain themselves through the social security system.

I don't believe in big government, but I believe in effective governmental action, and I think that's the only way that the United States is going to maintain its freedom; it's the only way that we're going to move ahead. I think we can do a better job. I think we're going to have to do a better job if we are going to meet the responsibilities which time and events have placed upon us.

We cannot turn the job over to anyone else. If the United States fails, then the whole cause of freedom fails, and I think it depends in great measure on what we do here in this country.

The reason Franklin Roosevelt was a good neighbor in Latin America was because he was a good neighbor in the United States, because they felt that the American society was moving again. I want us to recapture that image. I want people in Latin America and Africa and Asia to start to look to America to see how we're doing things, to wonder what the president of the United States is doing, and not to look at Khrushchev or look at the Chinese Communists. That is the obligation upon our generation.

In 1933 Franklin Roosevelt said in his inaugural that this generation of Americans has a "rendezvous with destiny." I think our generation of Americans has the same rendezvous. The question now is, Can freedom be maintained under the most severe attack it has ever known? I think it can be, and I think in the final analysis it depends upon what we do here. I think it's time America started moving again.

NIXON.   The things that Senator Kennedy has said, many of us can agree with. There is no question but that we cannot discuss our internal affairs in the United States without recognizing that they have a tremendous bearing on our international position. There is no question but that this nation cannot stand still, because we are in a deadly competition, a competition not only with the men in the Kremlin but the men in Peking. We're ahead in this competition, as Senator Kennedy, I think, has implied. But when you're in a race, the only way to stay ahead is to move ahead, and I subscribe completely to the spirit that Senator Kennedy has expressed tonight, the spirit that the United States should move ahead.

Where then do we disagree?

I think we disagree on the implication of his remarks tonight and on the statements that he has made on many occasions during his campaign to the effect that the United States has been standing still. We heard tonight, for example, the statement made that our growth and national product last year was the lowest of any industrial nation in the world.

Now, last year, of course, was 1958. That happened to be a recession year, but when we look at the growth of GNP this year—a year of recovery—we find that it is 6.9 percent and one of the highest in the world today. More about that later.

Looking then to this problem of how the United States should move ahead and where the United States is moving, I think it is well that we take the advice of a very famous campaigner, "Let's look at the record."

Is the United States standing still?

Is it true that this administration, as Senator Kennedy has charged, has been an administration of retreat, of defeat, of stagnation?

Is it true that as far as this country is concerned in the field of electric power, and all of the fields that he has mentioned, we have not been moving ahead?

Well, we have a comparison that we can make. We have the record of the Truman administration of 7½ years, and the 7½ years of the Eisenhower administration.

When we compare these two records in the areas that Senator Kennedy has discussed tonight, I think we find that America has been moving ahead.

Let's take schools. We have built more schools in these last 7½ years than we built in the previous 7½, for that matter in the previous 20 years.

Let's take hydroelectric power. We have developed more hydroelectric power in these 7½ years than we developed in any previous administration in history.

Let us take hospitals. We find that more have been built in this administration than in the previous administration. The same is true of highways.

Let's put it in terms that all of us can understand.

We often hear gross national product discussed, and in that respect may I say that when we compare the growth in this administration with that of the previous administration, that then there was a total growth of 11 percent over 7 years; in this administration there has been a total growth of 19 percent over 7 years.

That shows that there has been more growth in this administration than in its predecessor. But let's not put it there; let's put it in terms of the average family.

What has happened to you?

We find that your wages have gone up five times as much in the Eisenhower administration as they did in the Truman administration.

What about the prices you pay?

We find that the prices you pay went up five times as much in the Truman administration as they did in the Eisenhower administration.

What's the net result of this?

This means that the average family income went up 15 percent in the Eisenhower years as against 2 percent in the Truman years.

Now, this is not standing still, but good as this record is, may I emphasize it isn't enough. A record is never something to stand on, it's something to build on, and in building on this record I believe that we have the secret for progress. We know the way to progress and I think first of all our own record proves that we know the way.

Senator Kennedy has suggested that he believes he knows the way.

I respect the sincerity with which he makes that suggestion, but on the other hand, when we look at the various programs that he offers, they do not seem to be new. They seem to be simply retreads of the programs of the Truman administration which preceded him, and I would suggest that during the course of the evening he might indicate those areas in which his programs are new, where they will mean more progress than we had then.

What kind of programs are we for?

We are for programs that will expand educational opportunities, that will give to all Americans their equal chance for education, for all of the things which are necessary and dear to the hearts of our people.

We are for programs in addition which will see that our medical care for the aged is much better handled than it is at the present time.

Here again may I indicate that Senator Kennedy and I are not in disagreement as to the aim. We both want to help the old people. We want to see that they do have adequate medical care. The question is the means.

I think that the means that I advocate will reach that goal better than the means that he advocates.

I could give better examples but for whatever it is, whether it's in the field of housing or health or medical care or schools or the development of electric power, we have programs which we believe will move America, move her forward and build on the wonderful record that we have made over these past 7½ years.

Now, when we look at these programs, might I suggest that in evaluating them we often have a tendency to say that the test of a program is how much you are spending. I will concede that in all of the areas to which I have referred, Senator Kennedy would have the federal government spend more than I would have it spend.

I costed out the cost of the Democratic platform. It runs a minimum of $13.2 billion a year more than we are presently spending to a maximum of $18 billion a year more than we are presently spending.

Now, the Republican platform will cost more, too. It will cost a minimum of $4 billion a year more, a maximum of $4.9 billion a year more than we are presently spending.

Now, does this mean that his program is better than ours?

Not at all, because it isn't a question of how much the federal government spends. It isn't a question of which government does the most. It's a question of which administration does the right things, and in our case I do believe that our programs will stimulate the creative energies of 180 million free Americans.

I believe the programs that Senator Kennedy advocates will have a tendency to stifle those creative energies.

I believe, in other words, that his programs would lead to the stagnation of the motive power that we need in this country to get progress.

The final point that I would like to make is this: Senator Kennedy has suggested in his speeches that we lack compassion for the poor, for the old, and for others that are unfortunate.

Let us understand throughout this campaign that his motives and mine are sincere. I know what it means to be poor. I know what it means to see people who are unemployed.

~

Kennedy-Nixon
October 21, 1960

NIXON. Since this campaign began I have had a very rare privilege. I have traveled to forty-eight of the fifty states, and in my travels I have learned what the people of the United States are thinking about.

There is one issue that stands out above all the rest; one in which every American is concerned, regardless of what group he may be a member and regardless of where he may live. And that issue, very simply stated, is this: How can we keep the peace, keep it without surrender? How can we extend freedom, extend it without war?

Now, in determining how we deal with this issue, we must find the answer to a very important but simple question. Who threatens the peace? Who threatens freedom in the world?

There is only one threat to peace and one threat to freedom; that is presented by the international Communist movement, and, therefore, if we are to have peace, if we are to keep our own freedom and extend it to others without war, we must know how to deal with the Communists and their leaders.

I know Mr. Khrushchev. I also have had the opportunity of knowing and meeting other Communist leaders in the world. I believe there are certain principles we must find in dealing with him and his colleagues, principles, if followed, that will keep the peace and that also can extend freedom.

First, we have to learn from the past, because we cannot afford to make the mistakes of the past. In the 7 years before this administration came into power in Washington, we found that 600 million people went behind the Iron Curtain, and at the end of that 7 years we were engaged in a war in Korea which cost over 30,000 American lives. In the past 7 years, in President Eisenhower's administration, this situation has been reversed. We ended the Korean War by strong, firm leadership. We have kept out of other wars and we have avoided surrender of principle or territory at the conference table.

Now, why were we successful as our predecessors were not successful? I think there are several reasons. In the first place, they made a fatal error in misjudging the Communists in trying to apply to them the same rules of conduct that you would apply to the leaders of the free world.

One of the major errors they made was the one that led to the Korean War. In ruling out the defense of Korea, they invited aggression in that area. They thought they were going to have peace. It brought war. We learned from their mistakes. And so, in our 7 years, we find that we have been firm in our diplomacy.

We have never made concessions without getting concessions in return. We have always been willing to go the extra mile to negotiate for disarmament or in any other area, but we have never been willing to do anything that, in effect, surrendered freedom any place in the world. That is why President Eisenhower was correct in not apologizing or expressing regrets to Mr. Khrushchev at the Paris Conference as Senator Kennedy suggested he could have done. That is why President Eisenhower was also correct in his policy in the Formosa Straits where he declined and refused to follow the recommendations, recommendations which Senator Kennedy voted for in 1955, again made in 1959, again repeated in his debates that you have heard, recommendations with regard to again slicing off a piece of free territory and abandoning it, in effect, to the Communists.

Why did the president feel this was wrong, and why was the president right and his critics wrong? Because again, this showed a lack of understanding of dictators, a lack of understanding particularly of Communists, because every time you make such a concession, it does not lead to peace. It only encourages them to blackmail you. It encourages them to begin a war.

And so I say that the record shows that we know how to keep the peace, to keep it without surrender. Let us move now to the future.

It is not enough to stand on this record because we are dealing with the most ruthless, fanatical leaders that the world has ever seen. That is why I say that in this period of the sixties America must move forward in every area. First of all, although we are today, as Senator Kennedy has admitted, the strongest nation in the world militarily, we must increase our strength, increase it so that we will always have enough strength that regardless of what our potential opponents have, if they should launch a surprise attack we will be able to destroy their war-making capabilities.

They must know, in other words, that it is national suicide if they begin anything. We need this kind of strength because we're the guardians of the peace.

In addition to military strength, we need to see that the economy of this country continues to grow. It has grown in the past 7 years. It can and will grow even more in the next 4. And the reason that it must grow even more is because we have things to do at home, and also because we are in a race for survival, a race in which it isn't enough to be ahead; it isn't enough simply to be complacent. We have to move ahead in order to stay ahead. And that is why in this field I have made recommendations which I am confident will move the American economy ahead, move it firmly and soundly so that there will never be a time when the Soviet Union will be able to challenge our superiority in this field.

And so we need military strength. We need economic strength. We also need the right diplomatic policies. What are they? Again, we turn to the past. Firmness but no belligerence, and by "no belligerence" I mean that we do not answer insult by insult.

When you are proud and confident of your strength, you do not get down to the level of Mr. Khrushchev and his colleagues.

And that example that President Eisenhower has set we will continue to follow.

But all this, by itself, is not enough. It is not enough for us simply to be the strongest nation militarily, the strongest economically, and also to have firm diplomacy.

We must have a great goal, and that is not just to keep freedom for ourselves but to extend it to all the world. To extend it to all the world because that is America's destiny. To extend it to all the world because the Communist aim is not to hold their own but to extend Communism. And you cannot fight a victory for Communism or a strategy of victory for Communism with a strategy simply of holding the line.

And so I say that we believe that our policies of military strength, of economic strength, of diplomatic firmness, first will keep the peace and keep it without surrender.

We also believe that in the great field of ideals that we can lead America to the victory for freedom, victory in the newly developing countries, victory also in the captive countries, provided we have faith in ourselves and faith in our principles.

KENNEDY.   First let me again try to correct the record on the matter of Quemoy and Matsu. I voted for the Formosa resolution in 1955. I have sustained it since then. I have said that I agree with the administration policy. Mr. Nixon earlier indicated that he would defend Quemoy and Matsu even if the attack on these islands two miles off the coast of China were not part of a general attack on Formosa and the Pescadores. I indicated that

I would defend those islands if the attack were directed against Pescadores and Formosa, which is part of the Eisenhower policy. I have supported that policy.

In the last week, as a member of the Senate Foreign Relations Committee, I reread the testimony of General Twining, representing the administration in 1959, and the assistant secretary of state, before the Foreign Relations Committee in 1958, and I have accurately described the administration policy and I support it wholeheartedly. So that really isn't an issue in this campaign. It isn't an issue with Mr. Nixon, who now says that he also supports the Eisenhower policy.

Nor is the question that all Americans want peace and security an issue in this campaign. The question is, Are we moving in the direction of peace and security? Is our relative strength growing? Is—as Mr. Nixon says—our prestige at an all-time high, as he said a week ago, and that of the Communists at an all-time low? I don't believe it is. I don't believe that our relative strength is increasing, and I say that not as a Democratic standard bearer but as a citizen of the United States who is concerned about the United States.

I look at Cuba, ninety miles off the coast of the United States. In 1937 I was in Havana. I talked to the American ambassador there. He said that he was the second most powerful man in Cuba, and yet even though Ambassador Smith and Ambassador Gardner, both Republican ambassadors, both warned of Castro, the Marxist influences around Castro, the Communist influences around Castro, both of them have testified in the last six weeks that in spite of their warnings to the American government nothing was done.

Our security depends upon Latin America. Can any American, looking at the situation in Latin America, feel contented with what's happening today, when a candidate for the presidency of Brazil feels it necessary to call not on Washington during the campaign but on Castro in Havana in order to pick up the support of the Castro supporters in Brazil?

At the inter-American conference this summer, when we wanted them to join together in the denunciation of Castro and the Cuban Communists, we couldn't even get the inter-American group to join together in denouncing Castro. It was rather a vague statement that they finally made.

Do you know today that the Russians broadcast ten times as many programs in Spanish to Latin America as we do?

Do you know we don't have a single program sponsored by our government to Cuba to tell them our story, to tell them that we are their friends, that we want them to be free again?

Africa is now the emerging area of the world. It contains 25 percent of all the members of the General Assembly. We didn't even have a Bureau of African Affairs until 1957. In Africa, south of the Sahara, which is the major new section, we have less students from all of Africa in that area studying under government auspices today than from the country of Thailand. If there's one thing Africa needs, it's technical assistance, and yet last year we gave them less than 5 percent of all the technical assistance funds that we distributed around the world. We relied in the Middle East on the Baghdad Pact, and yet when the Iraqi government was changed, the Baghdad Pact broke down.

We relied on the Eisenhower doctrine for the Middle East which passed the Senate. There isn't one country in the Middle East that now endorses the Eisenhower doctrine.

~

Carter-Ford
September 23, 1976

Expectations about this debate were high, because it was the first presidential campaign confrontation since 1960, and because the country knew so little about the two candidates. Gerald R. Ford had been appointed vice president after Spiro Agnew's resignation and had reached the White House when Watergate forced Richard Nixon from office. He was the first appointed president in U.S. history. Jimmy Carter was a former governor of Georgia who had risen from obscurity during the brief 1976 primary season. Both men knew that their debate performances would provide many voters with their first—and probably most lasting—impression of the candidates.

Carter's approach was significant because the themes he chose—personal trust in himself as an individual and faith in the future—came back to haunt him when he ran for reelection four years later. Ford's approach—that government is too big—became an interesting prelude to the Reagan years.

CARTER.   Well, tonight we've had a chance to talk a lot about the past, but I think it's time to talk about the future. Our nation in the last eight years had been divided as never before. It's a time for unity. It's a time to draw ourselves together, to have a president and a Congress that can work together with mutual respect for a change, cooperating for a change, and open for a change, so that people can understand their own government. It's time for government, industry, labor, manufacturing, agriculture, education, other entities in our society to cooperate, and it's a time for government to understand and to cooperate with our people.

For a long time our American citizens have been excluded, sometimes misled, sometimes have been lied to. This is not compatible with the purpose of our nation. I believe in our country. It needs to be competent, the government needs to be well managed, efficient, economical. We need to have a government that's sensitive to our people's needs, to those who are poor, who don't have adequate health care, who have been cheated too long with our tax programs, who've been out of jobs, whose families have been torn apart. We need to restore the faith and the trust of the American people in their own government. In addition to that, we've suffered, because we haven't had leadership in this administration. We've got a government of stalemate. We've lost the vision of what our country can and ought to be. This is not the America that we've known in the past. It's not the America that we have to have in the future.

I don't claim to know all the answers, but I've got confidence in my country. Our economic strength is still there. Our system of government, in spite of Vietnam, Cambodia, CIA, Watergate, is still the best system of government on earth and the greatest resource of all of the 215 million Americans who still have within us the strength, the character, the intelligence, the experience, the patriotism, the idealism, the compassion, the sense of brotherhood on which we can rely in the future to restore the greatness to our country. We ought not to be excluded from our government any more. We need a president who can go in, who derives his strength from the people. I owe the special interests nothing. I owe everything to you, the people of this country, and I believe that we can bind our wounds. I believe that we can work together, and I believe that if we can tap the tremendous untapped reservoir of innate strength in this country, that we can once again have a government as good as our people, and let the world know what we still know and hope for, that we still live in the greatest and the strongest and the best country on earth.

FORD.   On November 2 all of you will make a very, very important decision. One of the major issues in this campaign is trust. A president should never promise more than he can deliver, and a president should always deliver everything that he's promised. A president can't be all things to all people. A president should be the same thing to all people. Another issue in this campaign: Governor Carter has endorsed the Democratic platform, which calls for more spending, bigger deficits, more inflation, or more taxes. Governor Carter has embraced the record of the present Congress, dominated by his political party. It calls for more of the same. Governor Carter in his acceptance speech called for more and more programs, which means more and more government. I think the real issue in this campaign and that which you must decide on November 2 is whether you should vote for his promises or my performance in two years in the White House.

On the Fourth of July we had a wonderful two-hundredth birthday for our great country. It was a superb occasion. It was a glorious day. In the first century of our nation's history our forefathers gave us the finest form of government in the history of mankind. In the second century of our nation's history, our forefathers developed the most productive industrial nation in the history of the globe. Our third century should be the century of individual freedom for all our 215 million Americans today and all that join us. In the last few years government has gotten bigger and bigger. Industry has gotten larger and larger. Labor unions have gotten bigger and bigger. And our children have been the victims of mass education. We must make this next century the century of the individual. We should never forget that a government big enough to give us everything we want is a government big enough to take from us everything we have.

The individual worker in the plants throughout the United States should not be a small cog in a big machine. The member of a labor union must have his rights strengthened and broadened, and our children in their education should have an opportunity to improve themselves based on their talents and their abilities. My mother and father, during the depression, worked very hard to give me an opportunity to do better in our great country. Your mothers and fathers did the same thing for you and others. Betty and I have worked very hard to give our children a brighter future in the United States, our beloved country. You and others in this great country have worked hard and done a great deal to give your children and your grandchildren the blessings of a better America. I believe we can all work together to make the individuals in the future have more. And all of us, working together, can build a better America.

~

Carter-Reagan
October 28, 1980

Jimmy Carter and Ronald Reagan met only once, less than a week before the polls opened. Each had something important to prove: Reagan, that he was well within the mainstream of American political opinion and could hold his own with the president of the United States, and Carter, that he deserved reelection despite high inflation and his inability to obtain the release of American diplomats by then held hostage in Iran for nearly a year.

Carter's summation, like his presentation in 1976, was very personal. Although he was leader of the nation's majority political party, he included neither the Democratic party nor Congress. Carter also did not mention Reagan by name but attempted to evoke fear of what might happen if the Republican won. Reagan, in turn, relied upon what became one of the most brilliant political questions in modern times, "Are you better off than you were four years ago?"

CARTER. I've been president now for almost four years. I've had to make thousands of decisions, and each one of those decisions has been a learning process. I've seen the strength of my nation, and I've seen the crises it approached in a tentative way. And I've had to deal with those crises as best I could.

As I've studied the record between myself and Governor Reagan, I've been impressed with the stark differences that exist between us. I think the result of this debate indicates that that fact is true. I consider myself in the mainstream of my party. I consider myself in the mainstream even of the bipartisan list of presidents who served before us. The United States must be a nation strong; the United States must be a nation secure. We must have a society that's just and fair. And we must extend the benefits of our own commitment to peace, to create a peaceful world.

I believe that since I've been in office, there have been six or eight areas of combat evolved in other parts of the world. In each case I alone have had to determine the interests of my country and the degree of involvement of my country. I've done that with moderation, with care, with thoughtfulness, sometimes consulting experts. But I've learned in this last three and a half years that when an issue is extremely difficult, when the call is very close, the chances are the experts will be divided almost 50-50. And the final judgment about the future of the nation—war, peace, involvement, reticence, thoughtfulness, care, consideration, concern—has to be made by the man in the Oval Office. It's a lonely job, but with the involvement of the American people in the process, with an open government, the job is a very gratifying one.

The American people now are facing, next Tuesday, a lonely decision. Those listening to my voice will have to make a judgment about the future of this country. And I think they ought to remember that one vote can make a lot of difference. If one vote per precinct had changed in 1960, John Kennedy would never have been president of this nation. And if a few more people had gone to the polls and voted in 1968, Hubert Humphrey would have been president; Richard Nixon would not.

There is a partnership involved in our nation. To stay strong, to stay at peace, to raise high the banner of human rights, to set an example for the rest of the world, to let our deep beliefs and commitments be felt by others in other nations is my plan for the future. I ask the American people to join me in this partnership.

REAGAN.   Next Tuesday all of you will go to the polls, will stand there in the polling place and make a decision. I think when you make that decision, it might be well if you would ask yourself, Are you better off than you were four years ago? Is it easier for you to go and buy things in the stores than it was four years ago? Is there more or less unemployment in the country than there was four years ago? Is America as respected throughout the world as it was? Do you feel that our security is as safe, that we're as strong as we were four years ago? And if you answer all of those questions "yes," why then, I think your choice is very obvious as to whom you will vote for. If you don't agree, if you don't think that this course that we've been on for the last four years is what you would like to see us follow for the next four, then I could suggest another choice that you have.

This country doesn't have to be in the shape that it is in. We do not have to go on sharing in scarcity with the country getting worse off, with unemployment growing. We talk about the unemployment lines. If all of the unemployed today were in a single line, allowing two feet for each of them, that line would reach from New York City to Los Angeles, California. All of this can be cured and all of it can be solved.

I have not had the experience the president has had in holding that office, but I think in being governor of California, the most populous state in the Union—if it were a nation, it would be the seventh-ranking economic power in the world—I, too, had some lonely moments and decisions to make. I know that the economic program that I have proposed for this nation in the next few years can resolve many of the problems that trouble us today. I know because we did it there. We cut the cost—the increased cost of government—in half over the eight years. We returned $5.7 billion in tax rebates, credits, and cuts to our people. We, as I have said earlier, fell below the national average in inflation when we did that. And I know that we did give back authority and autonomy to the people.

I would like to have a crusade today, and I would like to lead that crusade with your help. And it would be one to take government off the backs of the great people of this country and turn you loose again to do those things that I know you can do so well, because you did them and made this country great. Thank you.

~

Mondale-Reagan
October 7, 1984

Reagan, as president, once again utilized his "Are you better off than you were four years ago?" question. Its power to shape the candidates' strategies was confirmed when Mondale, too, used it as the basis for his remarks.

REAGAN. Four years ago, in similar circumstances to this, I asked you, the American people, a question. I asked, "Are you better off than you were four years before?" The answer to that, obviously, was "no." And as the result, I was elected to this office and promised a new beginning. Now, maybe I'm expected to ask that same question again. I'm not going to, because I think that all of you, or not everyone—those people that are in those pockets of poverty and haven't caught up—they couldn't answer the way I would want them to. But I think that most of the people in this country would say "yes," they are better off than they were four years ago.

The question, I think, should be enlarged. Is America better off than it was four years ago? And I believe the answer to that has to also be "yes."

I'd promised a new beginning. So far it is only a beginning. If the job were finished, I might have thought twice about seeking reelection for this job. But we now have an economy that, for the first time—well, let's put it this way. In the first half of 1980, gross national product was down minus 3.7 percent. First half of '84 it's up 8.5 percent. Productivity in the first half of 1980 was down, minus 2 percent. Today it is up plus 4 percent. Personal earnings after taxes, per capita, have gone up almost $3,000 in these four years. In 1980 or 1979 a person with a fixed income of $8,000 was $500 above the poverty line. And this maybe explains why there are the numbers still in poverty. By 1980 that same person was $500 below the poverty line.

We have restored much of our economy. With regard to business investment, it is higher than it has been since 1949. So there seems to be no shortage of investment capital. We have, as I said, cut the taxes, but we have reduced inflation, and for two years now it has stayed down there—not at double digit, but in the range of 4 [percent] or below.

We had also promised that we would make our country more secure. Yes, we have an increase in the defense budget. But back then we had planes that couldn't fly for lack of spare parts or pilots. We had Navy vessels that couldn't leave harbor because of lack of crew or again lack of spare parts. Today we're well on our way to a 600-ship Navy. We have 543 at present. [In] our military, the morale is high. I think the people should understand that two-thirds of the defense budget pays for pay and salary, or pay and pension. And then you add to that food and wardrobe and all the other things, and you have only a small portion going for weapons. But I am determined that if ever our men are called up, they should have the best that we can provide in the manner of tools and weapons.

There has been reference to expensive spare parts—hammers costing $500. Well, we are the ones who found those.

I think we've given the American people back their spirit. I think there's an optimism in the land and a patriotism. And I think that we're in a position once again to heed the words of Thomas Paine, who said, "We have it in our power to begin the world over again."

MONDALE. The president's favorite question is, Are you better off? Well, if you're wealthy, you're better off. If you're middle income, you're about where you were. And if you're of modest income, you're worse off. That's what the economists tell us, but is that really the question that should be asked? Isn't the real question will we be better off? Will our children be better off? Are we building the future that this nation needs?

I believe that if we ask those questions that bear on our future—not just congratulate ourselves, but challenge us to solve those problems—you'll see that we need new leadership. Are we better off with this arms race? Will we be better off if we start this "star wars" escalation into the heavens? Are we better off when we deemphasize our values in human rights? Are we better off when we load our children with this fantastic debt? Would fathers and mothers feel proud of themselves if they loaded their children with debts like this nation is now—over a trillion dollars on the shoulders of our children? Can we say, really say, that we will be better off when we pull away from sort of that basic American instinct of decency and fairness?

I would rather lose a campaign about decency than win a campaign about self-interest. I don't think this nation is composed of people who care only for themselves. And when we sought to assault social security and medicare, as the record shows we did, I think that was mean-spirited. When we terminated 400,000 desperate, hopeless, defenseless Americans who were on disability—confused and unable to defend themselves—and just laid them out on the street, as we did for four years, I don't think that's what America is all about.

America is a fair society, and it is not right that Vice President Bush pays less in taxes than the janitor who helps him. I believe there's fundamental fairness crying out that needs to be achieved in our tax system. I believe that we will be better off if we protect this environment. And contrary to what the president says, I think their record on the environment is inexcusable and often shameful. These laws are not being enforced, have not been enforced, and the public health and the air and the water are paying the price. That's not fair for our future.

I think our future requires a president to lead us in an all-out search to advance our education, our learning, and our science and training, because this world is more complex, and we're being pressed harder all the time.

I believe in opening doors. We won the Olympics in part because we've had civil rights laws and the laws that prohibit discrimination against women. I have been for those efforts all my life. The president's record is quite different.

The question is our future. President Kennedy once said, in response to similar arguments, "We are great, but we can be greater." We can be better if we face our future, rejoice in our strengths, face our problems, and, by solving them, build a better society for our children.

~

Anderson-Reagan
September 21, 1980

Third-party and independent candidates have been important throughout the era of the televised presidential debates. Disagreement about whether George Wallace—who ultimately received 13.5 percent of the popular vote and 46 electoral college votes—should be included in any debates sabotaged presidential debates in 1968. In 1976 Eugene McCarthy—who eventually received 0.9 percent of the vote and no electoral college votes, yet threatened to throw the close election to the House of Representatives—was excluded from all debates. Then, in 1980, John Anderson (who eventually received 6.6 percent of the popular vote and no electoral college votes) became the first non-major-party candidate to participate in a debate. Jimmy Carter, the incumbent president, chose not to attend.

REAGAN. Before beginning our closing remarks here, I would just like to remark a concern that I have that we have criticized the failures of the Carter policy here rather considerably, both of us this evening. And there might be some feeling of unfairness about this because he was not here to respond. But I believe it would have been much more unfair to have had John Anderson denied the right to participate in this debate. And I want to express my appreciation to the League of Women Voters for adopting a course with which I believe the great majority of Americans are in agreement.

Now, as to my closing remarks: I've always believed that this land was placed here between two great oceans by some divine plan. That it was placed here to be found by a special kind of people—people who had a special love for freedom and who had the courage to uproot themselves and leave hearth and homeland, and come to what, in the beginning, was the most undeveloped wilderness possible.

We came from 100 different corners of the earth. We spoke a multitude of tongues. We landed on this eastern shore and then went out over the mountains and the prairies and the deserts and the far western mountains to the Pacific, building cities and towns and farms and schools and churches. If wind, water, or fire destroyed them, we built them again. And in so doing, at the same time, we built a new breed of human called an American—a proud, an independent, and a most compassionate individual, for the most part.

Two hundred years ago, Tom Paine, when the thirteen tiny colonies were trying to become a nation, said, we have it in our power to begin the world over again. Today, we're confronted with the horrendous problem that we've discussed here tonight. And some people in high positions of leadership tell us that the answer is to retreat. That the best is over. That we must cut back. That we must share in an ever-increasing scarcity. That we must, in the failure to be able to protect our national security as it is today, we must not be provocative to any possible adversary.

Well, we, the living Americans, have gone through four wars. We've gone through a Great Depression in our lifetime that literally was worldwide and almost brought us to our knees. But we came through all of those things and we achieved even new heights and new greatness.

The living Americans today have fought harder, paid a higher price for freedom, and done more to advance the dignity of man than any people who ever lived on this earth. For 200 years, we've lived in the future, believing that tomorrow would be better than today, and today would be better than yesterday.

I still believe that. I'm not running for the presidency because I believe that I can solve the problems we've discussed tonight. I believe the people of this country can, and together we can begin the world over again. We can meet our destiny—and that destiny [is] to build a land here that will be, for all mankind, a shining city on a hill. I think we ought to get at it.

ANDERSON. President Carter was not right a few weeks ago when he said that the American people were confronted with only two choices, with only two men, and with only two parties.

I think you've seen tonight in this debate that Governor Reagan and I have agreed on exactly one thing—we are both against the reimposition of a peacetime draft. We have disagreed, I believe, on virtually every other issue. I respect him for showing tonight, for appearing here, and I thank the League of Women Voters for the opportunity that they have given me.

I am running for president as an independent because I believe our country is in trouble. I believe that all of us are going to have to begin to work together to solve our problems. If you think that I am a spoiler, consider these facts: Do you really think that our economy is healthy? Do you really think that 8 million Americans being out of work and the 50 percent unemployment among the youth of our country are acceptable? Do you really think that our armed forces are really acceptably strong in those areas of conventional capability where they should be? Do you think that our political institutions are working the way they should when literally only half of our citizens vote?

I don't think you do think that. And, therefore, I think you ought to consider doing something about it and voting for an independent in 1980.

You know, a generation of office-seekers has tried to tell the American people that they could get something for nothing. It's been a time, therefore, of illusion and false hopes, and the longer it continues, the more dangerous it becomes. We've got to stop drifting.

What I wish tonight so desperately is that we had had more time to talk about some of the other issues that are so fundamentally important. A great historian, Henry Steele Commager, said that in their lust for victory, neither traditional party is looking beyond November. And he went on to cite three issues that their platforms totally ignore. Atomic warfare, Presidential Directive 59 notwithstanding—if we don't resolve that issue, all others become irrelevant. The issue of our natural resources—the right of posterity to inherit the earth, and what kind of earth will it be? The issue of nationalism—the recognition, he says, that every major problem confronting us is global and cannot be solved by nationalism here or elsewhere—that is chauvinistic, that is parochial, that is as anachronistic as states' rights was in the days of Jefferson Davis.

Those are some of the great issues—atomic warfare, the use of our natural resources, and the issue of nationalism—that I intend to be talking about in the remaining six weeks of this campaign, and I dare hope that the American people will be listening and that they will see that an independent government of John Anderson and Patrick Lucey [former Democratic governor of Wisconsin who ran for vice president on Anderson's ticket] can give us the kind of coalition government that we need in 1980 to begin to solve our problems.

~

Bush-Ferraro
October 11, 1984

In 1960, during the exhilaration over the first presidential debates, few people noticed that the vice-presidential candidates, Lyndon B. Johnson and Henry Cabot Lodge, did not debate. In 1976 vice-presidential nominees did meet, but there were no vice-presidential debates in 1980. In 1984 the candidates for vice president met once.

Geraldine Ferraro was the first woman to be nominated by a major political party and the first female nominee to participate in a general-election debate. Her remarks are perhaps most noteworthy because she was also the first debate participant to draw voter attention to discrepancies between reality and what is shown in political commercials.

BUSH. In a couple of weeks, you, the American people, will be faced—three weeks—with a choice. It's the clearest choice in some fifty years. And the choice is, Do we move forward with strength and with prosperity, or do we go back to weakness, despair, disrespect? Ronald Reagan and I have put our trust in the American people. We've moved some of the power away from Washington, D.C., and put it back with the people. We're pulling together. The neighborhoods are safer because crime is going down. Your sons and daughters are doing better in school. Test scores are going up. There's a new opportunity lying out there in the future: science, technology, and space offering opportunity to everybody—all the young ones coming up. And abroad, there's new leadership and respect. And Ronald Reagan is clearly the strong leader of the free world. And I'll be honest with you: it's a joy to serve with a president who does not apologize for the United States of America.

Mr. Mondale, on the other hand, has one idea—go out and tax the American people. And then he wants to repeal indexing, to wipe out the one protection that those at the lowest end of the economic scale have—protecting them against being rammed into higher and higher tax brackets. We just owe our country too much to go back to that kind of an approach.

I'd like to say something to the young people. I started a business. I know what it is to have a dream and have a job and work hard to employ others and really to participate in the American dream. And some of you out there are finishing high school or college, and some of you are starting out in the working place. And we want for you America's greatest gift. And that is opportunity. And then on peace—yes, I did serve in combat. I was shot down when I was a young kid, scared to death, and saw friends die. But that heightened my convictions about peace. It is absolutely essential that we guarantee the young people that they will not know the agony of war. America's gift—opportunity and peace.

And now we do have some unfinished business. We must continue to go ahead. The world is too complex to go back to vacillation and weakness. There's too much going on to go back to the failed policies of the past. The future is too bright not to give it our best shot. Together, we can go forward and lift America up to meet her greatest dreams.

FERRARO. Being the candidate for vice president of my party is the greatest honor I have ever had. But it's not only a personal achievement for Geraldine Ferraro, and certainly not only the bond that I feel as I go across this country with women throughout the country. I wouldn't be standing here if Fritz Mondale didn't have the courage and my party didn't stand for the values that it does: the values of fairness and equal opportunity. Those values make our country strong. And the future of this country, and how strong it will be, is what this election is all about.

Over the last two months, I've been traveling all over the country, talking to the people about the future. I was in Kentucky and I spoke to the Deihaus family. He works for a car dealer, and he's worried about the deficits and how high interest rates are going to affect his job. Every place I go, I see young parents with their children, and they say to me, "What are you going to do to stop this nuclear arms race?" I was in Dayton, Ohio, a week and a half ago, and I sat with the Allen family, who live next door to a toxic dump, and they're very, very concerned about the fact that those toxics are seeping into the water that they and their neighbors drink.

And those people love this country, and they're patriotic. It's not the patriotism that you're seeing in the commercials as you watch television these days. Their patriotism is not only a pride in the country as it is, but a pride in this country that is strong enough to meet the challenges of the future.

Do you know, when we find jobs for the 8.5 million people who are unemployed in this country, you know we will make our economy stronger, and that will be a patriotic act. When we reduce the deficits, we cut interest rates. And I know the president doesn't believe that, but it's so. We cut those interest rates—young people can buy houses. That's pro-family. And that will be a patriotic act.

When we educate our children—oh, good Lord, they're going to be able to compete in a world economy, and that makes us stronger. And that's a patriotic act. When we stop the arms race, we make this a safer, saner world. And that's a patriotic act. And when we keep the peace, young men don't die, and that's a patriotic act.

Those are the keys to the future. And who can be the leader for the future? When Walter Mondale was attorney general of Minnesota, he led the fight for a man who could not afford to get justice because he couldn't afford a lawyer. When he was in the Senate, he fought for child nutrition programs. He wrote the Fair Housing Act. He even investigated the concerns and the abuses of migrant workers. And why did he do that? Those weren't popular causes. You know, no one had ever heard of Clarence Gideon, the man without a lawyer. Children don't vote, and migrant workers aren't exactly a powerful lobby in this country. But he did it because it was right. Fritz Mondale has said that he'd rather lose a battle over decency than win one over self-interest, and I agree with him.

FEDERAL DEFICIT

Overall, the federal deficit has been the most frequently debated topic in presidential debates. One basic reason is that federal spending—thus the question of deficit—touches upon taxes, unemployment, health care, education, national security, welfare, and dozens of other fundamental public policy issues.

Debate discussion of the deficit reveals a remarkable consistency from 1960 through 1984. Candidates of both parties regularly (1) blamed the deficit largely on national security needs; (2) said they want a balanced budget but that it would not be possible for a few years; and (3) explained that economic growth, not cuts in domestic programs, was key to deficit reduction. At the same time, partisan patterns are apparent. What Richard Nixon said to John F. Kennedy in 1960 is what Ronald Reagan said to Walter Mondale in 1984: when you talk about deficit, you're really talking about raising taxes.

The following excerpts also give some evidence of why this issue so confuses voters. To read what follows is not to become better informed.

~

Kennedy-Nixon
September 26, 1960

NOVINS. Senator Kennedy, in connection with these problems of the future that you speak of and the program that you enunciated earlier in your direct talk, you call for expanding some of the welfare programs, for schools, for teacher salaries, medical care, and so forth, but you also call for reducing the federal debt, and I am wondering how you, if you are president in January, would go about paying the bill for all this. Does this mean—

KENNEDY. I did not advocate reducing the federal debt because I don't believe that you're going to be able to reduce the federal debt very much in 1961, '2, or '3.

I think you have heavy obligations which affect our security which we're going to have to meet, and, therefore, I've never suggested we should be able to retire the debt substantially or even at all in 1961 or '2—

NOVINS. Senator, I believe in one of your speeches . . .

KENNEDY. No, never.

NOVINS. . . . you suggested reducing the interest rate would help toward a reduction of the federal debt—

KENNEDY. No, no, not reducing the interest rate. In my judgment, the hard money—tight money policy—fiscal policy of this administration has contributed to the slowdown in our economy which helped bring the recession of '54, which made the recession of '58 rather intense and which has slowed somewhat our economic activity in 1960.

The kinds of program that I talk about, in my judgment, are fiscally sound. Medical care for the aged I would put under social security. The vice president and I disagree on this. The program, the Javits-Nixon or Nixon-Javits program, would have cost, if fully used, $600 million by the government per year and $600 million by the states.

The program which I advocated, which failed by five votes in the United States Senate, would have put medical care for the aged in social security and would have been paid for through the social security system and the social security tax.

Secondly, I support federal aid to education and federal aid for teachers' salaries. I think that's a good investment. I think we're going to have to do it. And I think to heap the burden further on the property tax, which is already strained in many of our communities, will ensure, in my opinion, that many of our children will not be adequately educated and many of our teachers not adequately compensated. There is no greater return to an economy or to a society than an education system second to none.

On the question of the development of natural resources, I would pay-as-you-go in the sense that they would be balanced and the power revenues would bring back sufficient money to finance the projects, in the same way as the Tennessee Valley.

I believe in the balanced budget, and the only conditions under which I would unbalance the budget would be if there was a grave national emergency or a serious recession. Otherwise, with a steady rate of economic growth, and Mr. Nixon and Mr. Rockefeller in their meeting said a 5 percent economic growth would bring by 1962 $10 billion extra in tax revenues. Whatever is brought in, I think that we can finance essential programs within a balanced budget if business remains orderly.

NIXON. I think what Mr. Novins was referring to was not one of Senator Kennedy's speeches but the Democratic platform, which did mention cutting the national debt.

I think, too, that it should be pointed out that, of course, it is not possible, particularly under the proposals that Senator Kennedy has advocated, either to cut the national debt or to reduce taxes. As a matter of fact, it will be necessary to raise taxes.

Senator Kennedy points out that as far as his one proposal is concerned, the one for medical care for the aged, that that would be financed out of social security. That, however, is raising taxes for those who pay social security.

He points out that he would make pay-as-you-go be the basis for our natural resources development, where our natural resources development, which I also support, incidentally—however, whenever you appropriate money for one of these projects, you have to pay now and appropriate the money, and while they eventually do pay out, it doesn't mean that the government doesn't have to put out the money this year.

And so I would say that in all of these proposals Senator Kennedy has made, they will result in one of two things: either he has to raise taxes or he has to unbalance the budget. If he unbalances the budget, that means you have inflation, and that will be, of course, a very cruel blow to the very people—the older people—that we've been talking about.

As far as aid for school construction is concerned, I favor that, as Senator Kennedy did in January of this year when he said he favored that rather than aid to teachers' salaries. I favor that because I believe that's the best way to aid our schools without running any risk whatever of the federal government telling our teachers what to teach.

~

Carter-Ford
September 23, 1976

DREW. Governor Carter, you proposed a number of new or enlarged programs, including jobs, health, welfare reform, child care, aid to education, aid to cities, changes in social security, and housing subsidies. You've also said that you want to balance the budget by the end of your first term. Now, you haven't put a price tag on those programs, but even if we priced them conservatively, and we count for full employment by the end of your first term, and we count for the economic growth that would occur during that period, there still isn't enough money to pay for those programs and balance the budget by any estimates that I've been able to see. So, in that case, what would give?

CARTER. As a matter of fact, there is. If we assume a rate of growth of our economy equivalent to what it was during President Johnson, President Kennedy, even before the Vietnamese war, and if we assume that at the end of the four-year period we can cut our unemployment rate down to 4 to 4.5 percent, under those circumstances, even assuming no elimination of unnecessary programs and assuming an increase in the allotment of money to finance programs increasing as the inflation rate does. My economic projections, I think confirmed by the House and the Senate Committees, have been with a $60 billion extra amount of money that can be spent in fiscal year '81 which will be the last year of this next term. Within that $60 billion increase, they would benefit the programs that I promised the American people. I might say, too, that if these goals cannot be reached, and I believe they are reasonable goals, that I would cut back on the rate of implementation of new programs in order to accommodate a balanced budget by fiscal year '81, which is the last year of the next term. I believe that we ought to have a balanced budget during normal economic circumstances. And these projections have been carefully made. I stand behind them. And if they should be in error, slightly on the down side, then I'll phase in the programs that we've advocated more slowly.

DREW. Governor, according to the budget committees of the Congress that you referred to, if we get to the full employment, would they project, at a 4 percent unemployment, and as you say, even allowing for the inflation in the programs, there would not be anything more than a surplus of $5 billion by 1981? And conservative estimates of your programs would be that they'd be about $85 to $100 billion. So how do you say that you're going to be able to do these things and balance the budget?

CARTER. Well, the assumption that you have described is different, is in the rate of growth on our economy.

DREW. No, they took that into account in those figures.

CARTER. I believe that it's accurate to say that the committees to whom you refer, with the employment rate that you state, and with the 5 to 5.5 percent growth rate in our economy, that the projections would be a $60 billion increase in the amount of money that we have to spend in 1981 compared to now, and in that framework, would befit any improvements in the program.

Now, this does not include any extra control over unnecessary spending—the weeding out of obsolete or obsolescent programs. We'll have a safety version built in with complete reorganization of the executive branch of government which I have pledged to do. The present bureaucratic structure of the federal government is a mess. And if I'm elected president, that's going to be a top priority of mine to completely revise the structure of the federal government to make it economical, efficient, purposeful, and manageable for a change. And also, I'm going to institute zero-base budgeting, which I used four years in Georgia, which assesses every program every year and eliminates those programs that are obsolete or obsolescent. But with these projections, we will have a balanced budget by fiscal year 1981, if I'm elected president, keep my promises to the American people. And it's just predicated on very modest but, I think, accurate projections of employment increases and growth in our national economy equal to what was experienced under Kennedy and Johnson before the Vietnam War.

FORD.   If it is true that there will be a $60 billion surplus by fiscal year 1981, rather than spend that money for all the new programs that Governor Carter recommends and endorses, and which are included in the Democratic platform, I think the American taxpayer ought to get an additional tax break, a tax reduction of that magnitude.

I feel that the taxpayers are the ones that need the relief. I don't think we should add additional programs of the magnitude that Governor Carter talks about. It seems to me that our tax structure today has rates that are too high, but I am very glad to point out that since 1969, during a Republican administration, we have had 10 million people taken off of the tax rolls at the lower end of the taxpayer area. And at the same time, assuming that I sign the tax bill that was mentioned by Mr. Gannon, we will, in the last two tax bills, have increased the minimum tax on all wealthy taxpayers. And I believe that by eliminating 10 million taxpayers in the last eight years and by putting a heavier tax burden on those in the higher tax brackets, plus the other actions that have been taken, we can give taxpayers adequate tax relief. Now, it seems to me that as we look at the recommendations of the budget commitTees and our own projection, there isn't going to be any $60 billion dividend. I've heard of those dividends in the past. It always happens. We expected one at the time of the Vietnam War, but it was used up before we ever ended the war, and taxpayers never got the adequate relief they deserved.

~

Carter-Reagan
October 28, 1980

STONE.   Governor, we've been hearing that the defense buildup that you would associate yourself with would cost tens of billions of dollars more than is now contemplated. Assuming that the American people are ready to bear this cost, they nevertheless keep asking the following question: how do you reconcile huge increases in military outlays with your promise of substantial tax cuts and of balancing the budget, which in this fiscal year, the one that just ended, ran more than $60 billion in the red?

REAGAN.   I have submitted an economic plan that I have worked out in concert with a number of fine economists in this country, all of whom approve it, and believe that over a five-year projection this plan can permit the extra spending for needed refurbishing of our defensive posture, that it can provide for a balanced budget by 1983, if not earlier, and that we can afford—along with the cuts that I have proposed in government spending—we can afford the tax cuts I have proposed and probably mainly because Mr. Carter's economic policy has built into the next five years, and on beyond that, a tax increase that will be taking $82 billion more out of the people's pockets than was taken this year. And my tax cut does not come close to eliminating that $86 billion increase. I'm only reducing the amount of the increase. In other words, what I'm talking about is not putting government back to getting less money than government's been getting, but simply cutting the increase in spending.

~

Mondale-Reagan
October 7, 1984

WIEGHART.   Mr. President, in 1980 you promised the American people in your campaign a balanced budget by 1983. We've now had more and bigger deficits in the four years you've been in office. Mr. President, do you have a secret plan to balance the budget sometime in a second term? And if so, would you lay out that plan for us tonight?

REAGAN. I have a plan, not a secret plan. As a matter of fact, it is the economic recovery program that we presented when I took office in 1981. It is true that earlier, working with some very prominent economists, I had come up, during the campaign, with an economic program that I thought could rectify the great problems confronting us: the double-digit inflation, the high tax rates that I think were hurting the economy, the stagflation that we were undergoing.

Before even the election day, something that none of those economists had even predicted had happened: that the economy was so worsened that I was openly saying that what we had thought, on the basis of our plan, could have brought a balanced budget—no, that was no longer possible. So the plan that we have had and that we are following is a plan that is based on growth in the economy, recovery without inflation, and reducing the share that the government is taking from the gross national product, which has become a drag on the economy.

Already we have a recovery that has been going on for about twenty-one months, to the point that we can now call it an expansion. Under that, this year we have seen a $21 billion reduction in the deficit from last year, based mainly on the increased revenues the government is getting without raising tax rates. Our tax cut, we think, was very instrumental in bringing about this economic recovery. We have reduced inflation to about a third of what it was. The interest rates have come down about nine or ten points and, we think, must come down further. In the last twenty-one months more than 6 million people have gotten jobs. There have been created new jobs for those people, to where there are now 105 million civilians working, where there were only 99 million before, 107 [million] if you count the military.

So we believe that as we continue to reduce the level of government spending—the increase, rate of increase in government spending, which has come down from 17 to 6 percent—and at the same time as the growth in the economy increases the revenues the government gets without raising taxes, those two lines will meet. And when they meet, that is a balanced budget.

WIEGHART. Mr. President, the Congressional Budget Office has some bad news. The lines aren't about to meet, according to their projections. They project that the budget deficit will continue to climb. In the year 1989 they project a budget deficit of $273 billion. In view of that, and in view of the economic recovery we are now enjoying, would it make sense to propose a tax increase or take some other fiscal measures to reduce that deficit now, when times are relatively poor?

REAGAN. The deficit is the result of excessive government spending. I do not, very frankly, take seriously the Congressional Budget Office projections, because they have been wrong on virtually all of them, including the fact that our recovery wasn't going to take place to begin with. But it has taken place. But, as I said, we have the rate of increase in government spending down to 6 percent. If the rate of increase in government spending can be held at 5 percent—we're not far from there—by 1989 that would have reduced budget deficits down to a $30 or $40 billion level. At the same time, if we can have a 4 percent recovery continue through the same period of time, that will mean—without an increase in tax rates—that will mean $400 billion more in government revenues. And so I think that the lines can meet.

Actually, in constant dollars, in the domestic side of the budget, there has been no spending increase in the four years that we have been here.

WIEGHART. Mr. Mondale, the Carter-Mondale administration didn't come close to balancing the budget in its four years in office, either, despite the fact that President Carter did promise a balanced budget during his term. You have proposed a plan, combining tax increases and budgetary cuts and other changes in the administration of the government, that would reduce the projected budget deficit by two-thirds to approximately $87 billion in 1989. That still is an enormous deficit that we'll be running for these four years. What other steps do you think should be taken to reduce this deficit and position the country for economic growth?

MONDALE.   One of the key tests of leadership is whether one sees clearly the nature of the problems confronted by our nation. And perhaps *the* dominant domestic issue of our times is, What do we do about these enormous deficits? I respect the president. I respect the presidency, and I think he knows that. But the fact of it is, every estimate by this administration about the size of the deficit has been off by billions and billions of dollars. As a matter of fact, over four years they have missed the mark by nearly $600 billion. We were told we would have a balanced budget in 1983. It was [a] $200 billion deficit instead. And now we have a major question facing the American people as to whether we'll deal with this deficit and get it down for the sake of a healthy recovery. Virtually every economic analysis that I've heard of, including the distinguished Congressional Budget Office—which is respected by, I think, almost everyone—says that even with historically high levels of economic growth, we will suffer a $263 billion deficit. In other words, it doesn't converge, as the president suggests—it gets larger even with growth.

What that means is that we will continue to have devastating problems with foreign trade: this is the worst trade year in American history, by far. Our rural and farm friends will have continued devastation. Real interest rates, the real cost of interest, will remain very, very high. And many economists are predicting that we're moving into a period of very slow growth because the economy is tapering off, and maybe a recession.

I get it down to a level below 2 percent of gross national product with a policy that's fair. I've stood up and told the American people that I think it's a real problem, that it can destroy long-term economic growth, and I've told you what I think should be done. I think this is a test of leadership, and I think the American people know the difference.

WIEGHART.   Mr. Mondale, one other way to attack the deficit is further reductions in spending. The president has submitted a number of proposals to Congress to do just that and, in many instances, the House—controlled by the Democrats—has opposed them. Isn't it one aspect of leadership for a prominent Democrat such as yourself to encourage responsible reductions in spending and thereby reduce the deficit?

MONDALE.   Absolutely, and I have proposed over $100 billion in cuts in federal spending over four years. But I am not going to cut it out of social security and medicare and student assistance and things that people need. These people depend upon all of us for the little security that they have, and I'm not going to do it that way. The rate of defense spending increase can be slowed. Certainly, we can find a coffee pot that costs something less than $7,000. And there are other ways of squeezing this budget without constantly picking on our senior citizens and the most vulnerable in American life. And that's why the Congress, including the Republicans, have not gone along with the president's recommendations.

REAGAN.   I don't believe that Mr. Mondale has a plan for balancing the budget; [he] has a plan for raising taxes. And as a matter of fact, the biggest single tax increase in our nation's history took place in 1977. And for the five years previous to our taking office, taxes doubled in the United States, and the budgets increased $318 billion. So there is no ratio between taxing and balancing a budget. Whether you borrow the money or whether you simply tax it away from the people, you're taking the same amount of money out of the private sector unless and until you bring down government's share of what it is taking.

With regard to social security, I hope there will be more time than just this minute to mention that, but I will say this: a president should never say "never," but I'm going to violate that rule and say "never." I will never stand for a reduction of the social security benefits to the people that are now getting them.

MONDALE. That's exactly the commitment that was made to the American people in 1980—he would never reduce benefits. And of course, what happened right after the election is they proposed to cut social security benefits by 25 percent, reducing the adjustment for inflation, cutting out minimum benefits for the poorest on social security, removing educational benefits for dependents [of] widows [who] were trying to get them through college. Everybody remembers that. People know what happened. There is a difference. I have fought for social security and medicare and for things to help people who are vulnerable all my life. And I will do it as president of the United States.

VIETNAM

The single most important foreign policy issue facing the United States during the era of television debates has been the Vietnam War—especially when this war is seen as a case study in how the country can and should use force to stop its perceived enemies.

In 1960, at the time of the first presidential debates, the United States had fewer than ten thousand military advisers in Vietnam. By 1976, when debates were next held, several million Americans had served in Vietnam, and the war—which cost more than 300,000 American wounded, nearly 60,000 dead, and more than $200 billion—was over.

It is noteworthy that the debates between 1976 and 1984, to the degree that they even touched on the Vietnam War, focused on tangential—however important—issues such as prisoners of war and pardons for draft resisters. Debaters—and their questioners—ignored questions about why America had become involved in Vietnam, the efficacy and morality of our war strategy, the reasons the antiwar movement was so strong, and the lessons that could be learned from defeat.

The only exceptions are found in several Democratic prenomination debates that occurred between 1968 to 1976. Emotions generated by disagreement over Vietnam, and evident in these debates, help to explain some of the intraparty fissures visible in the Democratic party of the 1980s. In discussing Vietnam during debates, it should be noted, no Democrats went outside America's conventional post-World War II political wisdom: that not one inch of territory anywhere in the world should be "surrendered" to communism.

In the following speeches *Indochina* refers to Vietnam, Laos, and Cambodia.

~

Kennedy-Nixon
October 7, 1960

KENNEDY. We poured $300 million of surplus military equipment into Laos. We paid more military aid, more aid into Laos per person, than in any country in the world, and we ought to know now that Laos is moving from neutralism in the direction of the Communists. I believe instead of doing that we should concentrate our aid in long-term loans which these people can pay back either in hard money or in local currency.

This permits them to maintain their self-respect. It permits us to make sure that the projects which are invested in are going to produce greater wealth.

NIXON. In the Truman administration 600 million people were behind the Iron Curtain, including the satellite countries of eastern Europe and Communist China. In this administration we've stopped them at Quemoy and Matsu, we've stopped them in Indochina, we've stopped them in Lebanon, we've stopped them in other parts of the world.

~

Kennedy-Nixon
October 13, 1960

CATER. Critics have claimed that on at least three occasions in recent years, on the sending of American troops to Indochina in 1954, on the matter of continuing the U-2 flights in May, and that on this definition of our commitment to the offshore island, that you have overstated the administration position, that you have taken a more bellicose position than President Eisenhower.

Just two days ago you said that you called on Senator Kennedy to serve notice to Communist aggressors around the world that we're not going to retreat one inch more any place, whereas we did retreat from the Taichen Islands, or at least Chiang Kai-shek did. Would you say this was a valid criticism of your statement of foreign policy?

NIXON. As far as Indochina was concerned, I stated over and over again that it was essential during that period that the United States make it clear that we would not tolerate Indochina falling under Communist domination.

Now, as a result of our taking the strong stand that we did, the civil war there was ended, and today at least in the south of Indochina the Communists have moved out and we do have a strong free bastion there.

KENNEDY. On Indochina, Mr. Nixon talked before the newspaper editors in the spring of 1954 about putting, and I quote him, "American boys into Indochina." The reason Indochina was preserved was the result of the Geneva Conference which partitioned Indochina.

The vice president suggests that we should keep the Communists in doubt about whether we would fight on Quemoy and Matsu. That's not the position he's taking. He's indicating that we should fight for these islands, come what may, because they are, in his words, "in the area of freedom."

He didn't take that position on Tibet. He didn't take that position on Budapest. He doesn't take that position that I have seen so far in Laos. Guinea and Ghana have both moved within the Soviet sphere of influence on foreign policy. So has Cuba.

~

Kennedy-McCarthy
June 1, 1968

QUESTIONER. For both senators, really. You are presenting yourself tonight to the American people and to the voters of California as candidates for the presidency. If, in fact, you were president, what would you do at this time that President Johnson is not doing in order to bring peace in Vietnam?

McCARTHY. There are two or three things that I would be doing, or at least recommending, if I were president at this time. I would be de-escalating the war in Vietnam, drawing back from some of our advanced positions while still holding strength in Vietnam. I would not have the secretary of state making statements about how we would have no coalition government come out of the conference in Paris, nor have someone say that the vice president made a slip of the tongue when he talked about involving the National Liberation Front.

I think these are the important positions that have to be taken: one, a de-escalation of the war and, secondly, recognition that we have to have a new government in South Vietnam. I'm not particularly concerned whether it's called a coalition or a fusion or a new government of some kind.

And we have to recognize that the government would include the National Liberation Front. I think this is prerequisite to any kind of negotiations that may move on to talk about what the nature of that new government might be.

We've not really made any significant changes that I can see in terms of our activities or our words. We're calling up more troops. We say we're going to send more troops. We have intensified the bombing. Taken all together, I don't see either in action or in words any significant change on the part of the administration since the negotiations began.

KENNEDY. I'd pursue the negotiations in Paris at the same time and make it quite clear that we would expect Saigon, the government in Saigon, to begin their own negotiations with the National Liberation Front. I would be opposed to what I understand is Senator McCarthy's position to be of forcing a coalition government on the government of Saigon, a coalition with the Communists, even before we begin the negotiations.

I would make it quite clear that we are going to the negotiating table not with the idea that we want them to unconditionally surrender but—and that we expect that the National Liberation Front and the Vietcong have a place somewhere in the future political process of South Vietnam—but that should be determined by the negotiators and particularly by those people in South Vietnam.

I think that's terribly important that we accept that, because without accepting that what we're really asking for is unconditional surrender, and they're not going to turn over their arms—lay down their arms—live in peace if the government is going to be run by General Ky and General Thieu.

The next point: I would demand privately and publicly an end of public corruption, the official corruption that exists in Vietnam—a land reform program that's meaningful so that they can gain the support of the people themselves. I would pull back from the demilitarized zone—I think that's an important area—but I would permit the troops of South Vietnam to remain there rather than American troops where a third of our casualties have occurred—half really—and I would end the search and destroy missions by American troops and American marines and let the South Vietnamese soldiers and troops carry that burden of the conflict.

I would make it clear as we went along that the South Vietnamese are going to carry more and more of the burden of the conflict. I'm not going to accept the idea that we can draft the young man from the United States, send him to South Vietnam to fight and maybe to die while at the same time a young man, if he's wealthy enough, can buy his way out of the draft in South Vietnam.

McCARTHY. I didn't say I was going to force a coalition government on South Vietnam. I said we should make clear that we're willing to accept that. Now if the South Vietnamese want to continue the fight, work out their own negotiation, that is well and good. But I don't think there's much point in talking about reform in Saigon or land reform because we've been asking for that for at least five years and it hasn't happened.

QUESTIONER. Senator Kennedy, this week at his press conference in Texas, the president indicated he was not closing any of his options. Indeed, he was considering perhaps resuming bombing farther north around Hanoi and Haiphong if something didn't happen in Paris pretty soon. Was this a wise move? In the interest of peace?

KENNEDY. Well, I think that escalating the conflict again is not going to be a wise move. I think that the decision as I read about it in the newspapers as to why they de-escalated and went to the conference table was made on the basis that the bombing hadn't been successful.

I think that the reports of the intelligence community show quite clearly that, rather than having been successful, it strengthened the will of the people of North Vietnam to resist the United States and resist the outside—as they described it—the outside aggressor. So I think that to resume the bombing in that fashion is not going to be any more successful now than it has been in the past.

Third, Secretary McNamara has already testified before congressional committees that the bombing of the North does not stop the North from sending whatever men and materials they need into the South. What, in the last analysis, is needed in South Vietnam is for the people themselves to have the will to fight.

If they don't have that will, no matter how many men we send over there, how many bombs we drop—and we're dropping more now than we dropped in the Second World War—no matter how much we do with that, if they don't have the will and desire themselves, no matter what we do, we can't instill that in them.

And that's why I want to make it clear if I was president of the United States—and why I was critical back in 1965, because I felt we were making it America's war, we were militarizing the conflict—that this is the South Vietnamese war. I'm opposed to unilaterally withdrawing from there, but they have to carry the major burden of this conflict. It can't be carried by American soldiers.

QUESTIONER. Senator McCarthy, in commenting on Senator Kennedy's answer, would you also take into account the charge made by some critics of the administration, who are more hawkish, that we give the North Vietnamese a rather clear berth by telling them exactly what we're not going to do and that this doesn't increase the pressure for peace?

McCARTHY. I don't think it makes much difference because we are really doing enough to them in any case, and our saying we're not going to do more in this particular area doesn't really change the ratio, it seems to me, of force to any significant degree. As far as the bombing is concerned, for example, the question of what area you bomb is not as important, it seems to me, as how intensely you bomb the areas that you are bombing.

I look upon the bombing question really as one that has to be considered in relation to what we are doing with reference to other troop movements in South Vietnam. Where to resume or not to resume, I think, has now become really a tactical question—since negotiations have started—and also a practical question because we've had through the years testimony from many experts saying that it was wasteful, that it wasn't accomplishing anything, that we were losing planes and spending money and not breaking. I remember Secretary McNamara telling us in early '66 that if we resume the bombing and intensify it, he said, they will be able to infiltrate up to 4,500 men a month and supply them, and then we can wear them down in South Vietnam.

By June of that year, the report was they were infiltrating up to 7,000 a month after the bombing had been intensified. His explanation was that the number they could infiltrate had always been "X"—that's what it has been.

~

Humphrey-McGovern
May 30, 1972

NOVAK. Senator Humphrey, I would like to explore your contention that there is no real difference between you and Senator McGovern on Vietnam right now. Would you really be willing to cut off all the South Vietnamese troops fighting in the field without a dime, if you were president, as Senator McGovern would?

HUMPHREY. I consider, if I am the president of the United States, I shall put foremost what I believe to be the interests of this nation, and I think it is time that we had that kind of policy—put this country up front for a change. That means, to me, that it is no longer in our national interest, if it ever was, for us to be involved in the war in Vietnam.

We are not leaving those people as if they had nothing. They have equipment until they don't know what to do with it today. Frankly, sometimes they don't know what to do with it. It is my judgment that they are capable today of their own defense. It is also my judgment that if we will get out of there, with an agreement to get the release of our prisoners and to withdraw our forces—by the way, just as President Nixon outlined here the other night when he was outlining his speech on the mining of Haiphong Harbor; he said four months after the agreement upon the release of the prisoners of war, we will have all of our forces out of Vietnam. I think that is a sensible policy. It is one that I have been advocating for a good deal of time, and I think we ought to fulfill it.

NOVAK. Senator, you are familiar enough with that war to know that with all of these piles of equipment, as you call it, they can't exist for a month without our financing their day-to-day fighting. I just wonder, with the invading North Vietnamese army, considering your past positions on Vietnam, if you would really be willing to cut them off flat?

HUMPHREY. Yes, I would, because I believe that it is no longer in our interest to be there, and I believe it is imperative if we are going to halt the spiraling inflation here at home to get on with the job of meeting our needs here, of taking care of the needs of our cities, of taking care of the job requirements of our people, of reordering the social security structure of this country to provide decent care for our elderly, that we quit spending our resources in Vietnam and get back here to the United States and start to take care of the human needs and the physical needs of this country. That is my judgment.

NOVAK. Senator Humphrey, seven years ago in California when you were vice president, you said, "Have we the patience to work and bleed thousands of miles from home for months and years ahead?" Is your answer "no" now?

HUMPHREY. We have bled and we have sacrificed for better than ten years in South Vietnam. We have actually been involved in that part of the world since 1954. We have contributed 55,000 dead, 300,000 casualties, $200 billion in resources. No ally has ever done so much for so few over such a long, extended period of time, and I do believe that if you are president of the United States, the time comes when you must make the decision—which may take as much courage to make the decision to get out as it did to make the decision to get in.

JOHNSON. Senator McGovern, I have some questions about Vietnam, and particularly the aftermath of Vietnam. If you were president, and you do end the war as you say and our presence is withdrawn from there, what steps would you take if our prisoners over there are not released?

McGOVERN. The burden of proof is really the other way around. We haven't released any prisoners with the most massive kind of aerial bombardment. We didn't get any prisoners released with 500,000 American troops there. I think we have to begin with the assumption that the American prisoners are going to be held as long as military activities are in progress, so the time has come now to try something different.

I have no inside pipeline to Hanoi. I don't know what they are going to do if we stop the bombing and withdraw our forces. I assume at that point they no longer have any interest in holding American prisoners of war. I think it is clear now to the wives of these prisoners, dozens of whom have come to me and talked about their support for my candidacy, because they now realize they will never see their husbands again until the war ends. So we have to take whatever risk is involved now on the side of peace. We have taken all these risks on the side of war, and it has accomplished two things: it has killed more of our people, and the other side has taken more of our prisoners. Let's try now to see if ending the war isn't also the way to end the imprisonment of our soldiers.

JOHNSON. In other words, you really don't know what you would do.

McGOVERN. There is not an awful lot we can do other than to take our case to the international community, unless we want to go over there and obliterate North Vietnam, which would kill all of our prisoners.

JOHNSON. Another question, Senator, about Vietnam. What sort of obligation do you think this country has to the people, assuming the war ends and so forth? We have been there all these years. The country is ravaged, destitute people—forget how we got into the war, but what is the obligation of an American president and the American people to that country?

McGOVERN. I think the obligation is at least as great as it was to Germany and Japan at the end of World War II. Here were two countries that actually attacked us, and yet when the war was over, we saw that it was in our national interest to see that the suffering and the chaos was ended as quickly as possible, and we extended a helping hand.

I would hope, in concert with other countries, that we would join in an effort to rebuild the devastated areas of southeast Asia once the war comes to an end.

~

Carter-Ford
September 23, 1976

REYNOLDS. Mr. President, very early in your administration you went out to Chicago, and you announced a program of case-by-case pardons for draft resisters to restore them to full citizenship. Some 14,000 young men took advantage of your offer, but another 90,000 did not. In granting the pardon to former president Nixon, part of your rationale was to put Watergate behind us, to, if I may quote you again, "truly end our long national nightmare." Why does not the same rationale apply now, today, in our bicentennial year, to the young men who resisted in Vietnam, and many of them still in exile abroad?

FORD. The amnesty program that I recommended in Chicago in September of 1974 would give to all draft evaders and military deserters the opportunity to earn their good record back. About 14,000-15,000 did take advantage of that program. We gave them ample time. I am against an across-the-board pardon of draft evaders or military evaders.

Now, in the case of Mr. Nixon, the reason the pardon was given was that, when I took office, this country was in a very, very divided condition. There was hatred; there was divisiveness; people had lost faith in their governments in many, many respects. Mr. Nixon resigned, and I became president. It seemed to me that if I was to adequately and effectively handle the problems of high inflation, a growing recession, the involvement of the United States still in Vietnam, that I had to give 100 percent of my time to those two major problems. Mr. Nixon resigned; that is [a] disgrace—the first president out of thirty-eight that ever resigned from public office under pressure. So when you look at the penalty that he paid, and when you analyze the requirements that I had to spend all of my time working on the economy—which was in trouble—that I inherited, working on our problems in southeast Asia, which were still plaguing us, it seemed to me that Mr. Nixon had been penalized enough by his resignation and disgrace, and the need and necessity for me to concentrate on problems of the country fully justified the action that I took.

REYNOLDS.   I take it then that you do not believe that you are going to reconsider and think about those 90,000 who are still abroad. Have they not been penalized enough— many of them been there for years?

FORD.   Mr. Carter has indicated that he would give a blanket pardon to all draft evaders. I do not agree with that point of view. I gave, in September of 1974, an opportunity for all draft evaders, all deserters, to come in voluntarily, clear their records by earning an opportunity to restore their good citizenship. I think we gave them a good opportunity. I don't think we should go any further.

CARTER.   I think it's very difficult for President Ford to explain the difference between the pardon of President Nixon and his attitude toward those who violated the draft laws. As a matter of fact I don't advocate amnesty; I advocate pardon. There's a difference in my opinion and in accordance with the ruling of the Supreme Court and accordance with the definition in the dictionary. Amnesty means that what you did was right. Pardon means that what you did, whether right or wrong, you're forgiven for it. And I do advocate a pardon for draft evaders. I think it's accurate to say that two years ago when Mr. Ford put in this amnesty that three times as many deserters were excused as were the ones who evaded the draft.

But I think that now is the time to heal our country after the Vietnam War and I think that what the people are concerned about is not the pardon or the amnesty of those who evaded the draft, but whether or not our crime system is fair. We've got a sharp distinction drawn between white-collar crime—the big shots who are rich, who are influential very seldom go to jail; those who are poor and who have no influence quite often are the ones who are punished. And I believe that the fairness of it is a major problem that addresses our leader, and this is something that hasn't been addressed adequately by this administration. But I hope to have a complete responsibility on my shoulders to help bring about a fair criminal justice system and also to bring about an end to the divisiveness that has occurred in our country as a result of the Vietnam War.

~

Carter-Ford
October 6, 1976

TREWHITT.   Mr. President, if you get the accounting of missing-in-action you want from North Vietnam—or Vietnam, I'm sorry—now, would you then be prepared to reopen negotiations for restoration of relations with that country?

FORD.   Let me restate our policy. As long as Vietnam, North Vietnam, does not give us a full and complete accounting of our missing-in-action, I will never go along with the admission of Vietnam to the United Nations. If they do give us a bona fide complete accounting of the 800 MIA, then I believe that the United States should begin negotiations for the admission of Vietnam to the United Nations. But not until they have given us the full accounting of our MIA.

CARTER.   One of the most embarrassing failures of the Ford administration, and one that touches specifically on human rights, is his refusal to appoint a presidential commission to go to Vietnam, to go to Laos, to go to Cambodia and try to trade for the release of information about those who are missing in action in those wars. This is what the families of MIAs want. So far, Mr. Ford has not done it. We've had several fragmentary efforts by members of the Congress and by private citizens. Several months ago the Vietnam government said we are ready to sit down and negotiate for release of information on MIAs. So far, Mr. Ford has not responded.

I also would never normalize relationships with Vietnam, nor permit them to join the United Nations, until they have taken this action. But that's not enough. We need to have an active and aggressive action on the part of the president, the leader of this country, to seek out every possible way to get that information, which has kept the MIA families in despair and doubt. And Mr. Ford has just not done it.

CARTER. [Closing statement] We ought to be a beacon for nations who search for peace and who search for freedom, who search for individual liberty, who search for basic human rights. We haven't been lately. We can be once again. We'll never have that world leadership until we are strong at home. And we can have that strength if we return to the basic principle. It ought not to be a strength of bombast and threats. It ought to be a quiet strength based on the integrity of our people, the vision of the Constitution, and innate strong will and purpose, that God's given us in the greatest nation on earth, the United States.

During prenomination debates in February 1980, Republican Ronald Reagan mentioned Vietnam in passing, calling it a war "our government was afraid to let them win," and stating that we should never again abandon a "small country to godless Communist tyranny." In April 1984 Senator Gary Hart referred to Vietnam: "[T]here's also a struggle in our party over what those lessons were and how to save young American lives from unnecessary involvement abroad. And still, we can meet all of our commitments to our allies." Again in May 1984 he remarked that "the lesson from Vietnam is not whether we should be strong and dumb or weak and dumb, but how to be strong and smart. The question of how to be smart is when to know, when you should use those forces, and whether they are going to work when you use them." There was no response from other candidates to any of these statements.

RELIGION

Discussions of politics and religion offer a fascinating and provocative example of how values and modes of political expression have changed in the United States during the past quarter-century.

In 1960 the presidential candidates were reluctant, at best, to discuss religion. By 1984 questioners and candidates felt free—or perhaps obligated—to discuss personal religious beliefs as well as a litany of related issues such as abortion and prayer in school. Note that between 1960, when a Roman Catholic was first elected president of the United States, and 1984, when a Catholic earned a place on the Democratic ticket without attracting particular attention to her religion, there was no resolution of the issue of how independent from their church Catholic candidates could be.

~

Humphrey-Kennedy
May 3, 1960

CHILTON. The Roman Catholic church's position on truth versus error assumes a right to discriminate against Protestants in some countries where Catholics are in the majority. Do you agree with the church's reported attitude that where Protestants are a minority they shouldn't be permitted equal status?

KENNEDY. No, I wholly disagree. I couldn't disagree more. I think that using the power of the state against any group, using the state to force a group to be of one faith or another, is wholly repugnant to our experience. I wholly disagree with that.

Now, there are some states where there is no separation between church and state. The queen of England is the head of the Church of England as well as the state. There're other states in Europe where the relationship is intimate. In Spain the relationship between church and state has been intimate. I disagree with that. This country was founded on the principle of separation of church and state. This is a view that I hold against any other view, and it's the view that I subscribe to in the Constitution. Now, other countries have less fortunate experiences. I wish they all provided for the separation of church and state, but we do in this United States, and we're going to continue to do it, because I don't know of anyone who holds any position of responsibility that isn't devoted to that and wishes that that system could spread throughout the world.

HUMPHREY. That was stated very well; this obviously is my position. I have always believed in and will continue to believe in the separation of church and state because it is fundamental, to my mind, to the basic political democracy that this country enjoys and that it wants to enjoy in the years ahead.

~

Kennedy-Nixon
October 13, 1960

DRUMMOND. Adam Clayton Powell [Democratic representative from New York], in the course of his speaking tour in your behalf, is saying, and I quote, "The Ku Klux Klan is riding again in this campaign. If it doesn't stop, all bigots will vote for Nixon and all right-thinking Christians and Jews will vote for Kennedy rather than be found in the ranks of the Klan-minded." What is the purpose of this sort of thing? And how do you feel about it?

KENNEDY. Griffin, I believe, who is the head of the Klan—who lives in Tampa, Florida—indicated in a statement, I think, two or three weeks ago, that he was not going to vote for me and that he was going to vote for Mr. Nixon. I do not suggest in any way, nor have I ever, that that indicates that Mr. Nixon has the slightest sympathy, involvement, or in any way imply any inferences in regard to the Ku Klux Klan. That's absurd. I don't suggest that. I don't support it. I would disagree with it. Mr. Nixon knows very well that this whole matter has been involved—this so-called religious discussion in this campaign. I have never suggested even by the vaguest implication that he did anything but disapprove of it, and that's my view now. I disapprove of the issue. I do not suggest that Mr. Nixon does in any way.

NIXON. I welcome this opportunity to join Senator Kennedy completely on that statement and to say before this largest television audience in history something that I have been saying in the past and will always say in the future. Americans must choose the best man that either party could produce. We can't settle for anything but the best, and that means, of course, the best man that this nation can produce. And that means that we can't have any test of religion. We can't have any test of race. It must be a test of the man.

Also, as far as religion is concerned, I have seen Communism abroad. I see what it does. Communism is the enemy of all religions, and we who do believe in God must join together. We must not be divided on this issue. The worst thing that I think can happen in this campaign would be for it to be decided on religious issues. I, obviously, repudiate the Klan. I repudiate anybody who uses the religious issue. I will not tolerate it.

I have ordered all of my people to have nothing to do with it. And I say to this great audience, whoever may be listening, remember, if you believe in America, if you want America to set the right example to the world, that we cannot have religious or racial prejudice. We cannot have it in our hearts, but we certainly cannot have it in a presidential campaign.

~

Carter-Ford
October 22, 1976

KRAFT. Governor Carter, in the nearly 200-year history of the Constitution, there have been only, I think, twenty-five amendments, most of them on issues of the very broadest principle. Now we have proposed amendments in many highly specialized causes like gun control, school busing, balanced budget, school prayer, abortion—things like that. Do you think it's appropriate to the dignity of the Constitution to tack on amendments in a wholesale fashion, and which of the ones I listed—that is, balanced budget, school busing, school prayer, abortion, gun control—which of those would you work really hard to support if you were president?

CARTER. I would not work hard to support any of those. We have always had, I think, a lot of constitutional amendments proposed, but the passage of them has been fairly slow and few and far between. In the 200-year history, there has been a very cautious approach to this. Quite often we have a transient problem. I am strongly against abortion. I think abortion is wrong. I don't think the government ought to do anything to encourage abortion, but I don't favor constitutional amendment on the subject. But short of a constitutional amendment, and within the confines of the Supreme Court ruling, I will do everything I can to minimize the need for abortions with better sex education, family planning, with better adoptive procedures. I personally don't believe that the federal government ought to finance abortions, but I draw the line and don't support constitutional amendment. However, I honor the right of the people to seek the constitutional amendments on school busing, on prayer in the schools, and on abortion. But among those you named, I won't actively work for the passage of any of them.

FORD. I support the Republican platform which calls for a constitutional amendment that would outlaw abortions. I favor the particular constitutional amendment that would turn over to the states the individual right of the voters in those states the chance to make a decision by public referendum. I call that the people's amendment. I think if you really believe that the people of a state ought to make a decision on a matter of this kind, that we ought to have a federal constitutional amendment that would permit each one of the fifty states to make the choice.

I think this is a responsible and proper way to proceed. I believe also that there is some merit to an amendment that Senator Everett Dirksen proposed very frequently, an amendment that would change the Court decision as far as voluntary prayer in public schools. It seems to me that there should be an opportunity, as long as it's voluntary, as long as there is no compulsion whatsoever, that an individual have a right.

So, in those two cases, I think such a constitutional amendment would be proper. And I really don't think in either case they are trivial matters. I think they are matters of very deep conviction as far as many, many people in this country believe, and therefore they shouldn't be treated lightly, but they are matters that are important. And in those two cases I would favor them.

~

Anderson-Reagan
September 21, 1980

GOLDEN. This week, Cardinal Medeiros of Boston warned Catholics that it's sinful to vote for candidates who favor abortion. This did not defeat the two men he opposed, but it did raise questions about the roles of church and state.

You, Mr. Reagan, have endorsed the participation of fundamentalist churches in your campaign. And you, Mr. Anderson, have tried three times to amend the Constitution to recognize the "law and authority" of Jesus Christ.

My question: Do you approve of the church's actions this week in Boston? And should a president be guided by organized religion on issues like abortion, equal rights, and defense spending?

REAGAN. Whether I agree or disagree with some individual, or what he may say, or how he may say it, I don't think there's any way that we can suggest that, because people believe in God and go to church, that they should not want reflected in those people and those causes they support their own belief in morality and in the high traditions and principles which we've abandoned so much in this country.

Going around this country, I think that I have found a great hunger in America for a spiritual revival. For a belief that law must be based on a higher law. For a return to traditions and values that we once had. Our government, in its most sacred documents—the

Constitution and the Declaration of Independence and all—speak of man being created, of a creator, that we're a nation under God.

Now, I have thought for a long time that too many of our churches have been too re-luctant to speak up in behalf of what they believe is proper in government, and they have been too lax in interfering, in recent years, with government's invasion of the family itself, putting itself between parent and child. I vetoed a number of bills of that kind myself when I was in California.

Now, whether it is rightful, on a single issue, for anyone to advocate that someone should not be elected or not, I won't take a position on that. But I do believe that no one in this country should be denied the right to express themselves or to even try to persuade oth-ers to follow their leader. That's what elections are all about.

GOLDEN. I would point out that churches are tax-exempt institutions, and I'll repeat my question.

ANDERSON. Certainly, the church has the right to take a position on moral issues. But to try, as occurred in the case that you mentioned—that specific case—to try to tell the parishioners of any church, of any denomination, how they should vote or for whom they should vote, I think, violates the principle of separation of church and state.

On the amendment that you mentioned, I abandoned it fifteen years ago. And I have said freely, all over this country, that it was a mistake for me or anyone to ever try to put the Judeo-Christian heritage of this country, important as it is, and important as my religious faith is to me—it's a very deeply personal matter. But for me to try, in this very pluralistic society of ours, to try to frame any definition, whatever, of what that belief should be is wrong.

And so, not once, but twice—in 1971—I voted on the floor of the House of Representatives against a constitutional amendment that tried to bring prayer back into the public schools. I think mother ought to whisper to Johnny and to Susie, as they button their coats in the morning and leave for the classroom, "Be sure to say a prayer before you start your day's work." But I don't think that the state, the board of regents, a board of education, or any state official should try to compose that prayer for a child to recite.

~

Mondale-Reagan
October 7, 1984

BARNES. Would you describe your religious beliefs, noting particularly whether you consider yourself a born-again Christian, and explain how these beliefs affect your presidential decisions?

REAGAN. I was raised to have a faith and a belief, and have been a member of a church since I was a small boy. In our particular church we did not use that term, "born again," so I don't know whether I would fit that particular term. But I have, thanks to my mother—God rest her soul—the firmest possible belief and faith in God. I believe, as Lincoln once said, that I would be the most stupid man in the world if I thought I could confront the duties of the office I hold if I could not turn to someone who was stronger and greater than all others. And I do resort to prayer.

At the same time, however, I have not believed that prayer should be introduced into an election, or be a part of a political campaign, or religion a part of that campaign. As a matter of fact, I think religion became a part of this campaign when Mr. Mondale's running mate said I wasn't a good Christian. So it does play a part in my life. I have no hesitancy in saying so. And, as I say, I don't believe that I could carry on unless I had a be-lief in a higher authority and a belief that prayers are answered.

MONDALE. First of all, I accept President Reagan's affirmation of faith. I am sure that we all accept and admire his commitment to his faith, and we are strengthened, all of us, by that fact. I am the son of a Methodist minister. My wife is the daughter of a Presbyterian minister. I don't know if I've been born again, but I know I was born into a Christian family, and I believe I have sung at more weddings and more funerals than anybody ever to seek the presidency. Whether that helps or not, I don't know. I have a deep religious faith; our family does. It is fundamental. It's probably the reason that I'm in politics. I think our faith instructs us about the moral life that we should lead, and I think we are all together on that.

What bothers me is this growing tendency to try to use one's own personal interpretation of faith politically to question others' faith and to try to use the instrumentalities of government to impose those views on others. All history tells us that that's a mistake. When the Republican platform says that from here on out we're going to have a religious test for judges before they're selected for the federal court, and then Jerry Falwell [president, Moral Majority, Incorporated] announces that that means they get at least two justices of the Supreme Court, I think that's an abuse of faith in our country.

This nation is the most religious nation on earth. More people go to church and synagogues than any other nation on earth, and it's because we kept the politicians and the state out of the personal exercise of our faith. That's why faith in the United States is pure and unpolluted by the intervention of politicians. And I think if we want to continue, as I do, to have a religious nation, let's keep that line and never cross it.

~

Bush-Ferraro
October 11, 1984

QUARLES. [One] of the most emotional issues in this campaign has been the question of the separation of church and state. What are your views on the separation of church and state, specifically with regard to abortion, and do you believe it was right for the archbishop of Philadelphia to have a letter read in 305 churches urging Catholics to fight abortion with their votes?

BUSH. I do believe in pluralism. I do believe in separation of church and state. I don't consider abortion a religious issue; I consider it a moral issue. I believe the archbishop has every right to do everything he wants in that direction, just as I never faulted Jesse Jackson for taking his message to the black pulpits all across this country, just as I never objected when the nuclear arms freeze or the antinuclear people—many of those movements were led by priests. Suddenly, because a Catholic bishop or an evangelist feels strongly on a political issue, people are saying it's merging of church and state.

We favor—and I speak confidently for the president—we favor separation of church and state. We favor pluralism. Now, somebody says, "Well, you want to restore prayer in schools. You don't think it's right to prohibit a kid from praying in schools." For years, kids were allowed to pray in schools. We don't think that's a merger of church and state to have a nonmandatory, voluntary, nongovernment-ordered prayer. And yet, some are accusing us of injecting religion into politics. I have no problem with what the archbishop does. And I have no problems [with] what the evangelists have a right to do. And I have no problem [with] what the priests on the left do. And it didn't bother me when, during the Vietnam War, much of the opposition to the government—Democrat *and* Republican governments—was led by priests encouraging people to break the law. And the adage of, you know, the civil disobedience thing.

So our position—separation of church and state, pluralism, so no little kid with a minority religion of some sort is going to feel offended or feel left out or feel uncomfortable. But, yes, prayer in school—voluntary basis. It worked for many, many years, until the Supreme Court ruled differently. And I'm glad we got this question, because I think there has been too much said about religion and politics. We don't believe in denominationally moving in. It wasn't our side that raised the question about our president, whether he was a good Christian or not. And so that's our position—separation of church and state, pluralism, respect for all.

QUARLES. Vice President Bush, four years ago, you would have allowed federal financing of abortions in cases of rape and incest as well as when the mother's life was threatened. Does your position now agree with that of President Reagan, who in Sunday's debate came very close to saying that abortion is murder?

BUSH. You know, there has been—I have to make a confession—an evolution in my position. There's been 15 million abortions since 1973. And I don't take that lightly. There has been a million and a half this year. The president and I do favor a human rights amendment. I favor one that would have an exception for incest and rape, and he doesn't, but we both [agree] only for the life of the mother. And I agree with him on that. So, yes, my position's evolved. But I'd like to see the American who, faced with 15 million abortions, isn't rethinking his or her position. I'll just stand with the answer: I support the president's position—and comfortably, from a moral standpoint.

QUARLES. So you believe it's akin to murder?

BUSH. No, I support the president's position.

QUARLES. Congresswoman Ferraro, what are your views on the separation of church and state with regard to abortion, and do you believe it was right for the archbishop of Philadelphia to have those letters read in the pulpits in this city and urge the voters to fight abortion with their vote?

FERRARO. I believe very, very sincerely in the separation of church and state. I mean, taking it from the historical viewpoint, if you go back to the 1600s when people came here, the reason they came to this country was to escape religious persecution. And that's the same reason why people are coming here today, and in the 1940s to escape Nazism, and now in the 1980s and 1984—when they can get out of the country—to escape Communism so they can come here and practice their religion. Our country is founded on the principle that our government should be neutral as far as religion is concerned.

Now what's happened over the past several years—and quite frankly, I'm not going to let you lay on me the intrusion of state politics into religion, or religion into politics, by my comments with reference to the president's policies. Because it started in 1980, when this administration was running for office and the Reverend Jerry Falwell became very, very involved in the campaign. What has happened over the past four years has been, I think, a real fudging of that line with the separation of church and state. The archbishop has not only a right, but a responsibility, to speak up. And, even though I've been the person who they have been speaking up about, I feel that they do have the responsibility to do so, and I have no problem with it, no more than I did with the priest who marched at the time of Vietnam, and no more than I did at the time when Martin Luther King marched at the time of the civil rights marches. I have absolutely no problem with them speaking up. I think they have an obligation as well as a right.

But what I do have a problem with is when the president of the United States gets up in Dallas and addresses a group of individuals and said to them that anybody who doesn't support his constitutional amendment for prayer in the schools is intolerant of religion. Now, there are numerous groups who don't support prayer in the school—numerous religious groups. Are they intolerant of religion? Is that what the president is saying? I also object when I am told that the Reverend Falwell has been told that he will pick two of our Supreme Court justices. That's going a little bit far. In that instance, let me say to you, it is more than a fudging of the line. It is a total intrusion, and I think that it's in violation of our Constitution.

QUARLES.   As a devout Catholic, does it trouble you that so many of the leaders of your church disagree with you, and do you think that you're being treated unfairly in any way by the Catholic church?

FERRARO.   I did not come to my position on abortion very lightly. I am a devout Catholic. When I was running for Congress in 1978, I sat and met with a person I felt very close to, a monsignor, currently a bishop. I spoke to him about my personal feelings that I would never have an abortion. But I was not quite sure, if I were ever to become pregnant as a result of a rape, if I would be that self-righteous. I then spoke to him. He said, "Gerry, that's not good enough. You know you can't support that position." And I said, "O.K." That's my religious view. I will accept the teaching of the church, but I cannot impose my religious views on someone else.

I truly take an oath as a public official to represent all the people in my district, not only the Catholics. If there comes a time where I cannot practice my religion and do my job properly, I will resign my job.

MISTAKES

Fear that a slip of the tongue or some other mistake might help America's enemies or otherwise harm the national interest was a paramount concern about broadcast debates until 1960, when the concern suddenly disappeared. No nation-damaging mistake was made in any of the presidential debates from 1960 through 1984.

Richard Nixon did make two major personal mistakes—at least in the first 1960 debate—by not wearing makeup and by addressing remarks to his opponent more than to the invisible television audience. (Of course, had Nixon won the extremely close 1960 election, experts would have discovered serious errors made by John F. Kennedy.)

In subsequent debates, no one repeated Nixon's mistakes, but mistakes quickly became one of the most watched for, talked about, and analyzed features of presidential debates. Not surprisingly, avoiding mistakes thus became one of the candidates' chief goals. An examination of candidates' mistakes reveals that they occurred because of human foibles, not because of particularly wise or penetrating questions, and not because a debate format encouraged aggressive rebuttals or follow-through questioning.

~

Carter-Ford
September 23, 1976

Near the end of the first 1976 Carter-Ford encounter, the television picture suddenly went silent. For the next twenty-seven minutes, while technicians frantically sought the problem (it was a small, inexpensive piece of equipment), the two candidates—apparently frozen by fear of any action that might make them look unpresidential—stood silently and looked straight ahead. Then sound was restored, and the debate resumed. This was one of the few unrehearsed, surprising events to occur during any presidential debate.

DREW. Mr. President, the real problem with the FBI, in fact, all of the intelligence agencies, is there are no real laws governing them. Such laws as there are tend to be vague and open-ended. Now, you have issued some executive orders, but we've learned that leaving these agencies to executive discretion and direction can get them and, in fact, the country in a great deal of trouble. One president may be a decent man; the next one might not be. So, what do you think about trying to write in some more protection by getting some laws governing these agencies?

FORD.   You are familiar, of course, with the fact that I am the first president in thirty years who has reorganized the intelligence agencies in the federal government: the CIA, the Defense Intelligence Agency, the National Security Agency, and the others. We've done that by executive order, and I think we've tightened it up. We've straightened out their problems that developed over the last few years. It doesn't seem to me that it's needed or necessary to have legislation in this particular regard. I have recommended to the Congress, however—I'm sure you're familiar with this—legislation that would make it very proper and in the right way that the attorney general could go in and get the right for wiretapping under security cases. This was an effort that was made by the attorney general and myself working with the Congress. But even in this area, where I think new legislation would be justified, the Congress has not responded. So I feel in that case as well as in the reorganization of the intelligence agencies, as I've done, we have to do it by executive order, and I'm glad that we have a good director in George Bush. We have good executive orders, and the CIA and the DIA and NSA are now doing a good job under proper supervision.

CARTER.   One of the very serious things that's happened in our government in recent years, and it's continued up until now, there's a breakdown in the trust among our people in the—

[A twenty-seven-minute audio emergency occurred at this point.]

NEWMAN.   We very much regret the technical failure that lost the sound as it was leaving this theater. It occurred during Governor Carter's response to what would have been and what was the last question put to the candidates. That question went to President Ford. It dealt with the control of government intelligence agencies. Governor Carter was making his response and had very nearly finished it. He will conclude that response now, after which President Ford and Governor Carter will make their closing statements.

CARTER.   There has been too much government secrecy and not enough respect for the personal privacy of American citizens.

NEWMAN.   It is now time for the closing statements, which are to be up to four minutes long. Governor Carter, by the same toss of the coin that directed the first question to you, you are to go first now. [And the debate proceeded.]

All other "mistakes" were nontechnical. They did not, however, always look like mistakes when they happened, nor do they necessarily read like mistakes after the fact. Indeed, what made most of them mistakes was that journalists covering the debates called them mistakes. Reading them in context, it is possible to conclude that few errors really occurred.

~

Carter-Ford
October 6, 1976

Ford's 1976 "liberating eastern Europe" mistake has become a classic because for five days after the debate Ford refused to acknowledge that he had said anything wrong, thus helping to guarantee that the issue would remain in newspaper headlines.

Note that Ford's statement could easily be interpreted as exactly what he said it was before he admitted error: an assertion that the spirit of the people in eastern Europe cannot be dominated by the Soviets. Also note that the panelist who introduced the notion and the actual word *dominance* gave Ford an immediate opportunity to correct or clarify his statement during the debate and that Ford's opponent mentioned *dominance* but chose to focus on other aspects of Ford's statement.

FRANKEL. Mr. President, I'd like to explore a little more deeply our relationship with the Russians. They used to brag, back in Khrushchev's day, that because of their greater patience and because of our greed for business deals, that they would sooner or later get the better of us. Is it possible that despite some setbacks in the Middle East, they've proved their point?

Our allies in France and Italy are now flirting with Communism. We've recognized a permanent Communist regime in East Germany. We virtually signed, in Helsinki, an agreement that the Russians have dominance in eastern Europe. We've bailed out Soviet agriculture with our huge grain sales. We've given them large loans, access to our best technology, and if the Senate hadn't interfered with the Jackson amendment, maybe we would have given them even larger loans. Is that what you call a two-way street of traffic in Europe?

FORD. I believe that we have negotiated with the Soviet Union, since I've been president, from a position of strength. And let me cite several examples.

Shortly after I became president, in December of 1974 I met with General Secretary Brezhnev in Vladivostok, and we agreed to a mutual cap on the ballistic missile launchers at a ceiling of 2,400, which means that the Soviet Union, if that becomes a permanent agreement, will have to make a reduction in their launchers that they now have or plan to have. I negotiated at Vladivostok with Mr. Brezhnev a limitation on the MIRVing of their ballistic missiles at a figure of 1,320, which is the first time that any president has achieved a cap either on launchers or on MIRVs. It seems to me that we can go from there to the grain sales.

The grain sales have been a benefit to American agriculture. We have achieved a five and three-quarter year sale of a minimum of 6 million metric tons, which means that they have already bought about 4 million metric tons this year and are bound to buy another 2 million metric tons to take the grain and corn and wheat that the American farmers have produced in order to have full production, and these grain sales to the Soviet Union have helped us tremendously in meeting the costs of the additional oil and the oil that we have bought from overseas. If we turn to Helsinki—I'm glad you raised it, Mr. Frankel. In the case of Helsinki, thirty-five nations signed an agreement, including the secretary of state for the Vatican. I can't, under any circumstances, believe that His Holiness the Pope would agree by signing that agreement, that the thirty-five nations have turned over to the Warsaw Pact nations the domination of eastern Europe. It just isn't true. And if Mr. Carter alleges that His Holiness, by signing that, has done it, he is totally inaccurate.

Now what has been accomplished by the Helsinki agreement? Number one, we have an agreement where they notify us and we notify them of any military maneuvers that are to be undertaken. They have done it in both cases where they've done so. There is no Soviet domination of eastern Europe, and there never will be under a Ford administration.

FRANKEL. Did I understand you to say, sir, that the Russians are not using eastern Europe as their own sphere of influence in occupying most of the countries there in making sure with their troops that it's a Communist zone, whereas on our side of the line, the Italians and the French are still flirting with—

FORD. I don't believe, Mr. Frankel, that the Yugoslavians consider themselves dominated by the Soviet Union. I don't believe that the Rumanians consider themselves dominated by the Soviet Union. I don't believe that the Poles consider themselves dominated by the Soviet Union. Each of those countries is independent, autonomous. It has its own territorial integrity, and the United States does not concede that those countries are under the domination of the Soviet Union. As a matter of fact, I visited Poland, Yugoslavia, and Rumania to make certain that the people of those countries understood that the president of the United States and the people of the United States are dedicated to their independence, their autonomy, and their freedom.

CARTER. In the first place, I'm not criticizing His Holiness the Pope. I was talking about Mr. Ford. The fact is that secrecy has surrounded the decisions made by the Ford administration. In the case of the Helsinki agreement, it may have been a good agreement at the beginning, but we have failed to enforce the so-called Basket Three part which insures the right of people to migrate, to join their families, to be free, to speak out. The Soviet Union is still jamming Radio Free Europe. We've also seen a very serious problem with the so-called Bonnenfeldt document, which apparently Mr. Ford has just endorsed, which set it as an organic linkage between the eastern European countries and the Soviet Union. And I would like to see Mr. Ford convince the Polish-Americans and the Czech-Americans and the Hungarian-Americans in this country that those countries don't live under the domination and supervision of the Soviet Union behind the Iron Curtain.

We also have seen Mr. Ford exclude himself from access to the public. He hasn't had a tough cross-examination-type press conference in over thirty days. One press conference he had without sound. He's also shown a weakness in yielding to pressure. The Soviet Union, for instance, put pressure on Mr. Ford, and he refused to see a symbol of human freedom recognized around the world, Aleksandr Solzhenitsyn. The Arabs have put pressure on Mr. Ford, and he's yielded and has permitted a boycott by the Arab countries of American businesses who trade with Israel, who have American Jews owning or taking part in the management of American companies. His own secretary of commerce had to be subpoenaed by the Congress to reveal the names of businesses that are subject to this boycott. They didn't [give] the information. He had to be subpoenaed.

And I'd like to say this: this grain deal with the Soviet Union in '72 was terrible, and Mr. Ford . . . for it with three embargoes, one against . . . ally in Japan. That's not the way to run foreign policy, including international trade.

~

Dole-Mondale
October 15, 1976

During the third 1960 debate, Richard Nixon had attracted little attention when he said, "I would ask him [JFK] to name one Republican president who had led this nation into war. There were three Democratic presidents who led us into war." But by 1976, when Republican vice-presidential candidate Robert Dole made a similar charge, such rhetoric—as indicated by Democratic vice-presidential candidate Walter Mondale's response—was a mistake. Among other things, it alienated Democratic voters whom the Republican ticket was trying to woo. Dole repeated the charge later in the campaign and then had to read a statement conceding error.

MEARS. Senator Dole, ten days ago, when Senator Mondale raised the issues of Watergate and the Nixon pardon, you called it the start of the campaign mudslinging.

Two years ago, when you were running for the Senate, you said that the pardon was prematurely granted and that it was a mistake. You were quoted by the *Kansas City Times* as saying you can't ignore our tradition of equal application of the law. Did you approve of the Nixon pardon when President Ford granted it? Do you approve of it now? And if the issue was fair game in your 1974 campaign in Kansas, why is it not an appropriate topic now?

DOLE. It is an appropriate topic, I guess, but it's not a very good issue, any more than the war in Vietnam would be, or World War II or World War I or the war in Korea. All Democrat wars. All in this century. I figured up the other day, if we added up the killed and wounded in Democrat wars in this century, it would be about 1.6 million Americans, enough to fill the city of Detroit. Now, if we want to go back and rake that over and over and over, we can do that. I assume Senator Mondale doesn't want to do that. But it seems to me that the pardon of Richard Nixon is behind us. Watergate's behind us. If we have this vision for America, and if we're really concerned about those people out there, and their problems—yes, and their education and their jobs—we ought to be talking about that.

I know it strikes a responsive chord for some to kick Richard Nixon around. I don't know how long you can keep that up. How much mileage is there in someone who's been kicked; whose wife suffered a serious stroke; who's been disgraced in office and stepped down from that office? I think, after two years and some months, that it's probably a dead issue. But let them play that game. That's the only game they know.

~

Carter-Reagan
October 28, 1980

During preparation for this debate, Jimmy Carter told aides he might use a conversation with his daughter, Amy, as a way to personalize fear about nuclear war. Aides argued against it. The "Amy" speech occurred in the context of Carter's strong attacks on Reagan as irresponsible on nuclear issues. Thus, it did Carter double damage because it diverted attention from an issue where Reagan was supposedly weakest.

STONE. Governor Reagan—arms control: The president said it was the single most important issue. Both of you have expressed the desire to end the nuclear arms race with Russia, but by methods that are vastly different. You suggest that we scrap the SALT II treaty already negotiated and intensify the buildup of American power to induce the Soviets to sign a new treaty—one more favorable to us. President Carter, on the other hand, says he will again try to convince a reluctant Congress to ratify the present treaty on the grounds it's the best we can hope to get.

Now, both of you cannot be right. Will you tell us why you think you are?

REAGAN. Yes. I think I'm right because I believe that we must have a consistent foreign policy, a strong America, and a strong economy. And then, as we build up our national security to restore our margin of safety, we at the same time try to restrain the Soviet buildup, which has been going forward at a rapid pace and for quite some time.

The SALT II treaty was the result of negotiations that Mr. Carter's team entered into after he had asked the Soviet Union for a discussion of actual reduction of nuclear strategic weapons. And his emissary, I think, came home in twelve hours having heard a very definite *nyet*. But taking that one "no" from the Soviet Union, we then went back into negotiations on their terms, because Mr. Carter had canceled the B-1 bomber, delayed the

MX, delayed the Trident submarine, delayed the Cruise missile, shut down the Minute Man missile production line, and whatever other things that might have been done. The Soviet Union sat at the table knowing that we had gone forward with unilateral concessions without any reciprocation from them whatsoever.

Now, I have not blocked the SALT II treaty, as Mr. Carter and Mr. Mondale suggest that I have. It has been blocked by a Senate in which there is a Democratic majority. Indeed, the Senate Armed Services Committee voted 10-0, with seven abstentions, against the Salt II treaty and declared that it was not in the national security interests of the United States. Besides which it is illegal, because the law of the land, passed by Congress, says that we cannot accept a treaty in which we are not equal. And we are not equal in this treaty for one reason alone—our B-52 bombers are considered to be strategic weapons; their Backfire bombers are not.

SMITH. Governor, I have to interrupt you at that point. The time is up for that. But the same question now to President Carter.

STONE. Yes. President Carter, both of you have expressed the desire to end the nuclear arms race with Russia, but through vastly different methods. The governor suggests we scrap the SALT II treaty which you negotiated in Vienna—or signed in Vienna—intensify the buildup of American power to induce the Soviets to sign a new treaty, one more favorable to us. You, on the other hand, say you will again try to convince a reluctant Congress to ratify the present treaty on the grounds it is the best we can hope to get from the Russians.

You cannot both be right. Will you tell us why you think you are?

CARTER. Yes, I'd be glad to. Inflation, unemployment, the cities are all very important issues, but they pale into insignificance in the life and duties of a president when compared with the control of nuclear weapons. Every president who has served in the Oval Office since Harry Truman has been dedicated to the proposition of controlling nuclear weapons.

To negotiate with the Soviet Union a balanced, controlled, observable—and then reducing levels of atomic weaponry—there is a disturbing pattern in the attitude of Governor Reagan. He has never supported any of those arms-control agreements—the limited test ban, SALT I, nor the Antiballistic Missile treaty, nor the Vladivostok treaty negotiated with the Soviet Union by President Ford—and now he wants to throw into the wastebasket a treaty to control nuclear weapons on a balanced and equal basis between ourselves and the Soviet Union, negotiated over a seven-year period, by myself and my two Republican predecessors.

The Senate has not voted yet on the Strategic Arms Limitation Treaty. There have been preliminary skirmishings in the committees of the Senate, but the treaty has never come to the floor of the Senate for either a debate or a vote. It's understandable that a senator in the preliminary debates can make an irresponsible statement, or, maybe, an ill-advised statement. You've got ninety-nine other senators to correct that mistake, if it is a mistake. But when a man who hopes to be president says, take this treaty, discard it, do not vote, do not debate, do not explore the issues, do not finally capitalize on this long negotiation—that is a very dangerous and disturbing thing.

REAGAN. I'd like to respond very much. First of all, if I have been critical of some of the previous agreements, it's because we've been out-negotiated for quite a long time. And they have managed, in spite of all of our attempts at arms limitation, to go forward with the biggest military buildup in the history of man.

Now, to suggest that because two Republican presidents tried to pass the SALT treaty—that puts them on its side—I would like to say that President Ford, who was within 90 percent of a treaty that we could be in agreement with when he left office, is emphatically against this SALT treaty. I would like to point out also that senators like

Henry Jackson and [Ernest F.] Hollings of South Carolina—they are taking the lead in the fight against this particular treaty.

I am not talking of scrapping. I am talking of taking the treaty back and going back into negotiations. And I would say to the Soviet Union, we will sit and negotiate with you as long as it takes to have not only legitimate arms limitation but to have a reduction of these nuclear weapons to the point that neither one of us represents a threat to the other. That is hardly throwing away a treaty and being opposed to arms limitation.

CARTER. Governor Reagan is making some very misleading and disturbing statements. He not only advocates the scrapping of this treaty—and I don't know that these men that he quotes are against the treaty in its final form—but he also advocates the possibility—he said it's been a missing element—of playing a trump card against the Soviet Union of a nuclear arms race, and is insisting upon nuclear superiority by our own nation as a predication for negotiation in the future with the Soviet Union.

If President Brezhnev said, We will scrap this treaty, negotiated under three American presidents over a seven-year period of time, we insist upon nuclear superiority as a basis for future negotiations, and we believe that the launching of a nuclear arms race is a good basis for future negotiations, it's obvious that I, as president, and all Americans, would reject such a proposition. This would mean the resumption of a very dangerous nuclear arms race. It would be very disturbing to American people. It would change the basic tone and commitment that our nation has experienced ever since the Second World War, with all presidents, Democratic and Republican. And it would also be very disturbing to our allies, all of whom support this nuclear arms treaty. In addition to that, the adversarial relationship between ourselves and the Soviet Union would undoubtedly deteriorate very rapidly.

This attitude is extremely dangerous and belligerent in its tone, although it's said with a quiet voice.

REAGAN. I know the president's supposed to be replying to me, but sometimes I have a hard time in connecting what he's saying with what I have said or what my positions are. I sometimes think he's like the witch doctor that gets mad when a good doctor comes along with a cure that'll work.

My point I have made already, Mr. President, with regard to negotiating: it does not call for nuclear superiority on the part of the United States. It calls for a mutual reduction of these weapons, as I say, [so] that neither of us can represent a threat to the other. And to suggest that the SALT II treaty that your negotiators negotiated was just a continuation, and based on all of the preceding efforts by two previous presidents, is just not true. It was a new negotiation because, as I say, President Ford was within about 10 percent of having a solution that could be acceptable. And I think our allies would be very happy to go along with a fair and verifiable SALT agreement.

CARTER. I think, to close out this discussion, it would be better to put into perspective what we're talking about. I had a discussion with my daughter, Amy, the other day, before I came here, to ask her what the most important issue was. She said she thought nuclear weaponry—and the control of nuclear arms.

This is a formidable force. Some of these weapons have 10 megatons of explosion. If you put 50 tons of TNT in each one of railroad cars, you would have a carload of TNT—a trainload of TNT stretching across this nation. That's one major war explosion in a warhead. We have thousands, equivalent of [a] megaton, or million tons, of TNT warheads. The control of these weapons is the single major responsibility of a president, and to cast out this commitment of all presidents, because of some slight technicalities that can be corrected, is a very dangerous approach.

PRESIDENTS DEBATING VICE PRESIDENTS

Men who eventually served together as president and vice president have debated each other in the prenomination stages of two elections. During the 1968 Democratic convention, John F. Kennedy and Lyndon B. Johnson debated in front of a joint meeting of the Massachusetts and Texas delegations. The debates had no apparent impact on either the nomination or the relationship between the two men.

On April 23, 1980, after the Republican field had been narrowed, Ronald Reagan and George Bush met. In earlier group debates, Bush had attacked Reagan for being too old to be president, and Reagan had criticized Bush's handling of intelligence estimates as CIA chief. Bush had also attracted attention during the campaign by calling Reagan's plans for the economy "voodoo economics." But by late April, a time when each still hoped to win the Republican presidential nomination, a mutual desire to avoid conflict was clear.

~

Bush-Reagan
April 23, 1980

SMITH. You said you hoped to win because you had adopted the strategy of hammering away at the differences between you and Mr. Reagan. And one difference you mentioned was, in your words, Mr. Reagan was overpromising the American people. Could you explain that, and, if the spirit moves you, could you respond?

BUSH. A big difference, for example, that the governor and I have regards this tax cut. He feels—I don't want to put words in his mouth, and he is here to defend or explain his position—that you can cut taxes by $70 billion the first year. The *Wall Street Journal* attributed the figure to that tax cut idea to $90 billion the first year, cut inheritance and gift taxes—we computed that at $5.4 billion—and still balance the budget and still increase defense spending.

President Kennedy suggested this cut. It was implemented by Johnson. The cut was $11.4 billion. It resulted in a $4.4 billion revenue loss. Inflation then was 1.8 percent. Today it is 18 [percent]. Investor confidence was out there; today there is none.

So, in my judgment, that economic program would exacerbate the deficit. It would result in less stimulation of the economy because of the conditions. And I believe that before we can have massive across-the-board tax cuts, we've got to get the budget in balance.

So I am proposing a $20 billion, as opposed to $70 or $90 [billion], supply-side tax cut to stimulate savings for home to stimulate business. That is a major difference. There are plenty of others, but I do want to give the governor a chance to respond.

REAGAN. That is, indeed, a major difference; and I still believe firmly, and I think there are some differences of opinion about figures. Four times in this century we have had across-the-board tax cuts, all of which have resulted in such an increase in prosperity that the government even in the first year got increased revenues, not less. In the Kennedy year, the total revenues for government—and, of course, government was much smaller then—[were] about $109 billion instead of the $600 [billion] that will be coming up in '81, but according to the figures then, the federal government got some $5 billion in additional revenue and got about $1.1 billion additional revenue in the income tax.

But let me point something out. George mentioned the difference here. Under Jimmy Carter, the tax burden, as a percentage of the gross national product, has reached the highest level in the history of our nation. It is also the highest percentage of personal income that it has ever been in our history. Now, under the president's revised '81 budget, the total federal taxes are projected as $628 billion. Of that, $283 [billion] will be individual income tax. That's 115 percent increase in that tax since he took office.

Now, over the next ten years, if things aren't changed, it is estimated that the total tax increase on the people of America will be $1.5 trillion.

Now, rather than the Kemp-Roth bill, which I support, the idea of a 10 percent cut across the board, the income tax, administered over a three-year period to a total of 30 percent, I believe will stimulate the economy, will create jobs, but it will not reduce the increase in taxes, because we are going to be faced with an increase in taxes that is far beyond our comprehension right now. And if we figured that cut as a percentage of $628 billion, you would be reducing the first year less than 5 percent, perhaps about 4 percent, in the total tax revenues that the government is going to be getting. But I believe at the same time history has proven in all those other tax cuts, I believe that will stimulate the economy, more people will be working, and it will be contrary to the Carter policy now of fighting inflation by adding millions to the unemployment roles.

And so I support and stand by the idea of incentive taxes geared to the free-enterprise system that will provide incentive to increase productivity so we can compete in the international market, which we can't do on even terms today.

BUSH. I agree with that, but the difference we have is that it is my understanding the Kennedy tax cut, implemented by Lyndon Johnson, resulted in a $4.4 billion deficit; and inflation then was 1.8, not 18 percent. Investor confidence was high, not low; and it is my perception that that tax cut applied today in the same percentage, the same numbers, would result in an inflation rate of about 30 to 32 percent. I couldn't agree more about the percent of our gross national product taken by taxes, but I believe the first thing we must do is get in balance. Incidentally, not the way Jimmy Carter proposes, by higher and higher taxes. Get in balance by the reduction of expenditures; get in balance by a $20 billion supply-side tax cut and then begin to reduce rates.

But if we risk, with investor confidence where it is, a deficit that's going to be up already, I think, $37 billion, $30 billion on top of that, I'm afraid we can't break inflation, and we've got to do that and do it fast.

REAGAN. George, we've got to do that. And, of course, it goes without saying, and I certainly believe in reducing the cost of government far more than the phony decrease that Mr. Carter has proposed. But when you suggested, as you have, about a $20 billion tax cut, that is less than the federal government is going to get in a single year, undeserved, from people that just received cost-of-living pay raises and were pushed up into higher tax brackets. That amounts to more than $20 billion.

BUSH. But if we get that in balance and then do what I say, start reducing the rates, that is the key thing. Your plan in my judgment and the judgment of many economists would risk exacerbating that deficit. And today our creditors abroad, our economy is linked to foreign economies, and they take a look at us and see us living at deficit after deficit. You cite the Kennedy tax cut. There wasn't any surplus then. There was a deficit resulted from that scheme. Arthur Laffer, the economist that proposed it, he himself says, "I don't know whether it would work."

I don't believe we can take that kind of risk, Governor, and I would not propose it.

REAGAN.   George, how much more risk is there in just going along with what we've been doing?

BUSH.   That's not what I propose. I propose something very different than just going along.

REAGAN.   Let me just say one other thing. I have heard for a great many years that we can't possibly reduce taxes. This is Washington's cry.

BUSH.   I agree.

REAGAN.   We can't reduce taxes until we reduce government spending. And I have to point out that government does not tax to get the money it needs; government always needs the money it gets. Now, your son can be extravagant with his allowance, and you can lecture him day after day about saving money and not being extravagant, or you can solve the problem by cutting his allowance.

BUSH.   But the program I'm putting forward cuts the allowance, cuts on the spending side. It doesn't risk this "promise everybody everything," because you cut taxes $210 billion, and you favor increasing defense, and you favor cutting out inheritance and gift taxes; and I believe that you're going to end up with a much bigger deficit. And that's where you and I differ.

Listen, you talk to me about gross national product and percent of taxes. My whole program is based on getting tax relief. But I am not going to do it in a way, popular though it may be, if it's going to, in my view, make that deficit—

REAGAN.   There is one last point I want to make. There is one last point we haven't touched on. We are talking as if those dollars that are saved in taxes are not going to have any effect, no multiplier effect, when they are in the people's pockets and they're used out there in society. And it has been proven that there is a far greater multiplier effect and creation of prosperity in money spent by the people and invested by the people than there is when it is spent by government; and, therefore, we've got to recognize that that money isn't going to be buried in a tin can in the backyard. It's going to be used to buy things. And when we buy things, productivity is going to increase; people are going to put it in the savings account; then we're going to have the capital to invest in new plant and equipment and research and development. We have the highest percentage today of outmoded industrial plants and equipment of any of the industrial nations of the world. We can't compete evenly with them because we don't have the capital investment to put into business anymore.

BUSH.   That's why my cut is a supply-side tax cut. That's what will stimulate production. That's the cut I want.

FORMAT

Much of the controversy surrounding debates concerns format: Should there be a moderator? How about eliminating the panel of questioners? Why not just put the candidates on stage alone and let them confront each other? Those who ask such questions usually assume that more truth and better information will emerge from a face-to-face meeting without intermediaries.

But in the real world candidates do not want—and have not accepted—face-to-face confrontations. Such confrontations, they fear, could force them to appear unpresidential or overly aggressive. A confrontation also might divert them from their well-rehearsed answers. From 1960 through 1984, no primary or general-election presidential debate took place without a moderator or panel, and no general-election debate occurred with just a moderator.

Most formats *have* included a follow-through question or an opportunity for an opponent's rebuttal. Experience shows, however, that presidential candidates can dominate any format and can avoid revealing anything about their positions they do not wish to reveal. Two techniques candidates have most commonly used are the quick dismissal and the answer to a different question. Debates also document the fact that face-to-face meetings (whatever potential virtues they may offer) can easily digress into distracting pettiness.

On June 1, 1968, Democrats Robert F. Kennedy and Eugene McCarthy met under rules that did not allow them to question each other.

~

Kennedy-McCarthy
June 1, 1968

CLARK. Senator McCarthy, the McCarthy for President Committee has been running full-page ads in California papers in recent days saying that Senator Kennedy must bear part of the responsibility for the decision to intervene in Vietnam, and the implication seems to be that even though he has been a war critic for the past three years, he should be ruled out as president because of his participation in that decision in the Kennedy administration.

Is that what you mean?

McCARTHY. I don't think we said it should be ruled out at all, Bob. He has said he would take some responsibility for it. The question is, How much responsibility?

I was talking more about the process. I said one of the things we ought to talk about is the process by which decisions were made with reference to this war, because one of our problems has been to find out who decides and who is responsible and on what kind of evidence did we have this kind of escalation?

KENNEDY. It also said that I intervened in the Dominican Republic.

McCARTHY. That's right.

KENNEDY. Now how did they get that?

McCARTHY. Well, I think what they did, I had—

KENNEDY. I wasn't even in the government at the time.

McCARTHY. Well you weren't out very long.

KENNEDY. But I—

McCARTHY. I don't want to fault you on that.

KENNEDY. And then it ran again today.

McCARTHY. We stopped it—it may have run in two papers, but I don't think it ran twice.

KENNEDY. I saw it again this morning. I wasn't involved in the Dominican Republic. I wasn't even in the government, and I criticize this.

McCARTHY. What I said was that this was a process that was involved in our going into Cuba, involved in our going into the Dominican Republic, and also into Vietnam, and that I wanted to talk about the process. In any case, I had not seen the ad. When I saw it I said, "Stop it," and they stopped it as soon as they could.

KENNEDY. I appreciate that.

Some experts argue that only a moderator can force answers out of recalcitrant and slippery candidates; others say that a moderator has too much power. A confrontation during the February 23, 1984, Democratic debate shows what can happen when a moderator decides to pursue a point. It is impossible to generalize about whom such exchanges help or hurt. Much depends on the issue and the constituency involved and on whether the public and press see any candidate being treated unfairly.

~

Askew-Cranston-Glenn-Hart-Hollings-Jackson-McGovern-Mondale
February 23, 1984

WALTERS. [Addressing Jesse Jackson] Much of your press coverage this week has dealt with charges that you are anti-Semitic, and you have charged that Jewish groups are hounding you. You are accused by the *Washington Post* as referring to New York Jews as "heimies," and you have said that you cannot recall saying that. But on September 28, 1979, the *New York Times* reported your having said, and I quote, "I'm sick and tired about hearing constantly about the Holocaust. The Jews don't have a monopoly on suffering." That same month, on the program "60 Minutes," in speaking of terrorist attacks, you put the PLO [Palestine Liberation Organization] and Israel in the same basket.

Let's try to clear some of this up and give you an opportunity to answer. Is it unreasonable to think that such statements might be interpreted as being anti-Israel and anti-Semitic?

JACKSON. That's unfortunate, really. I'm convinced that, first of all, we ought to put this matter in context, have a major dialogue with leaders, and then put the matter to rest and move on to the higher agenda of social justice. I am not anti-Semitic. It is unfortunate that there is this continuous struggle, as it were, between black leadership and Jewish leadership. During the course of this campaign, I expect to meet with some leaders and presidents of Jewish organizations very soon. I am not anti-Semitic. And I do hope that during these next few months that the charges can be put to rest.

WALTERS. Let's put them to rest here. Have you made these statements?

JACKSON. These statements are out of context. First of all, I am not one inclined to call people by names that would be insulting. I intend to insult nobody.

WALTERS. Did you ever make that statement? Did you call any New York Jews "heimies" or New York "heimietown" or anything like that?

JACKSON. I have no recollection of that, and, furthermore, I have indicated that those who've said it—I've not seen them make that statement face to face. And during the course of this dialogue, perhaps even tonight, it will become even clearer. I am not anti-Semitic. I've proven to desire dialogue. I think the constant confrontations have irreparable damage, both to blacks and to Jews.

WALTERS. I would just like to stick to the question. Do you recall making either of the other two statements. I have exactly what was said, if you want me to read it, but—

JACKSON. Do read that again.

WALTERS. All right. "I'm sick and tired of hearing constantly about the Holocaust. The Jews don't have a monopoly on suffering." And in speaking with Dan Rather [anchor and managing editor, "CBS Evening News"], when he talked about the PLO engaged in terrorism, you said, "One could easily say. . . ." He said, "How can you compare it to Israel?" And you say, "Well, one could identify with Israel with the continuous violations they express in dropping their bombs in south Lebanon and using U.S. equipment. It's also terrorism."

JACKSON. The point is, the context of that is that both groups—blacks and Jews—have known suffering. That's what we really have in common, and we have known suffering. We have, should have, a real sensitivity one toward the other. That statement really was taken out of context. I have been a supporter of Israel's right to exist. But I'm also a human rights activist. I support Palestinians' right to exist also. I support a mutual recognition policy. Furthermore, I am convinced that so long as Israel is in a posture where it has to occupy and expand on the West Bank, it has a way of undercutting Israel's ability to be a democracy and to, in fact, have the moral authority that she needs. If our nation in fact uses its moral authority, it can expand upon Camp David. It can raise peace in that troubled region.

Several times, during both primary and general-election debates, candidates have had the opportunity to question each other. This invariably exposes their desire to remain nonconfrontational and does not necessarily make for a livelier or more informative debate.

~

Hart-Jackson-Mondale
April 5, 1984

HART.   Fritz, under the previous Democratic administration, unemployment went up in this state, the steel industry declined, and dozens, if not hundreds, of plants were closed. There was relief in isolated incidents of one or two plants, but overall I think in this state there are more than 50,000 workers in that industry who lost their jobs. What do you think? In very specific terms, what new proposals do you think we ought to adopt to put the entire industry back on its feet and put a state like this back on its feet?

MONDALE.   First of all, we were working very hard on problems in the steel industry through the years of our administration and probably did more to try to help that industry than any administration in American history. We put the price mechanism in place. For the first time, we set up the tripartite commissions: labor, management, and government.

We were going to do for steel what we did for Chrysler, and we were making progress. We were also beginning to take a proper stand on trade because the industry has been characterized as being a victim of a broad range of foreign predatory practices that were really being very, very unfair. And finally, we were helping industries to get back on their feet.

For example, Wheeling-Pittsburgh Steel's an example of the future. That was a company that was losing its competitive edge. It had some severe environmental problems that it wasn't able to solve, and I helped work out an arrangement where you get back on your feet. They're now producing the most advanced, highly competitive steel rails, and they're in very good shape now, and over a thousand jobs were saved. That's something I stood up for.

And what we need to do is go back to that approach, help the steel industry modernize, get competitive, work together. The key word is cooperation. When labor and management and government work together, as we did in Chrysler, the potential is unlimited.

DREW.   Mr. Hart will put a question to Mr. Jackson.

HART.   Mr. Jackson, a related subject to foreign policy is, of course, defense. You have taken a different position from that of Vice President Mondale and myself. You want deep cuts in the military. My position is, if we do that, two things will happen: we will lose the skilled personnel that additional benefits are needed to retain; the country will be weaker as a result of that. Many people, including many minority people who see the military service as a way out, would abandon that. I think the country would then be forced to go back to the draft. What are your views on that, and would you still support the cuts under those conditions?

JACKSON.   I accept the first premise that you and Mr. Mondale are alike on that question. Let's get that quite clear. All right?

On a serious note, we can cut this budget without cutting our defense and running us into a crisis. That is to say, 90 percent of all of the defense contracts are no-bid. That leaves the way for a lot of corruption, and waste, and abuse. We need to challenge that arrangement and break up that degree of socialism within that billion-dollar racket.

Number two, forty years later, we're paying $150 billion a year to defend Japan and Europe, about half of our military budget. Now, Japan is bragging about, "We'll only pay 1 percent." Europe at about 3.3 percent. We're paying about 6+ to 7 percent. We should have a serious commitment to troop reduction in Europe and begin to cut back on those costs. Japan and Europe are on their feet now. They can either accept that peace through us, or they can use some of their own money to help defend themselves. We cannot very well run a wartime budget for Japan and Europe during peace. And if it were wartime, we'd have to close down America just to defend Japan and Europe. So, we can cut that because they have been able to share that burden.

Lastly, if we cut the MX and the B-1, we seem to have enough money to cut the defense budget without cutting our defense. I do not think we'd, therefore, run into an emergency. If, however, we were in an emergency, I would use the draft, but if we were in an emergency, most Americans are so patriotic they wouldn't need to be drafted. History has shown people volunteer if it's an emergency. Going to Lebanon, going to Honduras, that's not an emergency. That's a tragedy of leadership.

DREW. A question from Mr. Jackson to Mr. Mondale.

JACKSON. South Africa represents a great source of shame in the world today. It operates as if it were a democracy, but, of course, blacks have to have passbooks. There's racial oppression. They have nuclear capability. Westinghouse is aiding them with the nuclear capability which threatens the entire human race. And then, beyond that, South Africa, of course, becomes a great recipient of jobs, because it's a slave labor market. What would you do to break off or change that relationship with South Africa and therefore make it compatible with America's highest and best values?

MONDALE. This gets back to the earlier question about human rights. The practice of apartheid in South Africa is exactly the way you described it. It is vicious, it is profound, it is an insult to human rights and to our values. We've tried for years to get them to change; I think we now have to start turning that screw tighter and tighter.

I have made several suggestions of what I would do. Number one, I would expand the restraint which now embargoes arms to cover all police equipment. Secondly, I would support—I think it is the Bill Gray amendment [amendment proposed by William H. Gray III of Pennsylvania]—which would prohibit any new investments by American businesses in South Africa. Third, I would support the IMF [International Monetary Fund] provision, which would prohibit any international loans to South Africa. Next, I would prohibit the sale of Krugerrands into the United States. I would finally—if that didn't make any progress—prohibit the flights of South African Airlines into the United States and begin to work multilaterally to make it known that our country cannot stand by and permit this profound abuse of human dignity to continue.

DREW. Now, Mr. Mondale, you ask a question to Mr. Hart.

MONDALE. The issue hasn't come up yet, but I believe that the control of nuclear weapons is the issue, because if those god-awful things go off, nothing else will matter. That's why I support the freeze and the other things. What's your view?

HART. Well, Fritz, you know from the period of the 1970s, when we worked very closely together on the SALT II treaty and other arms-control initiatives, that I share that fundamental belief with you, and, in fact, it's one of the reasons I'm in politics today and running for the presidency. I have teenage children, as I know you do; Reverend Jackson does. I think it unites us, doesn't divide us. I think the question is how to get that freeze and what to do in addition to the freeze as quickly as possible.

My view is that the freeze is a major contribution to the arms-control debate. I think we have to go beyond it, not after it, and do a number of things all at the same time: ban weapons in space, freeze the production of plutonium, stop proliferation of nuclear technology and materials to Third World nations to stop the horizontal arms race, set up a system whereby neither we nor the Soviets, in a period of crisis, start World War III. And I know that you agree with that.

We will not do that, however, unless we defeat Ronald Reagan. I hate to keep bringing it back to that, but what frightens me the most about Ronald Reagan is not only dividing this society along economic lines, but the unrestrained four more years of a nuclear arms race that I believe would bring this world—and I know you do, too—right to the very brink of nuclear war, and perhaps over that brink in a period of crisis and misunderstanding. This president frightens me to death.

On occasion, questioners have attempted to get candidates to confront one another, even given a format in which direct questions by one candidate to the other were not allowed. These attempts have failed.

~

Mondale-Reagan
October 7, 1984

SAWYER. What do you think is the most outrageous thing your opponent said in the debate tonight?

MONDALE. Do you want to give me some suggestions? I'm going to use my time a little differently. I'm going to give the president some credit. I think the president has done some things to raise the sense of spirit, morale, good feeling in this country. And he's entitled to credit for that. What I think we need, however, is not just that, but to move forward, not just congratulating ourselves, but challenging ourselves to get on with the business of dealing with America's problem.

I think in education, when he lectured the country about the importance of discipline, I didn't like it at first, but I think it helped a little bit. But now we need both that kind of discipline and the resources and the consistent leadership that allows this country to catch up in education and science and training. I like President Reagan. And this is not personal. These are deep differences about our future, and that's the basis of my campaign.

SAWYER. Follow up in a similar vein then. What remaining question would you most like to see your opponent forced to answer?

MONDALE. Without any doubt, I have stood up and told the American people that that $263 billion deficit must come down. And I've done what no candidate for president's ever done: I told you before the election what I'd do. As you saw tonight, President Reagan takes the position it will disappear by magic. It was once called "voodoo economics." I wish the president would say, "Yes, the CBO [Congressional Budget Office] is right. Yes, we have a $263 billion deficit. This is how I'm going to get it down." Don't talk about growth, because even though we need growth, that's not helping. It's going to go in the other direction, as they've estimated.

And give us a plan. What will you cut? Whose taxes will you raise? Will you finally touch that defense budget? Are you going to go after social security and medicare and student assistance and the handicapped again, as you did last time? If you'd just tell us what you're going to do, then the American people could compare my plan for the future with your plan. And that's the way it should be. The American people would be in charge.

SAWYER. Mr. President, the most outrageous thing your opponent has said in the debate tonight?

REAGAN. I have to start with a smile, since his kind words to me. I'll tell you what I think has been the most outrageous thing in political dialogue, both in this campaign and the one in '82. And that is the continued discussion and claim that somehow I am the villain who is going to pull the social security checks out from those people who are dependent on them. And why I think it is outrageous—first of all, it isn't true—but why it is outrageous is because, for political advantage, every time they do that, they scare millions of senior citizens who are totally dependent on social security, have no place else to turn. And they have to live and go to bed at night thinking, "Is this true? Is someone going to take our check away from us and leave us destitute?" And I don't think that that should be a part of political dialogue.

Now social security, let's lay it to rest once and for all. I told you, never would I do such a thing. But I tell you also now: social security has nothing to do with the deficit. Social security is totally funded by the payroll tax levied on employer and employee. If you reduce the outgo of social security, that money would not go into the general fund to reduce a deficit. It would go into the social security trust fund. So social security has nothing to do with balancing a budget or erasing or lowering the deficit.

Now, to get to whether I am depending on magic, I think I have talked in straight economic terms about a program of recovery that I was told wouldn't work. And then after it worked, I was told that lowering taxes would increase inflation. And none of these things happened. It is working, and we're going to continue on that same line.

As to what we might do and find in further savings cuts, no, we're not going to starve the hungry. But we have 2,478 specific recommendations from a commission of more than 2,000 businesspeople in this country, through the Grace Commission, that we're studying right now—and we've already implemented 17 percent of them—that are recommendations as to how to make government more efficient, more economic.

SAWYER. And, to keep it even, what remaining question would you most like to see your opponent forced to answer?

REAGAN. Why the deficits are so much of a problem for him now, but that in 1976, when the deficit was $52 billion and everyone was panicking about that, he said "no," that he thought it ought to be bigger, because a bigger deficit would stimulate the economy and would help do away with unemployment. In 1979 he made similar statements [to] the same effect. That there was nothing wrong with having deficits. Remember, there was a trillion dollar debt before we got here. That's got to be paid by our children and grandchildren, too, if we don't do it. And I'm hoping we can start some payments on it before we get through here. That's why I want another four years.

WALTERS. We have time now, if you'd like to answer the president's question, or whatever rebuttal.

MONDALE. We've just finished almost the whole debate, and the American people don't have the slightest clue about what President Reagan will do about these deficits. And yet that's the most important single issue of our time.

I did support the '76 measure that he told about, because we were in a deep recession and we needed some stimulation. But I will say, as a Democrat, I was a real piker, Mr. President. In 1979 we ran a $29 million deficit all year. This administration seems to run that every morning. And the result is exactly what we see. This economy is starting to run downhill. Housing is off. Last report on new purchases—it's the lowest since 1982. Growth is a little over 3 percent now. Many people are predicting a recession. And the flow of imports into this country is swamping the American people.

We've got to deal with this problem. And those of us who want to be your president should tell you now what we're going to do, so you can make a judgment.

~

Bush-Ferraro
October 11, 1984

BOYD. What is the single question you would most like to ask your opponent here on foreign policy?

FERRARO. I don't have a single most question. I guess the concern I have is a concern not only as the vice presidential candidate, but as a citizen in this country. My concern is that we are not doing anything to stop the arms race. And it seems to me that if we keep talking about military inferiority, which we do not have—we are at a comparable level with the Soviet Union. Our joint chiefs of staff have said they'd never exchange our military for theirs. I guess the thing is that I'd want a commitment that, you know—pretty soon they're going to do something about making this a safer world, you know, for all of us.

BUSH. I have none I'd like to ask of her. But I'd sure like to use the time [to] talk about the World Series or something of that nature.

Let me put it this way. I don't have any questions. The Reagan-Bush administration is so different from the Carter-Mondale administration that the American people are going to have the clearest choice. It's a question of going back to the failed ideas of the past, where we came in: 21.5 percent on those interest rates, inflation, despair, malaise, no leadership, blaming the American people for failed leadership. Or another option—keep this recovery going till it benefits absolutely everybody. Peace at home, peace abroad, prosperity, opportunity—I'd like to hear her talk on those things, but I think the yellow light is flashing, and so we'll leave it there.

Part IV

BROADCAST DEBATES
AND GALLUP POLLS

BROADCAST PRESIDENTIAL DEBATES
1948-1984

Republican Primary Debate
May 17, 1948

Governor Thomas E. Dewey and former governor Harold E. Stassen

Date of upcoming election—May 21, 1948; location—KEX-ABC radio studio, Portland, Oregon; time—10:00-11:00 p.m. EST; moderator—Donald R. Van Boskirk, chairman of the Multnomah County Republican Central Committee; format—20-minute opening arguments, followed by 8½-minute rebuttal statements; sponsored by KEX-ABC radio; broadcast nationwide on ABC, NBC, and Mutual Radio and heard by approximately 40-80 million listeners. Source: *New York Times*.

Democratic and Republican Candidates Forum,
"View of 52," May 1, 1952

Former governor W. Averell Harriman, Paul Hoffman
for Dwight D. Eisenhower, Senator Estes Kefauver,
Senator Robert S. Kerr, former governor Harold Stassen,
Governor Earl Warren

Date of upcoming election—November 4, 1952; location—Taft Auditorium, Cincinnati, Ohio; time—7:00-8:00 p.m. EST; invitees who did not participate— Senator Robert A. Taft and Senator Richard B. Russell; moderator—John Daly, ABC Radio; format—two questions, preselected from a poll of League of Women Voters members, asked of each candidate, and a reply from each; then questions from the audience; sponsored by the League of Women Voters and *Life* magazine; broadcast nationwide on ABC, picked up by 38 affiliates, and also heard on 130 NBC radio stations and Voice of America and Radio Free Europe. Source: *New York Times*.

Democratic Primary Debate
May 21, 1956

Senator Estes Kefauver and former governor Adlai E. Stevenson

Date of upcoming election—May 28, 1956; location—WTVJ studio, Miami, Florida; time—9:00-10:00 p.m. EST; moderator—Quincy Howe, ABC; format—candidates made 3-minute opening statements, asked each other one question, and made 5-minute closing statements; sponsored by ABC; broadcast nationwide on ABC television and ABC radio. Sources: *New York Times, Washington Star.*

Democratic Primary Debate
May 3, 1960

Senator Hubert H. Humphrey and Senator John F. Kennedy

Date of upcoming election—May 10, 1960; location—WCHS studios, Charleston, West Virginia; time—7:30-8:30 p.m. EST; moderator—William Ames, WCHS-TV; panelists—Ned Chilton, *Charleston Gazette;* Dale Schussler, WTRF; format—5-minute opening statements followed by straight questions and answers, with order of questions alternating, and opportunity to make 5-minute rebuttals; sponsored by WCHS-TV; broadcast on regional Westinghouse television stations KDKA in Pittsburgh, WNEW in New York, KDIX in San Francisco, WTOP in District of Columbia, WBZ in Boston, and KWY in Cleveland; broadcast later by Canadian Broadcasting Company. Sources: *New York Times, Washington Star.*

Democratic Convention Debate
July 12, 1960

Senator Lyndon B. Johnson and Senator John F. Kennedy

Location—Biltmore Hotel ballroom, Los Angeles, California, at Democratic party nominating convention; time—3:00-3:30 p.m. CST; format—10-minute opening statements, 5-minute rebuttals, and closing statements; sponsored by the Texas and Massachusetts delegations; broadcast nationwide on CBS television. Sources: *New York Times, Los Angeles Times, Washington Post.*

General Election Debate
September 26, 1960

Senator John F. Kennedy and Vice President Richard M. Nixon

Date of upcoming election—November 8, 1960; location—WBBM studio, Chicago, Illinois; time—7:30-8:30 p.m. EST; moderator—Howard K. Smith, CBS News; panelists—Robert Fleming, ABC; Stuart Novins, CBS; Charles Warren, Mutual Broadcasting System; Sander Vanocur, NBC; format—8-minute opening statements, followed by alternating questions from panelists with 2½ minutes to respond, other candidate has option to rebut or comment; sponsored by CBS; broadcast nationwide on ABC, NBC, and CBS; Nielsen ratings—66.4 for all three networks combined, 30 million households or 54 percent of television sets in use tuned to the debate. Sources: *New York Times; The Making of the President 1960,* White.

General Election Debate
October 7, 1960

Senator John F. Kennedy and Vice President Richard M. Nixon

Date of upcoming election—November 8, 1960; location—NBC studio, Washington, D.C.; time—7:30-8:30 p.m. EST; moderator—Frank McGee, NBC; panelists—Paul Niven, CBS; Edward P. Morgan, ABC; Alvin Spivak, UPI; Harold Levy, *Newsday;* format—questions from panelists, with opponent given opportunity to rebut or comment; sponsored by NBC; broadcast nationwide on NBC, ABC, and CBS; Nielsen ratings—61.9 for all three networks combined, 28 million households, 38 percent of television sets in use tuned to the debate. Source: *New York Times.*

General Election Debate
October 13, 1960

Senator John F. Kennedy and Vice President Richard M. Nixon

Date of upcoming election—November 8, 1960; location—Nixon in Hollywood, California, and Kennedy in New York City; time—7:30-8:30 p.m. EST; moderator—Bill Shadel, ABC; panelists—Charles Von Fremd, CBS; Frank McGee, NBC; Roscoe Drummond, *New York Herald Tribune;* Douglass Cater, *Reporter* magazine; format—questions from panelists to candidates, with opponent given time to comment before being asked the next question; sponsored by ABC; broadcast nationwide on ABC, CBS, and NBC; Nielsen ratings—63.7, 29 million households; 50.5 percent of television sets in use tuned to the debate. Sources: *New York Times; The Making of the President 1960,* White.

General Election Debate
October 21, 1960

Senator John F. Kennedy and Vice President Richard M. Nixon

Date of upcoming election—November 8, 1960; location—ABC studio, New York City; time—7:30-8:30 p.m. EST; moderator—Quincy Howe, ABC News; panelists—John Edwards, ABC; Walter Cronkite, CBS; Frank Singiser, Mutual Broadcasting System; John Chancellor, NBC; format—8-minute opening statements, followed by alternating questions from panelists with opportunity for other candidate to comment, and 3-minute closing statements; sponsored by ABC; broadcast nationwide on ABC, CBS, and NBC; Nielsen ratings—60.4 for all three networks combined. Sources: *New York Times; The Making of the President 1960,* White.

Democratic Primary Debate
June 1, 1968

Senator Robert Kennedy and Senator Eugene McCarthy

Date of upcoming election—June 4, 1968; location—San Francisco, California; time—6:30-7:30 PST, broadcast live at 9:30 p.m. EST and shown delayed at 9:30 PST; invitee who did not participate—Vice President Hubert H. Humphrey; moderator—Frank Reynolds, ABC News; panelists—Bill Lawrence, ABC News; Bob Clark, ABC News; format—alternating questions from panelists to candidates seated at table, first one candidate responding, then the second candidate responding to the first; sponsored by ABC; broadcast nationwide on ABC, carried on 171 ABC stations and 825 radio stations. Sources: *New York Times; 85 Days,* Witcover.

Democratic Primary Debate
May 28, 1972

Senator Hubert H. Humphrey and Senator George McGovern

Date of upcoming election—June 6, 1972; location—Los Angeles, California; 6:00-7:00 p.m. EST, shown at different times in different markets; moderator—George Herman, CBS News; panelists—David Schoumacher, CBS; David Broder, *Washington Post;* format—questions by panelists, candidates taking turns responding first; sponsored by "Face the Nation," CBS; broadcast nationwide on CBS. Sources: *Washington Star; The Making of the President 1972,* White.

Democratic Primary Debate
May 30, 1972

Senator Hubert H. Humphrey and Senator George McGovern

Date of upcoming election—June 6, 1972; location—NBC studios, Burbank, California; time—9:30-10:30 p.m. EST; moderator—Lawrence E. Spivak, NBC News; Robert Novak, *Chicago Sun-Times*; Haynes Johnson, *Washington Post*; Tom Pettit, NBC News; Richard Bergholz, *Los Angeles Times*; format—questions to each candidate in turn with followup questions; sponsored by NBC; broadcast on television nationwide on NBC-TV, radio broadcast at 10:05-11:00 p.m. EST. Source: "Meet the Press" transcript.

Democratic Primary Debate
June 4, 1972

Congresswoman Shirley Chisholm from a studio in New York;
Senator Hubert H. Humphrey; Senator George McGovern;
General George Taylor, representing Governor George C. Wallace;
Mayor Sam Yorty of Los Angeles

Date of upcoming election—June 6, 1972; location—ABC studio, Los Angeles, California; time—5:00-6:00 p.m. EST, seen at different times in different markets; panelists—"Issues and Answers" panel; format—not available; sponsored by ABC; broadcast nationwide on ABC. Sources: *New York Times, Los Angeles Times.*

Democratic Primary Debate
February 23, 1976

Senator Birch Bayh, former governor Jimmy Carter,

**former senator Fred Harris, Senator Henry Jackson,
Governor Milton Shapp, Sargent Shriver, Representative Morris Udall**

Date of upcoming election—February 24, 1976; location—John Hancock Auditorium, Boston, Massachusetts; 8:30-10:30 p.m. EST; invitee who did not participate—Governor George C. Wallace; moderator—Elie Abel, dean, Columbia University graduate School of Journalism; panelists—Carolyn Shaw Bell, professor of economics, Wellesley College; Robert Hall, professor, Massachusetts Institute of Technology; Karen Horn, assistant vice president of First National Bank of Boston; format—question and followup from panelists for specific candidates in turn, followed by questions from audience read by moderator or questioner in audience; sponsored by the League of Women Voters; broadcast nationwide on PBS and NPR. Source: League of Women Voters Education Fund.

Democratic Primary Debate
March 29, 1976

**Former governor Jimmy Carter, Senator Frank Church,
former senator Fred Harris, Senator Henry Jackson,
Representative Morris Udall**

Date of upcoming election—April 6, 1976; location—Waldorf-Astoria Hotel, New York City; time—8:30-10:00 p.m. EST; invitee who did not participate—Governor George C. Wallace; moderator—Elie Abel, dean, Columbia University Graduate School of Journalism; panelists—Neal R. Pierce, *National Journal;* Frank H. Blatz, Jr., former mayor of Plainfield, New Jersey; Lucille Rose, commissioner of New York City Department of Employment; format—question and followup from panelist to specific candidates in turn, followed by audience questions to candidates; sponsored by the League of Women Voters; broadcast nationwide on PBS and NPR. Sources: *New York Times;* League of Women Voters Education Fund, debate transcripts.

Democratic Primary Debate
May 3, 1976

Senator Frank Church and Representative Morris Udall

Location—Ambassador West Hotel, Chicago, Illinois; time—8:30-9:00 p.m. CST; invitees who did not participate—former governor Jimmy Carter, Senator Henry Jackson, Governor George C. Wallace; moderator—Elie Abel, dean, Columbia University Graduate School of Journalism; panelists—Phil Odeen, former director of program analysis, National Security Council; Richard Kosobud, economist and author; David Mellon, vice president, Chicago Council on Foreign Relations; format—question and followup from panelist to a specific candidate, question from member of audience; sponsored by the League of Women Voters; debate scheduled for 90 minutes but cut short because of small number of candidates participating; broadcast nationwide on PBS and NPR. Source: League of Women Voters Education Fund.

General Election Debate
September 23, 1976

Former governor Jimmy Carter and President Gerald R. Ford

Date of upcoming election—November 2, 1976; location—Walnut Theater, Philadelphia, Pennsylvania; time—9:30-11:00 p.m. EST; moderator—Edwin Newman, NBC News; panelists—Frank Reynolds, ABC News; Elizabeth Drew, *New Yorker* magazine; James Gannon, *Wall Street Journal;* format—question from panelist to be answered by candidate in 3 minutes, follow-up question from same panelist to be answered in 2 minutes, then another panelist questioning other candidate, 3-minute closing statements at end; sponsored by League of Women Voters; broadcast nationwide on ABC, NBC, CBS, and PBS; Nielsen ratings—72.5 for all networks combined, watched by 51.6 million households or 146 million persons. Source: *1976 Presidential Debates,* publication of League of Women Voters Education Fund.

General Election Debate
October 6, 1976

Former governor Jimmy Carter and President Gerald R. Ford

Date of upcoming election—November 2, 1976; location—Palace of Fine Arts, San Francisco, California; time—6:30-8:00 p.m. PST; moderator—Pauline Frederick, National Public Radio; panelists—Richard Valeriani, NBC News; Henry Trewhitt, *Baltimore Sun;* Max Frankel, *New York Times;* format— question from panelist to be answered by candidate in 3 minutes, follow-up question from same panelist with 2 minutes to respond, then another panelist questioning other candidate, 3-minute closing statements; sponsored by League of Women Voters; broadcast nationwide on ABC, CBS, NBC, and PBS at 9:30 p.m. EST; Nielsen ratings—65.3, watched by 46.5 million households, 131 million persons. Source: *1976 Presidential Debates,* publication of League of Women Voters Education Fund.

Vice-presidential Debate
October 15, 1976

Senator Robert Dole and Senator Walter Mondale

Date of upcoming election—November 2, 1976; location—Alley Theater, Houston, Texas; time—9:30-10:45 p.m. EST; moderator—James Hoge, *Chicago Sun-Times;* panelists—Marilyn Berger, NBC News; Walter Mears, Associated Press; Hal Bruno, *Newsweek;* format—2-minute opening statements, followed by alternating questions from panelists, with 2½-minute responses from candidates, and 3-minute closing statements; sponsored by the League of Women Voters; broadcast nationwide on ABC, CBS, and NBC; Nielsen ratings—50.0 on all three networks combined; 35.6 million households, with 100 million persons tuned to debate. Sources: *New York Times,* League of Women Voters Education Fund.

General Election Debate
October 22, 1976

Former governor Jimmy Carter and President Gerald R. Ford

Date of upcoming election—November 2, 1976; location—Phi Beta Kappa Hall, College of William and Mary, Williamsburg, Virginia; time—9:30-11:00 p.m. EST; moderator—Barbara Walters, ABC News; panelists—Joseph Kraft, syndicated columnist; Jack Nelson, *Los Angeles Times;* Robert Maynard, *Washington Post;* format—alternating questions to candidates from panelists, each candidate having 2 minutes for response, and second candidate a 2-minute comment on that response, panelist with optional follow-up question, 3-minute closing statements; broadcast nationwide on ABC, CBS, NBC, and PBS; Nielsen ratings—59.7 on all three commercial networks combined, 42.5 million households, with 120 million persons tuned to the debate. Source: *1976 Presidential Debates,* publication of League of Women Voters Education Fund.

Republican Primary Debate
January 5, 1980

Representative John Anderson, Senator Howard Baker, former ambassador George Bush, former governor John Connally, Representative Philip Crane, Senator Robert Dole

Date of upcoming election—January 21, 1980, caucuses; location—Des Moines Civic Center, Des Moines, Iowa; time—7:30-9:30 CST; invitee who did not participate—Ronald Reagan; moderator—James P. Gannon, executive editor of the *Des Moines Register and Tribune;* panelists—George Anthan, *Des Moines Register and Tribune;* Richard Doak, *Des Moines Tribune,* Walter Mears, Associated Press; Mary McGrory, *Washington Star;* format—question from panelist to candidate who has 2 minutes to respond, other candidates have 1 minute each to rebut answer, followed a 20-minute period of questions from audience with 1 minute for each response, 3-minute closing statements for each candidate; sponsored by *Des Moines Register;* broadcast nationwide on live radio on ABC, CBS, NBC, and NPR; broadcast in Iowa live on WHO, KDIN, Iowa Public Broadcasting Network; delayed and shown January 5 at 10:30 p.m. on KCCI, and 12:30 p.m. on January 6 on WOI. Source: *Des Moines Register.*

Republican Primary Debate
February 20, 1980

Representative John Anderson, Senator Howard Baker, former ambassador George Bush, former governor John Connally, Representative Philip Crane, Senator Robert Dole, former governor Ronald Reagan

Date of upcoming election—February 26, 1980; location—St. Anselm's College, Manchester, New Hampshire; time—8:30-10:00 p.m. EST; moderator—Howard K. Smith; panelists—Joseph Kraft, syndicated columnist; Eileen Shanahan, *Washington Star;* format—in the first hour each candidate answering a question in 2 minutes, with other candidates having 1 minute to respond; in the second hour questions from members of the audience, with 1½ minutes to respond; 1-minute closing statements; broadcast nationwide on PBS and NPR. Source: *1980 Presidential Debates: Behind the Scenes,* publication of League of Women Voters Education Fund.

Republican Primary Debate
February 23, 1980

Former ambassador George Bush and former governor Ronald Reagan

Date of upcoming election—February 26, 1980; location—Nashua High School, Nashua, New Hampshire; time—8:15-9:45 p.m. EST; moderator—Jon Breen, *Nashua Telegraph*; format—questions from moderator with 2 minutes to answer, other candidate has 2 minutes to respond or rebut; then alternating questions from audience read by the moderator with same time limits; 2-minute closing statements; broadcast live statewide on PBS. Source: *Nashua Telegraph.*

Republican Primary Debate
February 28, 1980

Senator Howard Baker, former ambassador George Bush, former governor John Connally, former governor Ronald Reagan

Date of upcoming election—March 8, 1980; location—Longstreet Theatre, University of South Carolina, Columbia, South Carolina; time—9:00-10:30 p.m. EST; moderator—Jim Lehrer, PBS; panelists—Jack Germond, syndicated columnist; William Raspberry, syndicated columnist; Ken Krell, *Columbia Record;* Lee Bany, *The State* newspaper; format—question from panelist to first candidate with 2 minutes to respond and 1 minute each for other candidates to rebut; question from panelist for each candidate with 1 minute to respond; question and followup from moderator with 1 minute for response; 2-minute closing statements; sponsored by the University of South Carolina and Columbia Newspapers, Inc.; broadcast nationwide on PBS. Source: University of South Carolina.

Republican Primary Debate
March 13, 1980

Representative John Anderson, former ambassador George Bush, Representative Philip Crane, former governor Ronald Reagan

Date of upcoming election—March 18, 1980; location—Chicago, Illinois; time—8:00-9:30 p.m. CST; moderator—Howard K. Smith, ABC News; format—question from moderator for specific candidate, then discussion of issue by other candidates (90 minutes); questions from audience to specific candidate followed by discussion of issue by other candidates; a 1-minute closing statement from each candidate; sponsored by the League of Women Voters; broadcast nationwide on PBS and NPR. Source: League of Women Voters Education Fund.

Republican Primary Debate
April 23, 1980

Former ambassador George Bush and former governor Ronald Reagan

Date of upcoming election—May 3, 1980; location—Grapevine, Texas; time—8:00-9:00 p.m. CST; moderator—Howard K. Smith, ABC News; format—question from moderator for specific candidate, then discussion of issue by other candidate for 1¾ minutes each; questions from audience to specific candidate followed by discussion of issue by other candidate (13 minutes); 1-minute closing statements; sponsored by the League of Women Voters; broadcast nationwide on PBS and NPR. Source: *1980 Presidential Debates: Behind the Scenes*, publication of League of Women Voters Education Fund.

General Election Debate
September 21, 1980

Representative John Anderson and former governor Ronald Reagan

Date of upcoming election—November 4, 1980; location—Baltimore Convention Center, Baltimore, Maryland; time—10:00-11:00 p.m. EST; invitee who did not participate—President Jimmy Carter; moderator—Bill Moyers, PBS; panelists—Charles Corddry, *Baltimore Sun;* Soma Golden, *New York Times;* Daniel Greenberg, syndicated columnist; Carol Loomis, *Fortune* magazine; Lee May, *Los Angeles Times;* Jane Bryant Quinn, *Newsweek;* format—questions from panelists with 2½ minutes to respond, then 1 minute, 15 seconds for each candidate to challenge the other's response, 3-minute closing statements; sponsored by the League of Women Voters; broadcast nationwide on NBC, CBS, and CNN. Source: *1980 Presidential Debates: Behind the Scenes,* publication of League of Women Voters Education Fund.

General Election Debate
October 28, 1980

President Jimmy Carter and former governor Ronald Reagan

Date of upcoming election—November 4, 1980; location—Convention Center Music Hall, Cleveland, Ohio; time—9:30-11:00 p.m. EST; moderator—Howard K. Smith, ABC News; panelists—Harry Ellis, *Christian Science Monitor;* William Hilliard, *Portland Oregonian;* Marvin Stone, *U.S. News & World Report;* Barbara Walters, ABC News; format—question from panelist to one candidate with 2 minutes to respond, follow-up question with 1 minute to respond, then same question asked of other candidate with same time limits; each candidate given 1 minute to challenge the other's response (40 minutes); followed by question from panelist to each candidate, with 2 minutes to respond and 1½ minutes to rebut; 3-minute closing statements; broadcast nationwide on ABC, CBS, NBC, and CNN; Nielsen ratings—71.2 for all three commercial networks combined, 55.4 million households or 150 million persons. Source: *1980 Presidential Debates: Behind the Scenes,* a publication of the League of Women Voters Education Fund.

Democratic Primary Debate
January 15, 1984

**Former governor Reubin O. Askew, Senator Alan Cranston,
Senator John H. Glenn, Senator Gary Hart, Senator Ernest F. Hollings,
Reverend Jesse L. Jackson, former senator George McGovern,
former vice president Walter F. Mondale**

Date of upcoming election—New Hampshire primary, February 28, 1984; location—Spaulding Auditorium, Dartmouth College, Hanover, New Hampshire; time—3:00-6:00 p.m. EST; moderators—Ted Koppel, ABC News, and Phil Donahue, "Donahue" syndicated TV show; format—questions from Koppel and free-wheeling discussion for 90 minutes, followed by questions from members of the audience selected by Donahue and free-wheeling discussion for another 90 minutes; no closing statements; sponsored by the Democratic Caucus; broadcast nationwide on PBS. Sources: Dartmouth College, Democratic Caucus.

Democratic Primary Debate
January 31, 1984

**Senator Alan Cranston, Senator John Glenn, Senator Gary Hart,
Senator Ernest F. Hollings, Reverend Jesse Jackson,
former senator George McGovern, former vice president Walter Mondale**

Date of upcoming election—New Hampshire primary, February 28, 1984; location—Harvard University, Cambridge, Massachusetts; time—7:30-8:30 p.m. EST; invitee who did not participate—former governor Reubin O. Askew; moderator—Peter Mehegan, "Chronicle"; panelists—Karen Elliot House, *Wall Street Journal;* William Beecher, *Boston Globe;* Ezra Vogel, professor of sociology, Harvard University; Gregory Treverton, lecturer in public policy, Harvard University; format—questions from audience, then panelist question with follow-up and clean-up questions; candidate questions with clean-up questions; closing statements; sponsored by Harvard Institute of Politics, JFK School of Government, and the *Boston Globe;* broadcast locally on "Chronicle," fed to Metromedia network in New York City, Washington, D.C., and Chicago; aired on C-SPAN February 4. Source: JFK School of Government, Harvard University.

Democratic Primary Debate
February 3, 1984

**Senator John Glenn, Senator Gary Hart, Senator Ernest F. Hollings,
Reverend Jesse Jackson, former senator George McGovern**

Date of upcoming election—New Hampshire primary, February 28, 1984; location—Emmanuel College, Boston, Massachusetts; time—1½ hours; invitees who did not participate—former governor Reubin O. Askew, Senator Alan Cranston; moderator—Liz Walker, WBZ-Boston; panelists—Ellen Goodman, *Boston Globe;* Carole Simpson, ABC; Eileen Shanahan, *Pittsburgh Post-Gazette;* format—question and followup from panelist, addressed to one or all candidates, followed by closing statements; sponsored by Emmanuel College and Women in

Politics '84; broadcast on WBZ-Boston, made available to other stations via satellite, also on radio. Sources: Emmanuel College *Quarterly, New York Times.*

Democratic Primary Debate
February 11, 1984

Former governor Reubin O. Askew, Senator Alan Cranston, Senator John Glenn, Senator Gary Hart, Senator Ernest F. Hollings, Reverend Jesse Jackson, former senator George McGovern, former vice president Walter Mondale

Date of upcoming election—Iowa caucuses, February 20, 1984; location—Des Moines Civic Center, Des Moines, Iowa; time—2:00-4:30 p.m. CST; moderator—James P. Gannon, editor, *Des Moines Register;* panelists—James O. Freedman, president, University of Iowa; Matthew Bucksbaum, president, General Growth Companies; Denise O'Brien, farmer; Martha Nash, former director, Martin Luther King Center for Education and Vocational Training; Laurisa Sellers, former director, Young Women's Resource Center; James Risser, *Des Moines Register;* format—2-minute opening statements followed by three rounds of cross-questioning in which each candidate directed a question to three of the other candidates; moderator then questioned each candidate and panelists asked questions; 2-minute closing statements; sponsored by *Des Moines Register;* broadcast live nationwide on CNN and on statewide radio in Iowa; PBS delayed broadcast at 8:00 p.m. February 11; C-SPAN delayed broadcast at 6:00 p.m. on February 13. Source: *Des Moines Register.*

Democratic Primary Debate
February 23, 1984

Former governor Reubin O. Askew, Senator Alan Cranston, Senator John Glenn, Senator Gary Hart, Senator Ernest F. Hollings, Reverend Jesse Jackson, former senator George McGovern, former vice president Walter Mondale

Date of upcoming election—New Hampshire primary, February 28, 1984; location—St. Anselm's College, Manchester, New Hampshire; time—8:00-9:30 p.m. EST; moderator—Barbara Walters, ABC News; format—moderator put different question to each candidate, allowing a 1-minute answer; moderator asked a question any candidate could answer after the initial response; then same question put to each candidate with 1½-minute response; 1½-minute closing statements; sponsored by the League of Women Voters; broadcast nationwide on PBS; delayed broadcast on C-SPAN. Source: *Debates '84,* League of Women Voters Education Fund final report.

Democratic Primary Debate
March 11, 1984

Senator John Glenn, Senator Gary Hart, Reverend Jesse Jackson, former senator George McGovern, former vice president Walter Mondale

Date of upcoming election—March 13, 1984; location—Fox Theater, Atlanta, Georgia; time—5:00-6:00 p.m. EST; moderator—John Chancellor, NBC News; format—moderator asked question of each candidate, followed by questions to candidates at random with cross-talk after initial response, then closing statements; sponsored by League of Women Voters; broadcast nationwide on PBS, CNN, and delayed on C-SPAN. Source: League of Women Voters Education Fund files.

Democratic Primary Debate
March 18, 1984

Senator Gary Hart, Reverend Jesse Jackson, former vice president Walter Mondale

Date of upcoming election—March 20, 1984; location—Westin Hotel, Chicago, Illinois; time—7:00-8:00 p.m. CST; moderator—Thomas Hayward, Jr., president of Chicago Bar Association; panelists—Ron Magers and Carol Marin, WMAQ-TV; Walter Jacobson and Mike Flannery, WBBM; D. Michael Cheers, *Jet* magazine; format—question and followup from panelist for each candidate, with question open for other candidates, followed by closing statements; sponsored by Environmental Law Committee, Chicago Bar Association; broadcast on WBBM in Chicago and C-SPAN nationwide. Sources: *New York Times, Chicago Tribune,* and Chicago Bar Association.

Democratic Primary Debate
March 28, 1984

Senator Gary Hart, Reverend Jesse Jackson, former vice president Walter Mondale

Date of upcoming election—New York primary, April 3, 1984; location—Columbia University, New York; time—8:00-9:00 p.m. EST; moderator—Dan Rather, CBS News; format—same question addressed to all candidates, then a different question addressed to each candidate, with other candidates allowed to comment after the response, followed by 2-minute closing statements; all candidates seated at same table; sponsored by CBS; broadcast nationwide on CBS and delayed on C-SPAN. Source: *New York Times.*

Democratic Primary Debate
April 5, 1984

Senator Gary Hart, Reverend Jesse Jackson, former vice president Walter Mondale

Date of upcoming election—Pennsylvania primary, April 10, 1984; location—David Lawrence Convention Center, Pittsburgh, Pennsylvania; time—8:00-9:00 p.m. EST; moderator—Elizabeth Drew, *The New Yorker;* format—different question asked of each candidate with 1 minute to answer, then a question any candidate could answer after initial response, followed by cross-talk in which each candidate posed one question to another candidate; 1-minute closing statements; sponsored by League of Women Voters; broadcast on PBS and KDKA CBS affiliate and delayed on C-SPAN. Source: *Debates '84,* League of Women Voters Education Fund final report.

Democratic Primary Debate
May 2, 1984

Senator Gary Hart, Reverend Jesse Jackson, former vice president Walter Mondale

Date of upcoming election—Texas primary, May 8, 1984; location—Dallas/Fort Worth AMFAC Hotel, Texas; time—8:00-9:00 CST; moderator—Sander Vanocur, ABC News; format—moderator asked different question of each candidate, then asked questions of specific candidate that any candidate could answer after the initial response; closing statements; sponsored by the League of Women Voters; broadcast nationwide on PBS and affiliate KERA and delayed on C-SPAN. Source: *Debates '84,* League of Women Voters Education Fund final report.

Democratic Primary Debate
June 3, 1984

Senator Gary Hart, Reverend Jesse Jackson, former vice president Walter Mondale

Date of upcoming election—California primary, June 5, 1984; location—NBC studio, Los Angeles, California; time—7:00-8:00 p.m. EST; moderator—Tom Brokaw, NBC News; format—moderator asked questions with optional followup, then asked one candidate a question that the other candidates could respond to after initial response; 1½-minute closing statements; sponsored by NBC; broadcast nationwide on NBC. Source: NBC debate transcript.

General Election Debate
October 7, 1984

Former vice president Walter Mondale and President Ronald Reagan

Date of upcoming election—November 2, 1984; location—Kentucky Center for Arts, Louisville, Kentucky; time—9:00-10:30 p.m. EST; moderator—Barbara Walters, ABC News; panelists—Fred Barnes, *Baltimore Sun;* Diane Sawyer, CBS News; James Wieghart, Scripps-Howard News Service; format—panelist question to candidate, with a 2½-minute reply, follow-up question with 1-minute reply, same question and followup to second candidate, followed by 1-minute rebuttal by opponent; 4-minute closing statements; sponsored by the League of Women Voters; broadcast nationwide on ABC, CBS, NBC, PBS, and CNN; Nielsen ratings—59.1 for all three commercial networks combined, 50.2 million households or 132 million persons. Source: *Debates '84,* League of Women Voters Education Fund final report.

General Election Vice-presidential Debate
October 11, 1984

Vice President George Bush and Representative Geraldine Ferraro

Date of upcoming election—November 2, 1984; location—Philadelphia Civic Center, Philadelphia, Pennsylvania; time—9:00-10:30 p.m. EST; moderator—Sander Vanocur, ABC News; panelists—Robert Boyd, Knight-Ridder Newspapers; John Mashek, *U.S. News & World Report;* Norma Quarles, NBC News; Jack White, *Time* magazine; format—panelist question to candidate with a 2½-minute reply and follow-up question to same candidate with a 1-minute reply; same question to opponent with same amount of time for reply and followup; candidates could rebut one another for 1 minute; 4-minute closing statements; sponsored by the League of Women Voters; broadcast nationwide on ABC, CBS, NBC, and CNN, and delayed on C-SPAN; Nielsen ratings—56.4 for all three commercial networks combined, 47.9 million households or 125 million persons. Source: *Debates '84,* League of Women Voters Education Fund final report.

General Election Debate
October 21, 1984

Former vice president Walter Mondale and President Ronald Reagan

Date of upcoming election—November 2, 1984; location—Music Hall, Kansas City, Missouri; time—8:00-9:30 p.m. EST; moderator—Edwin Newman, retired NBC News; panelists—Georgie Anne Geyer, Universal Press Syndicate; Marvin Kalb, NBC; Morton Kondracke, *New Republic;* Henry Trewhitt, *Baltimore Sun;* format—panelist question to candidate, with a 2½-minute reply and a follow-up question to same candidate with a 1-minute reply; candidates could rebut one another for 1 minute; 4-minute closing statements; sponsored by the League of Women Voters; broadcast nationwide on ABC, CBS, NBC, PBS, CNN, and delayed on C-SPAN. Source: *Debates '84,* League of Women Voters Education Fund final report.

GALLUP POLLS
ON PRESIDENTIAL DEBATES
1960-1987

Kennedy-Nixon
August 25-30, 1960

Population: National
Sample size: 3,337
Survey #634

Have you heard or read about the TV debates planned between Kennedy and Nixon in the election campaign this fall?

Yes 66%
No 34

Would you say that you have a lot of interest in watching these TV debates, or not much interest?

A lot 56%
Not much 39
No opinion 4

From your own personal point of view, what issue or problem would you most like to have debated?

Racial segregation and civil rights, how to live in peace
without integration, the sit-in strikes, housing equality 12%
Social security benefits, social welfare program, care of
the aged, medical care, lower social security age 4
The farm problem, getting better prices for farm produce,
price of grain, subsidies—control, surpluses 8
High cost of living, taxes, high prices 5
Religion and politics, Kennedy and Catholicism, separation
of church and state, the religious issue 1
Unemployment 3
Trend towards big government, creeping socialism, federal
government power 1
Labor problem, labor unions, what to do about labor 2
States' rights . . . . *
Foreign problems; foreign relations, general; foreign policy;
international situation 17
Relations with Russia, what to do about Russia, danger of
Russia, how to handle Russia 6

National defense, self-defense of our government, our security,
our country's welfare 2
The war, the cold war, atomic warfare 1
How to keep the peace, general 3
Disarmament 1
Internal communism, communist infiltrations, keep communists
out of the country 1
Cuban situation, relations with Cuba 2
Congo situation, African situation . . . . *
Foreign aid 2
Fiscal policy, tariff laws, economics 1
Education, schools, teachers 1
Domestic problems, general 1
Space problems, missiles, etc. . . . . *
Miscellaneous other 3
Don't know 25
* = less than .5 percent

Kennedy-Nixon
September 28-October 2, 1960

Population: National
Sample size: 3,614
Interview method: Personal
Survey #636

Did you happen to see or hear the television debate between Nixon and Kennedy last Monday night?

Yes 62%
No 38

In your opinion, what man did a better job in this debate?

Kennedy 44%
Nixon 23
Same 29
No opinion 3

Kennedy-Nixon
November 17-22, 1960

Population: National
Sample size: 3,123
Survey #638

In the election this November, did things come up which kept you from voting, or did you happen to vote?

If "yes, voted"

Did you happen to vote for Kennedy or Nixon?

Yes, voted 2%
No, did not vote 25
No, too young 1
Kennedy 37
Nixon 35
Other 1

For the U.S. House of Representatives, did you vote for the Republican candidate, or for the Democratic candidate?

Republican 45%
Democratic 53
Other 2

For the various political offices, did you vote for all the candidates of one party—that is, a straight ticket—or did you vote for the candidates of different parties?

Straight 66%
Different 34

What was the MAIN REASON why you voted for (Kennedy) (Nixon)—that is, why did you think he was the best man?

Liked him (Nixon) (Kennedy) better—general 6%
Respondent is a (Democrat) (Republican) 12
Liked the (Democratic) (Republican) candidates' ticket better 3
He would make a better president—general 4
He did better in campaign, personal appearances, debates 7
He did better in TV appearances—specifically mentioned 2
He is more experienced, more training—general 28
He is more experienced in foreign policy 5
He would move ahead—would accomplish things, has new ideas,
  would do something 5
He would reduce taxes . . . . *
He would continue policies of present administration 3
He is more conservative 2
He would do some good for the farmers, the farm problem . . . . *
He would do some good for the working class, labor 7
He would do some good for business . . . . *
Respondent was dissatisfied with present administration—
  needed a change 6
Because he is a Catholic 1
Because he is not a Catholic 3
He would be good for integration problem 1
Misc. others (keep list) 1
* = less than .5 percent

When did you make up your mind definitely to vote for (Kennedy) (Nixon)?

When he got the nomination for president, at the convention,
  when he was chosen as a candidate, at the very beginning of the
  campaign, early this summer. 56%
During the TV debates 14
Have always voted for the (Democrats) (Republicans) 7
Just a short time before the elections (one day up to one week) 9
A few weeks or a month before the election (no mention of TV
  debates) 8
Sometime before the convention 7

At any time did you intend to vote for the OTHER candidate—that is, (Kennedy) (Nixon)?

Yes 12%
No 88

1976 Campaign
July 17-20, 1976

Population: National adult
Sample size: 1,518
Interview method: Personal
Survey #955

> *Would you like to have the presidential candidates in the campaign this (1976) fall participate in nationally televised debates, or not?*

Yes, would 69%
No, would not 23
No opinion 9

Carter-Ford
September 24-27, 1976

Population: National adult
Sample size: 1,498
Interview method: Personal
Survey #959

> *Did you happen to see or hear the (1976 presidential) television debate between Ford and Carter Thursday night?*

Yes 67%
No... 33

> *In your opinion, which man did a better job in this (1976 presidential) debate (between Ford and Carter)?*

Subpopulation: Saw/heard Ford-Carter debate (67%)

Ford 32%
Carter 25
Same 33
No opinion 10

1980 Campaign
November 12-15, 1976

Population: National adult
Sample size: 1,541
Interview method: Personal
Survey #962

> *Would you favor or oppose having televised presidential debates in the next presidential campaign in 1980?*

Favor 66%
Oppose 20
No opinion 14

> *If (presidential) debates were to be held in 1980, do you think there should be any changes in the format of the debates—that is, in the way they are presented?*

Yes 35%
No... 44
No opinion 21

Carter-Kennedy
November 16-19, 1976

Population: National adult
Sample size: 1,528
Interview method: Personal
Survey #1143

If a series of nationally televised debates between President Jimmy Carter and Senator Edward Kennedy are held during the (1980) presidential campaign, do you think you would be likely to watch any of these debates, or not?

Yes 78%
No 16
Don't know 6

What specific issues would you like to see Carter and Kennedy debate (if there were a series of nationally televised debates held during the 1980 presidential campaign)?

Energy crisis (general) 23%
Fuel shortages, high fuel prices 13
Nuclear energy, nuclear plants 3
References to gas and oil companies, fuel profits 2
National defense 5
Foreign affairs: policies and issues 25
Iranian situation: about hostages in Iran 12
Middle East: Arab-Israeli conflict 1
Inflation, high cost of living: medical costs,
   interest rates, utilities 38
National health insurance 12
Unemployment 7
Reference to government spending 3
Foreign aid 1
Taxes (tax reduction) 6
Domestic issues: social security, abortion,
   welfare, civil rights 19
Trade balance, tariffs . . . . *
Don't care 3
Their honesty, leadership 1
Miscellaneous 1
Don't know 16
Adds to more than 100% due to multiple responses

Anderson-Carter-Reagan
September 12-16, 1980

Population: National adult
Sample size: 508
Subpopulation: Registered voters (75%)
Interview method: Telephone
Survey #921

What issues would you most like to have the candidates (Reagan and Anderson) debate (in the first 1980 presidential debate)?

High cost of living, inflation 51%

Foreign affairs 17
Unemployment 15
Tax cut 12
Energy matters 10
Conservation and the environment 3
Race relations, minority rights 2
Abortion 2
Women's rights/ERA (Equal Rights Amendment) 2
All other 31
Don't know 22
Adds to more than 100 percent due to multiple responses

As you may know, the first of the debates by the presidential candidates will be on TV on Sunday, Sept. 21 (1980). How likely are you to watch this debate (between Reagan and Anderson)? Would you say you are very likely, fairly likely, not very likely, or not at all likely to watch it?

Very likely 41%
Fairly likely 29
Not very likely 17
Not at all likely/don't know 13

Do you happen to know which of the presidential candidates will be participating in this (first 1980 presidential) debate?

Carter 25%
Reagan 78
Anderson 60
Others/don't know 22
Correctly named both Reagan and Anderson 50

President Carter has said that he will not take part in the first (1980 presidential) debate. Do you think he should or should not have made this decision?

Should 25%
Should not 61
No opinion 14

Anderson-Carter-Reagan
November 7-10, 1980

Population: National adult
Sample size: 1,556
Interview method: Personal
Survey #1164

What was the MAIN REASON why you voted for (Carter/Reagan/Anderson)— that is, why do you think he was the best man (for president)?

Liked economic policy: inflation too high, economics,
  expresses my views in economics, his economic policies
  tighter with the money. I feel he will better the economy 6%
Dissatisfied with Carter: Carter's failure, disgusted
  with Carter, voted against Carter, didn't want Carter in 6
Need a change: we need a change, felt it was time for a
  change—we needed it bad and we needed it in a hurry 7
He can't be any worse: he couldn't do worse than Carter,
  I didn't think things could get worse 1

Carter has not accomplished anything: we feel like Carter
hasn't done anything; Carter couldn't do it in 4 years, he
won't do it in 8; Carter wasn't getting job done 2
Would make a stronger president/better leader: we needed a
stronger person, he's more forceful, Carter is just a too
easy man 4
Like his policies (general): I agree with what he said,
politically I support his feelings, has good platform
policies 6
Like his foreign policy: his foreign policy, we think he
can better handle foreign policy, I like his position on
foreign relations 1
Carter's handling of hostage problem: Carter didn't settle
hostage situation, thought Carter did wrong in working so
hard to get the hostages home just before the election . . . . *
Conservative: Carter's too liberal 2
Because of the debate: did better in the debate, debate
showed he wasn't a fool, incompetent 1
Lesser of 2 evils 3
Experienced: he's had the experience, more experienced 3
Voted against Reagan: didn't like Reagan at all, against
Reagan 5
Honest man/religious/moral. straight and honest man, he's
honest, Carter was truthful man 3
Reagan would get us into war: afraid Reagan would start a
war, Carter's military position will send me to war, Reagan
would get into war more than Carter 2
He tried to do good job: the way he handled things, I think
he was doing a good job, did right thing, I think he has tried 3
Afraid of Reagan: I'm scared to death of Reagan, Reagan
scared me 1
Didn't need a change: needed more time, could have done
better in more time 2
Didn't like Reagan's stand on some issues: I don't believe
in all the things Reagan was for, I did not care for Reagan's
unreality approach on the issues 1
For the working man/middle class: I think the Democrat is
for the working man, for the farmer, think he did all right
for farmer, didn't think Reagan was for the farmer, the
Republicans have never been for the middle class, I'm a
little man, I think Carter better understands the little man 2
Like him/good man: I like him, a good man 4
Handling of Iran situation: I liked the way he handled
the hostages . . . . *
Reagan's age: I think Reagan is too old for the job 1
Should get campaign expenses paid: felt he should get his
money out of it, because he was refused campaign money and I
think that's wrong 1
Stay with my party 5
Abortion issue 1
Miscellaneous 1
Don't know 3
Not asked—didn't vote for Carter, Reagan, or Anderson 38

Adds to more than 100 percent due to multiple responses
* = less than .5 percent

When did you make up your mind definitely to vote for (Carter/Reagan/ Anderson) (for president)?

Subpopulation: voted for Carter, Reagan, or Anderson 62%
Election Day: at last minute, when in voting booth 10
Sunday, when Iranians' demands for release of hostages
were announced (specific) . . . . *
Last 2 or 3 days before Election Day 7
More than 3 days (unspecific) 12
As soon as he announced his candidacy, when he said he was
running 12
After watching debate (Oct. 28) 6
After convention, when Kennedy didn't get the nomination 11
Any date or month, July/Sept./no event mention 11
Any date or month, earlier than July 27
Miscellaneous . . . . *
Don't know 6
* = less than .5 percent

Why did you change your mind (about who you were going to vote for for president)?

Liked economic policy: inflation too high, economics,
expressed my views in economics, his economic policies,
tighter with the money, I feel he will better the economy 1%
Dissatisfied with Carter: Carter's failure, disgusted with
Carter, voted against Carter, didn't want Carter in 1
Need a change: we need a change, felt it was time for a
change, needed a change—we needed it bad and we needed it
in a hurry . . . . *
He can't be any worse: he couldn't do worse than Carter, I
didn't think things could get worse . . . . *
Carter has not accomplished anything: we feel like Carter
hasn't done anything; Carter couldn't do it in 4 years, he
won't do it in 8; Carter wasn't getting job done . . . . *
Would make a stronger president/better leader: we needed a
stronger person, he's more forceful, Carter is just a too
easy man . . . . *
Like his policies (general): I agree with what he said,
politically I support his feelings, has good platform policies 1
Like his foreign policy: his foreign policy, we think he can
better handle foreign policy, I like his position on foreign
relations . . . . *
Carter's handling of hostage problem: Carter didn't settle
hostage situation, thought Carter did wrong in working so
hard to get the hostages home just before the election . . . . *
Because of the debate: did better in the debate, debate
showed he wasn't a fool, incompetent 1
Experienced: he's had the experience, more experienced 1
Voted against Reagan: didn't like Reagan at all, against
Reagan 1
Honest man/religious/moral: straight and honest man, he's
honest, Carter was truthful man . . . . *

Reagan would get us into war: afraid Reagan would start a
war, Carter's military position will send me to war, Reagan
would get into war more than Carter .... *
Afraid of Reagan: I'm scared to death of Reagan, Reagan
scared me .... *
Didn't need a change: needed more time, could have done
better in more time .... *
Didn't like Reagan's stand on some issues: I don't like some
of the issues Reagan was for, I don't believe in all the things
Reagan is for, I did not care for Reagan's unreality approach
on the issues 1
For the working man/middle class: I think the Democrat is
for the working man, for the farmer, think he did all right
for farmer, didn't think Reagan was for the farmer, the
Republicans have never been for the middle class, I'm a little
man and I think Carter better understands the little man .... *
Like him/good man: I like him, a good man .... *
Should get campaign expenses paid: felt he should get his
money out of it, because he was refused campaign money and I
think that's wrong .... *
Because he wasn't nominated 2
He could not win/no majority/did not want to waste a vote:
didn't have a chance, afraid no one would have majority of
electoral votes, the election would be too close, giving Carter
a better chance 4
Stay with my party 1
Miscellaneous 1
Don't know 1
Not asked—didn't change mind or didn't vote for Reagan,
Carter, or Anderson 83
* = less than .5 percent

Mondale-Reagan and Bush-Ferraro
September 7-10, 1984

Population: National adult
Sample size: 1,521
Interview method: Personal
Survey #1241

*As you may know, the (1984) presidential and vice-presidential candidates will
hold televised debates later this fall. First, how likely are you to watch the
debates between Ronald Reagan and Walter Mondale? Would you say you are
very likely, fairly likely, or not very likely, to watch them?*

Very 38%
Fairly 31
Not very 29
Don't know 2

*How about a televised debate between the (1984) vice-presidential candidates,
George Bush and Geraldine Ferraro? Would you say you are very likely, fairly
likely, or not very likely to watch it?*

Very 35%
Fairly 26

Not very 36
Don't know 3

Who do you think is likely to do a better job in the (1984) presidential debates, Ronald Reagan or Walter Mondale?

Reagan 59%
Mondale 22
No difference (volunteered) 8
Can't say 11

And who do you think is likely to do a better job in a debate between the (1984) vice-presidential candidates, George Bush or Geraldine Ferraro?

Bush 35%
Ferraro 38
No difference (volunteered) 10
Can't say 18

What issues would you most like to have the presidential candidates debate?

	First choice	Second choice
High cost of living, inflation	3%	3%
Unemployment, recession, depression	11	7
High interest rates	1	1
Poverty, hunger (in general or in U.S.)	1	1
Food costs (specific)	*	*
Housing costs (specific)	*	*
Technology, automation, loss of jobs	—	*
Economy (general)	11	5
Other economic issues	1	*
Excess government spending (unspecified)	1	1
Excess military spending	2	1
Excess spending for social programs to help the poor	1	1
Federal budget deficit, failure to balance budget	8	5
Taxation: too high, reform, system unfair, too many loopholes	6	5
"Fairness" issue: government policies favor rich	*	*
Cuts in spending for social programs, welfare	1	1
Government's/president's economic policies in general	*	*
Other political economics	*	*
(Nuclear) war threat/fear of: world peace	7	3
Arms race	4	3
Arms talks: breakdown in disarmament negotiations	3	2
U.S. defense capability: inadequate, unready	1	1
National security/defense (general)	1	2
Other war, defense, military	1	1
Relations with Soviet Union	1	1
Central America situation	*	*
Middle East	*	*
Africa	—	*
China	*	—
Western Europe: NATO alliance	—	*
Southeast Asia	—	*

Foreign affairs, policy, international problems (general)	5	5
Other international, foreign affairs	*	*
Crime	1	1
Alcohol abuse	*	—
Drug abuse	*	*
Abortion (anti)	1	*
Moral, religious decline	1	*
School prayer	1	1
Energy costs, shortages	*	*
Pollution: environment	*	*
Immigration: illegal aliens	*	*
Health care: cost, health insurance, Medicare, Medicaid	*	*
Education: cost, quality, tuition tax credits	2	3
Civil rights: racial equality, affirmative action	*	*
Women's rights, ERA	*	1
Organized labor	*	*
Problems of elderly; social security	3	4
Agriculture: food exports, farm price supports	*	*
Imports: loss of U.S. sales, jobs, "dumping"	1	*
Other domestic problems	1	*
Dissatisfaction with government	*	*
Waste, corruption in government	—	*
President Reagan: Reagan administration	*	*
Religion and politics	*	1
Other government problems	*	*
Miscellaneous	4	1
None/don't know/no answer	15	39

* = less than .5 percent

Population: National adult
Sample size: 1,525
Interview method: Personal
Survey #484

As you may know, the presidential and vice-presidential candidates will hold televised debates later this fall (1984). Who do you think is likely to do a better job in the presidential debates—Ronald Reagan or Walter Mondale?

Reagan 61%
Mondale 22
No difference (volunteered) 7
No opinion 10
Based on registered voters

As you may know, the presidential and vice-presidential candidates will hold televised debates later this fall (1984). And who do you think is likely to do a better job in a debate between the vice-presidential candidates—George Bush or Geraldine Ferraro?

Ferraro 38%
Bush 36
No difference 9
No opinion 17
Based on registered voters

As you may know, the presidential and vice-presidential candidates will hold televised debates later this fall (1984). What issues would you most like to have the presidential candidates (Ronald Reagan and Walter Mondale) debate?

Unemployment 18%
Economy (general) 16
High cost of living 6
Hunger, poverty 2
High interest rates 2
Other economic issues 1
Problems of elderly 6
Education 4
Abortion 2
Other domestic problems 11
Federal budget deficit 13
Taxation 11
Excess defense spending 3
Cuts in social spending 2
Excess government spending (general) 2
Threat of war 10
Arms race 7
Arms talks 4
National security 3
Defense capability 2
Other war, defense issues 1
Relations with USSR 2
Foreign affairs (general) 9
Other international, foreign affairs issues 2
All other 5
No opinion 15
Adds to more than 100 percent because of multiple responses
Subtotal: Economic issues, 40 percent; domestic problems, 21 percent; political problems, 29 percent; war/defense, 27 percent; international/ foreign, 13 percent

Mondale-Reagan
September 28-30, 1984

Population: National adult
Sample size: 1,219
Interview method: Personal
Survey #1011

Regardless of which man you happen to prefer (in the 1984 presidential election), please tell me whether you feel each phrase applies more to Ronald Reagan or more to Walter Mondale in the (first) debate?

Seemed thoughtful and well-informed

Reagan 37%
Mondale 45
Neither (volunteered), no opinion 18

Seemed confident and self-assured

Reagan 33%
Mondale 55
Neither (volunteered), no opinion 12

Came closer to reflecting your point of view on the issues

Reagan 57%
Mondale 38
Neither (volunteered), no opinion 5

Seemed more capable of dealing with the problems facing this country

Reagan 58%
Mondale 36
Neither (volunteered), no opinion 6

Came across as more likable

Reagan 50%
Mondale 40
Neither (volunteered), no opinion 10

Presented better ideas for keeping the country prosperous

Reagan 55%
Mondale 36
Neither (volunteered), no opinion 9

Regardless of which candidate (for president in 1984) you happen to support, who do you think did a better job in the (first) debate—Ronald Reagan or Walter Mondale?

Mondale 54%
Reagan 35
Neither (volunteered) 8
No opinion 3

Mondale-Reagan
October 21, 1984

Population: Registered voters who watched the second presidential debate, Oct. 21, 1984, drawn from a pool of those in a predebate Gallup Poll who said they might watch the debate
Sample size: 446
Interview method: Telephone
Survey #1025

Does the following phrase apply more to Reagan or to Mondale (with regard to the second presidential debate)?

Seemed thoughtful and well-informed

Reagan 44%
Mondale 38
Both (volunteered), not sure 18

Seemed confident and self-assured

Reagan 46%
Mondale 36
Both (volunteered), not sure 18

Came closer to your point of view on the issues

Reagan 57%
Mondale 38
Both (volunteered), not sure 5

Came closer to your point of view on foreign policy issues

Reagan 57%
Mondale 38
Both (volunteered), neither (volunteered), not sure 5

More capable of handling relations with Soviet Union

Reagan 55%
Mondale 38
Both (volunteered), neither (volunteered), not sure 7

Has best judgment on needed defense expenditures

Reagan 53%
Mondale 39
Both (volunteered), neither (volunteered), not sure 8

More likely to keep United States out of war

Reagan 49%
Mondale 39
Both (volunteered), neither (volunteered), not sure 12

Regardless of which candidate you happen to support, who do you think did a better job in the (second presidential) debate—Ronald Reagan or Walter Mondale?

Reagan 43%
Mondale 40
Neither (volunteered), not sure 17

Did the (second presidential) debate make you more likely to vote for Ronald Reagan or against him (in 1984)?

Vote for Reagan 47%
Vote against Reagan 33
Had no effect (volunteered) 18
No opinion 2

Did the (second presidential) debate make you more likely to vote for Walter Mondale or against him (in 1984)?

Vote for Mondale 37%
Vote against Mondale 44
Had no effect (volunteered) 16
No opinion 3

Mondale-Reagan
October 26-29, 1984

Population: National adult
Sample size: 1,520
Interview method: Personal
Survey #1244

Did you happen to watch any of the three nationally televised (presidential and vice-presidential) political debates in October (1984)?

Yes 78%
No 22

All things considered, did the (1984 presidential and vice-presidential) debates make you more likely to vote FOR Ronald Reagan or more likely to vote AGAINST him?

Subpopulation: Saw any of the debates (78%)

For 28%
Against 31
Did not affect (volunteered) 39
Don't know 2

All things considered, did the (1984 presidential and vice-presidential) debates make you more likely to vote FOR Walter Mondale or more likely to vote AGAINST him?

Subpopulation: Saw any of the debates (78%)

For 34%
Against 27
Did not affect (volunteered) 38
Don't know 2

How important would you say the (1984 presidential and vice-presidential) debates were in determining how you will vote in the presidential election—very important, fairly important, or not at all important?

Subpopulation: Saw any of debates (70%)

Very 16%
Fairly 32
Not at all 50
Don't know 2

Mondale-Reagan
November 9-12, 1984

Population: National adult
Sample size: 1,509
Interview method: personal
Survey #1245

When did you make up your mind definitely to vote for (Reagan/Mondale) (in the 1984 presidential election)?

Subpopulation: Voted for Reagan or Mondale (69%)

Election Day: at last minute, when I went into voting
booth 4%
Last 2 or 3 days before Election Day 2
More than 2 or 3 days (unspecific) to one month 6
As soon as he announced his candidacy, when he said
he was running 27
After first debate 1
After last debate 1
After debates 2
After convention, when Jackson dropped out of race 3
Any date or month (no event mentioned) from July to
Sept., 1-4 months 9
Any date or month earlier than July, 5 months or
more, a year ago 26

When Mondale/Reagan was nominated 8
Before the debates 2
Miscellaneous 3
Don't know 6

1988 Campaign
February 9-15, 1987

Population: National adult
Sample size: 503
Interview method: Telephone
Survey #2423

Would you favor or oppose having televised debates in the next presidential campaign in 1988?

Favor 72%
Oppose 16
Undecided 12

CONTRIBUTORS

Tom Brokaw is managing editor, anchor, and chief of correspondents of "NBC Nightly News," which he has hosted since 1983. Brokaw is a graduate of the University of South Dakota and began his journalism career in 1962 at KMTV in Omaha, Nebraska. He has covered every presidential campaign since 1968; he moderated a live debate between Democratic presidential aspirants Walter Mondale, Gary Hart, and Jesse Jackson in 1984.

Douglass Cater is president of Washington College, Chestertown, Maryland. He served as special assistant to President Lyndon B. Johnson and collaborated on much education legislation, such as the Higher Education Act. He assisted in the creation of the Corporation for Public Broadcasting and the Teacher Corps. A graduate of Harvard College and the Harvard School of Public Administration, he was Washington editor and later national affairs editor for *Reporter* magazine from 1950 to 1964. Cater has written several books, including *Power in Washington* (1964) and *The Fourth Branch of Government* (1959). More recently he has coauthored several studies of the media's role in society.

Edwin Diamond is director of the News Study Group at New York University, where he is also a member of the Faculty of Arts and Sciences. A critic and journalist, he is coauthor of *The Spot: The Rise of Political Advertising on Television* (1988) and is media critic for *New York* magazine.

Frank J. Donatelli is assistant to the president for political and intergovernmental affairs in the Reagan administration. He also served as deputy assistant to the president for public liaison at the White House and assistant administrator for African affairs, Agency for International Development (AID). A graduate of the University of Pittsburgh, he received a J.D. from American University and was a partner in the Washington, D.C. law firm of Patton, Boggs & Blow. He was part of the White House negotiating team for the 1984 presidential debates.

Charles M. Firestone is a communications lawyer with Mitchell, Silberberg & Knupp of Los Angeles. A visiting member of the law faculty at UCLA, he was formerly director of the school's communications law program. He has served as director of litigation of Citizens Communications Center, Washington, D.C., and as an attorney with the office of the general counsel, Federal Communications Commission.

Leslie C. Francis is founder and president of Francis, McGinnis & Rees, Inc., a public affairs consulting firm based in Washington, D.C. During the Carter administration he was deputy assistant to the president for congressional liaison and deputy White House chief of staff. Francis was national staff director of the Carter/Mondale campaign and executive director of the Democratic National Committee in 1980. He was a key adviser and project manager during the Mondale campaign in 1984.

Kathleen Friery is assistant to the executive producer for ABC's television news show, "20/20." A graduate of the State University of New York at Potsdam, she received her master's degree in journalism from New York University, where she was a research associate of The News Study Group.

George Gallup, Jr., is president of The Gallup Poll and cochairman of The Gallup Organization, Inc. He is a graduate of Princeton University and has authored and collaborated on numerous books and articles, among them *The Great American Success Story* (1985) and *Who Do Americans Say That I Am?* (1986).

Victoria Harian is the presidential debates director for the League of Women Voters Education Fund. She was responsible for all League-sponsored debates during the 1984 presidential campaign and has directed other debate-related projects, including election television specials, issue debates, conferences, and publications. A former congressional press secretary and staff assistant, she earned a journalism degree from Indiana University.

Kathleen Hall Jamieson is G.B. Dealey Professor of Communication at the University of Texas at Austin. She has cochaired the Speech Communication Association's Task Force on Presidential Debates and has served on the Twentieth Century Fund's Task Force on Presidential Debates. During the 1984 general election, she was a debate analyst for Cable News Network. Her books include *Packaging the Presidency* (1984) and *Eloquence in an Electronic Age* (1988).

Newton N. Minow is a partner in the law firm of Sidley & Austin and director of the Annenberg Washington Program in Communications Policy Studies of Northwestern University. A former chairman of the Federal Communications Commission and of the Public Broadcasting System, he is on the advisory board of the political parties' Commission on Presidential Debates. He served as cochairman of the advisory committee of the League of Women Voters' presidential debates in 1976 and 1980 and has written numerous books and articles about television and presidential politics.

Nancy M. Neuman is president of the League of Women Voters of the United States and chair of the League of Women Voters Education Fund. A member of the League's national board since 1978, she serves on the executive committee of the Leadership Conference on Civil Rights and on the University of Virginia's Miller Center Commission on Presidential Disability and the Twenty-fifth Amendment. A graduate of Pomona College, she received her master's degree in political science from the University of California at Berkeley.

Norman J. Ornstein is resident scholar at the American Enterprise Institute. He is a political contributor to the "MacNeil-Lehrer Newshour" and an election consultant to CBS News. He was also a series editor of public television's "Congress: We the People." Ornstein served as a congressional fellow (1969-1970) and worked to reorganize the Senate's committee system in 1976-1977. His books include *Congress in Change: Evolution and Reform* (1975), *Interest Groups, Lobbying and Policymaking* (1978), and *Vital Statistics on Congress,* currently in its fourth edition.

Clifford M. Sloan is associate counsel to Lawrence Walsh, the independent counsel investigating the Iran-contra affair. He was law clerk to Supreme Court Justice John Paul Stevens and U.S. Court of Appeals Judge J. Skelly Wright and was also a congressional executive assistant. Sloan served as director of the Twentieth Century Fund/Institute of Politics Presidential Debates Project.

Joel L. Swerdlow is program and publications adviser to the Annenberg Washington Program for Communications Policy Studies of Northwestern University. He received his Ph.D. from Cornell University and has been a broadcast and print journalist. He has written several books, including *Beyond Debate* (1984) and, with Jan Scruggs, *To Heal a Nation: The Vietnam Veterans Memorial* (1985). He conceived and wrote "Getting the Picture: The Growth of Television in American Life," an exhibition distributed by the Smithsonian Institution.

INDEX

Presidential debates : 1988 and
beyond / Joel L. Swerdlow, editor ;
[in cooperation with the] League of
Women Voters Education Fund. --
Washington, D.C. : Congressional
Quarterly, c1987.
  xiv, 191 p. ; 23 cm.

  Includes index.

  ISBN: 0871874466 (pbk.) : $12.95
    1. Presidents - United States -
Election. 2. Campaign debates -
United States. 3. Television in

(Continued on next card)